A GUIDE TO
MUSICAL
ANALYSIS

Nicholas Cook

GEORGE BRAZILLER

NEW YORK

First published in the United States in 1987
by George Braziller, Inc.

Originally published in Great Britain by J.M. Dent & Sons Ltd
Aldine House 33 Welbeck Street London W1M 8LX

For information address the publisher:

George Braziller, Inc.
60 Madison Avenue
New York, New York 10010

Library of Congress Cataloging-in-Publication Data

Cook, Nicholas.
  A guide to musical analysis.

  Includes index.
  1. Musical analysis. I. Title.
MT6.C775G8   1987   780'.1'5   87–727
ISBN 0–8076–1172–7

Printed in the United States of America
First Printing, March 1987

CONTENTS

ACKNOWLEDGMENTS

Dr Nicholas Routley, Professor Peter Evans and Professor Ian Bent read chapters of this book in draft form. Each made many corrections and suggestions, and I am grateful to all of them. My thanks go to Tabitha Collingbourne for preparing the figures; and I am also grateful to Malcolm Butler for pointing out errors of fact and infelicities of expression.

Acknowledgment is due to the copyright holders for agreeing to the reprinting of the following copyright material:

Fig. 11 from Heinrich Schenker (ed. Salzer), *Five Graphic Analyses*, Dover, 1969, pp. 36–7.

Fig. 12 from Allen Forte and Steven E. Gilbert, *An Introduction to Schenkerian Analysis*, Copyright © 1982 by W. W. Norton & Company, Inc., p. 202.

Fig. 15 as Fig. 11, pp. 32–3.

Fig. 18 chart by W. J. Mitchell, from *The Music Forum*, I, Columbia University Press, 1967, pp. 166–7.

Fig. 20 from Thomas Clifton, *Music as Heard: a study in applied phenomenology*, Yale University Press, 1983, p. 177.

Fig. 21 from L. B. Meyer, *Explaining Music*, University of California Press, Berkeley, 1973, Ex. 79 (adapted).

Fig. 22 as Fig. 21, Ex. 80.

Fig. 25 as Fig. 21, adaptation of Exx. 141, 150, 148 and 153.

Fig. 27 as Fig. 21, Ex. 155.

Fig. 28 from G. Perle, *Serial Composition and Atonality*, Faber, London/University of California Press, Berkeley, 5th edn, 1981, Ex. 7.

Fig. 34 from Rudolph Reti, *The Thematic Process in Music*, Greenwood Press, London, 1978, Exx. 318–21 (with minor alterations and additions).

Fig. 35 as Fig. 34, Ex. 324.

Fig. 36 as Fig. 34, Ex. 331.

Fig. 37 as Fig. 34, Ex. 338.

Fig. 39 as Fig. 34, Ex 340.

Fig. 41 Rudolph Reti, *Thematic Patterns in Sonatas of Beethoven*, Faber, 1965, Ex. 12.

Fig. 87 from M. Kassler, 'Explication of the Middleground of Schenker's Theory of Tonality', *Miscellanea Musicologica: Adelaide Studies in Musicology*, 1977, p. 80.

Fig. 88 as Fig. 87, pp. 78–9 (adapted).

Fig. 90 song collected by Norma McLeod and reproduced in 'Analysis: The Herding of Sacred Cows?' by M. Herndon, *Ethnomusicology*, Vol. 18, pp. 219–62. Copyright © 1974 by the Society for Ethnomusicology, Inc.

Fig. 92 from C. Adams, 'Melodic Contour Typology', *Ethnomusicology*, Vol. 20, pp. 179–215. Copyright © 1976 by the Society for Ethnomusicology, Inc.

Fig. 93 from article by M. Herndon (see Fig. 90).

Fig. 94 from A. Lomax (ed.), *Folk Song Style and Culture*. Copyright 1968 by the American Association for the Advancement of Science, Washington D.C., Pub. No. 88, Fig. 29, p. 131.

Fig. 95 adaptation of various exx. in J. Blacking, 'Tonal Organization in the music of two Venda initiation schools', *Ethnomusicology*, Vol. 14, pp. 1–56. Copyright © 1970 by the Society for Ethnomusicology, Inc.

Fig. 96 from article by M. Herndon (see Fig. 90).

Fig. 98 re-aligned version of Fig. 90.

Fig. 108 from C. Seeger, *Studies in Musicology 1935–75*, University of California Press, Berkeley, 1977, Table 4, pp. 298–9 (part).

Fig. 122 Britten, 'Pan' (No. 1 of *Six Metamorphoses after Ovid*). © Copyright 1952 by Hawkes & Son (London) Ltd. Reproduced by permission of Boosey & Hawkes Music Publishers Ltd, London.

Fig. 143 Webern, Piano piece from a 1925 sketchbook, bars 1–9. Universal Edition (Alfred A. Kalmus Ltd).

Fig. 147 Webern, *Piano Variations*, first movement (with additions), Universal Edition (Alfred A. Kalmus Ltd.).

Fig. 150 Stravinsky, *Movements* for Piano and Orchestra, No. 4 (with additions). © Copyright 1960 by Hawkes & Son (London) Ltd. Reproduced by permission of Boosey & Hawkes Music Publishers Ltd, London.

Fig. 161 Schoenberg, *Klavierstuck* Op. 33a, bars 26–8 (with additions), Universal Edition (Alfred A. Kalmus Ltd.).

Fig. 164 as Fig. 161, bars 35–9.

Fig. 168 Schoenberg, Op. 19/3 (*Six Little Piano Pieces*), Universal Edition (Alfred A. Kalmus Ltd).

Fig. 175 Stockhausen, *Klavierstuck III* (bar numbers and segmentations added), Universal Edition (Alfred A. Kalmus Ltd).
Fig. 178 as Fig. 175.
Fig. 181 form scheme from Stockhausen, *Stimmung*, Universal Edition (Alfred A. Kalmus Ltd).
Fig. 182 as Fig. 181.

Wherever possible the music discussed is reproduced in full. But this cannot be done in the case of the more extended scores, so here is a list of what is required.

Chapter	2	Wagner, *Tristan* Prelude
		Debussy, *Puck's Dance* (from Preludes, Book 1)
Chapter	3	Beethoven, *Pathétique* Sonata
Chapter	8	Mozart, *Marriage of Figaro* (No. 1)
		Beethoven, Sonata Op. 49/2 (first movement)
		Beethoven, Quartet Op. 18/2 (first movement)
		Beethoven, Fifth Symphony (first movement)
		Berlioz, *Symphonie Fantastique* (first movement)
Chapter	9	Schoenberg, Piano Piece Op 33a.
Chapter	10	Chopin, *Polonaise-Fantaisie*

Chapter 10 also requires a sound recording of Stockhausen's *Stimmung* (see p. 365 for details).

INTRODUCTION

There is something fascinating about the very idea of analyzing music. For music is surely among the most baffling of the arts in its power to move people profoundly whether or not they have any technical expertise or intellectual understanding of it. It moves people involuntarily, even subliminally, and yet all this is done by means of the most apparently precise and rational techniques. If a few combinations of pitches, durations, timbres and dynamic values can unlock the most hidden contents of man's spiritual and emotional being, then the study of music should be the key to an understanding of man's nature. Music is a code in which the deepest secrets of humanity are written: this heady thought assured musical studies their central place in ancient, medieval and renaissance thought. And though the study of music no longer occupies quite so elevated a role in intellectual circles, some of today's most important trends in the human sciences still owe it a debt. Structuralism is an example: you don't have to read a lot of Levi-Strauss to realize how great an influence music has had upon his thinking.

This book is altogether more modest in its purview, however. It is about the practical process of examining pieces of music in order to discover, or decide, how they work. And this is fascinating, because when you analyze a piece of music you are in effect recreating it for yourself; you end up with the same sense of possession that a composer feels for a piece he has written. Analyzing a Beethoven symphony means living with it for a day or two, much as a composer lives with a work in progress: rising with the music and sleeping with it, you develop a kind of intimacy with it that can hardly be achieved in any other way. You have a vivid sense of communicating directly with the masters of the past, which can be one of the most exhilarating experiences that music has to offer. And you develop an intuitive knowledge of what works in music and what doesn't, what's right and what isn't, that far exceeds your capacity to formulate such things in words or to explain them intellectually. This kind of immediacy gives analysis a special value in compositional training, as against the old books of theory and stylistic exercises that reduced the achievements of the past to a set of pedagogical rules and regulations. No wonder, then, that analysis has become the backbone of composition teaching.

Although analysis allows you to get directly to grips with pieces of music, they won't unfold their secrets unless you know what questions to ask of them. This is where analytical methods come in. There are a large number of analytical methods, and at first sight they seem very different; but most of them, in fact, ask the same sort of questions. They ask whether it is possible to chop up a piece of music into a series of more-or-less independent sections. They ask how components of the music relate to each other, and which relationships are more important than others. More specifically, they ask how far these components derive their effect from the context they are in. For example, a given note has one effect when it is part of chord X and a quite different effect when it is part of chord Y; and the effect of chord X in turn depends on the harmonic progression it forms part of. Or again, a particular motif may be unremarkable in itself but acquire a striking significance in the context of a given movement as a whole. And if you can work out how this comes about, then you have an understanding of how the music works which you didn't have before.

It's difficult to imagine that there could be an analytical method that didn't ask questions about these things – about division into sections, about the importance of different relationships, and about the influence of context. But in spite of such unity of purpose, the various methods of analysis are frequently pursued in isolation from each other or, what is worse, in acrimonious rivalry with each other. As often as not an analyst will adopt one method and ignore or denigrate the others: so that you get the motivic analyst, the Schenkerian analyst, the semiotic analyst and so forth. Each applies his particular method to whatever music comes his way, and at its worst the result is the musical equivalent of a sausage machine: whatever goes in comes out neatly packaged and looking just the same. This especially happens when the analyst has come to believe that the purpose of a piece of music is to prove the validity of his analytical method, rather than the purpose of the analytical method being to illuminate the music: in other words, when he has become more interested in the theory than in its practical application. I don't think it can be denied that this is true of some analysts. Rudolph Reti is a good example: he is always anxious above everything else to prove his theory right, regardless of the particular qualities of the music he's talking about. And you only have to look through today's specialist analytical journals to realize what a high premium is generally put on the formulation of increasingly precise and sophisticated analytical methods more or less as an end in itself. Over the last twenty years musical analysis has become professionalized: it has become to a large degree the preserve of music analysts rather than, simply, of musicians who happen to analyze.

Personally I dislike the tendency for analysis to turn into a quasi-scientific discipline in its own right, essentially independent of the practical concerns of musical performance, composition or education. Indeed I do not believe that analysis stands up to close examination when viewed this way: it simply doesn't have a sufficiently sound theoretical basis. (Chapter 6 goes into this in more detail.) I think that the emphasis many analysts place on objectivity and impartiality can only discourage the personal involvement that is, after all, the only sensible reason for anyone being interested in music. And I see no intrinsic merit in the development of ever more rigorous and sophisticated analytical methods: though there are areas which are analytically under-developed (early music is an important one), in general I think that our present analytical techniques are rather successful. As I see it, the important thing is not so much to invent new techniques, nor to go on endlessly refining those we already have, but rather to make the fullest possible *use* of them. One way in which the techniques can be made more useful is through their being employed in combination with one another, and some important steps have been taken in this direction during the past few years. (I am thinking for instance of Epstein's synthesis of Schenkerian and motivic techniques, of Lerdahl and Jackendoff's formalization of techniques drawn from Schenker and Meyer, and of Forte and Gilbert's Schenkerian treatment of the traditional forms of tonal music: it is no accident that Schenkerian analysis is the common factor in all of these.) But the most important way in which today's techniques of analysis can become more useful is through more people using them. I would like to see the analytical skills outlined in this book becoming part of the taken-for-granted professional equipment of the historical musicologist and the ethnomusicologist. And this is something that can happen only if analysis is seen as a central component of musical education, and not as some kind of esoteric specialism.

This book, then, is essentially pragmatic in its orientation. It is primarily a practical guide to musical analysis as it is, rather than a theoretical tract about musical analysis as it ought to be. And this means that the book reflects the prejudices and limitations of current analytical practice. For instance, it reflects the overriding interest most analysts have in what gives unity and coherence to musical masterpieces, with the answers being sought mainly in the formal and harmonic structures of individual compositions. It's possible to argue that these prejudices and limitations are perfectly justified; for instance, if analysts are less interested in timbral structure than in harmony and form, this may simply be because timbral structure is less interesting, or – what comes to the same thing – less amenable to rational comprehension. But it is undeniable that there are tacit assumptions here about the nature of musical analysis, and this book is cast more or less within the framework of these assumptions.[1]

The pragmatic orientation of the book is also reflected in the way it is organized. The first part sets out what I consider the most important analytical methods current in the English-speaking world, dealing with each in turn. The presentation is method-by-method (rather than being organized, for example, by musical parameters) because each method involves a characteristic set of beliefs about music and the purposes of analyzing it, and it is important to be clear what these beliefs are: otherwise you are likely to apply the techniques associated with any given method in an indiscriminate manner, and so bury yourself under a mound of data that do not actually mean anything to you. Whether the beliefs embodied in an analytical method are true, in a theoretical sense, isn't however so important: what matters is how useful the method based on them is, and under what circumstances.

The question of how you should decide what method to adopt under any particular circumstances – or for that matter whether you should improvise a new technique – is addressed in the second part of the book, in which given compositions rather than given analytical methods form the starting point. The analyses in this section are each designed to highlight some different aspect of analytical procedure, and the idea is that each chapter should be read as a whole.

---

[1] For critical views of analysis in relation to the entire field of musical studies see Joseph Kerman's *Musicology* (Fontana/Collins 1985), Chapter 3, and Leo Treitler's 'Structural and Critical Analysis', in Holoman and Palisca (eds.), *Musicology in the 1980s*, Da Capo Press 1982, pp. 67–77.

Part One

ANALYTICAL METHODS

CHAPTER ONE

TRADITIONAL METHODS OF ANALYSIS

I

I don't suppose there has ever been a time when music did not attract some kind of intellectual speculation. However, until some two hundred years ago such speculations bore little affinity to what we nowadays mean by the term 'musical analysis'. From the ancient world up to the Renaissance, as also in classical India and China, music was studied intellectually, but the music wasn't being studied for its own sake. Instead it was seen as a reflection of cosmic order or as an instrument of moral education; which meant that it was approached from a theoretical rather than an analytical point of view. Technical aspects of musical structure were not ignored, but they were looked at in the most general light, rather than in the context of individual pieces of music. For instance, theorists would write on the properties of the modal system as such, rather than on the modal characteristics of any particular composition. In fact these theorists were only really interested in individual pieces of music to the extent that the most general principles of musical structure could be derived from them. Once these principles had been discovered, they had no further interest in the individual piece, and that is why these people were not really analysts at all in the sense that we use the term nowadays.

Nevertheless these early theorists were classifying what they found in music – scales, chords, forms, even the instruments of music – and classification forms the indispensable basis of musical analysis. In his article on analysis in the *New Grove Dictionary of Music and Musicians*, Ian Bent describes musical analysis as a 'natural science' approach to music, and the rise of scientific thinking in general had an effect on the way

7

music was studied. Instead of looking everywhere for universal principles and ultimate explanations, people tried to describe and categorize music in a more neutral, scientific manner than before – trying to do the same for music as people such as Linnaeus were doing for the natural sciences. There is a more specific parallel to be made with the natural sciences, too. The discovery of the amazing variety of musical cultures throughout the world encouraged nineteenth-century theorists to apply evolutionary thinking to music. Basically these theorists explained music as they found it by deriving it from supposed origins of some sort. These origins might be historical; showing how chromatic harmony developed stage by stage from diatonic harmony, and diatonic harmony from the modal system, is an example of this. Or the origins might be biological, as when Riemann explained all the various types of phrase structure to be found in music in terms of patterns of inhalation and exhalation in breathing. This concept of what it means to explain something was very characteristic of the time, and you could compare it not only to what was happening in the natural sciences but in other branches of the humanities as well, for instance philology.

Theories of this kind, and analytical applications of them to music, reached a high level of sophistication by the end of the nineteenth century. But in this book we shall hardly be concerned with them at all. The reason is that, apart from the basic idea of explaining music by means of deriving it from something, these evolutionary approaches are more or less obsolete. By this I mean that they are not indispensable for an understanding of current analytical practice, which is what this book is about. This doesn't of course mean that there is no point in getting to know about nineteenth-century and, indeed, earlier musical analysis; it is interesting particularly as a background to the composition of the period, and the article by Ian Bent that I mentioned is the best starting point for such a study. But for our purposes all we need to know about is the basic terminology which twentieth-century analysts inherited from their predecessors and which remains the starting point for a great deal of analysis even now. The vocabulary that was traditionally used for the description of music and the notations that were used to repres-ent it are the topics of this chapter and, simple though these things are, they raise issues that attract analytical controversy to this day.

II

There were two main ways in which people approached pieces of music. One was their overall form and the other was their melodic, harmonic or rhythmic content. We'll consider each of these in turn.

Form was viewed in traditional terms. This means that analyzing the form of a new piece basically consisted of assimilating it into one existing formal prototype or another. The simplest of such analytical prototypes were purely sectional – binary form, ternary form – but forms of any complexity were described historically. This means not only that the familiar textbook forms (sonata, rondo, da capo aria) had a specific historical provenance, but also that they incorporated stylistic presuppositions of various sorts. The most important of these is that forms like rondo or sonata are by definition thematic. Certain parts of the music are picked out and identified as themes (and accordingly labelled A, B, B1 and so forth) whereas the rest of the music is regarded as non-thematic – or, to use the old-fashioned and rather unsatisfactory term, 'transitional'. And each of the various historical forms was defined as a specific permutation of these thematic units, sometimes in a specific association with a tonal area – though the bias of analytical interest at the beginning of this century was heavily weighted towards thematic rather than tonal structure.

Now this doesn't mean that music was seen just as a succession of tunes. Although 'theme' and 'tune' can mean the same thing, when applied in this kind of analysis 'theme' is really a technical term. It refers to some readily recognizable musical element which serves a certain formal function by virtue of occurring at structural points. A tune can be a 'theme' in this sense; but so also can a striking chord progression, a rhythm, or indeed any kind of sonority. So if there is something unduly restrictive about this traditional way of looking at musical form – if, that is, it doesn't express the experience of music very adequately – it is not simply because of the emphasis on themes. It has more to do with the function that the traditional approach to musical form ascribes to themes in music. I said that the term 'transition' was an unsatisfactory one: it implies that the function of all the sections in a piece of music that are not thematic is simply to link up the thematic ones – to create 'transitions' between them. But this isn't really how people experience music. Often – probably more often than not – it is the transitional passages of a sonata that are the most intense and expressive, not the themes; and this is especially true of Beethoven, who was traditionally regarded as the great master of sonata form. Why, then, did analysts lay so much emphasis on the thematic aspects of musical form? There are two possible reasons. The first involves the kind of evolutionary thinking I described earlier. Analysts emphasized thematic patterns because it was these that defined the traditional forms, and they emphasized the traditional forms because they believed that people's responses to music were largely conditioned by the past. Either, they may have thought, people derived aesthetic pleasure from music because the musical form developed in accordance with their expectations. Or else people might derive pleasure from just the opposite – from the music being unpredictable, from its doing something other than what the listener expected. These two interpretations of how music gives pleasure are diametrically opposed, but as usual with diametric opposites they have a lot in common. They both agree that expectation plays an important role in music, and how could people have expectations about musical form if not on the basis of the forms they had previously encountered? This is one possible reason for thinking it appropriate to formulate standard patterns corresponding to 'the' classical sonata, 'the' classical rondo and so forth – models from which analysts could derive any particular sonata or rondo by showing the respects in which it conformed to the model and those in which it deviated from it. But there is also a second reason, and a more basic one. This has to do with the purposes for which this kind of analysis was being done. During the nineteenth century it had become normal for composition to be taught in classes at music schools, rather than through private lessons as had been the case till then. Teaching composition in this way meant that teachers relied increasingly on textbooks to guide their students in their attempts at composition. And the standard patterns of form I have described were primarily textbook models; they were meant to be copied, in the same way as student painters used to copy old masters at that time. In a sense, then, they don't primarily belong to the history of musical analysis as such: they belong to the history of composition teaching.

Yet people did try to explain existing music in terms of these textbook models, and there was a good deal of so-called analysis which consisted of no more than fitting compositions into the straightjacket of traditional form and ignoring the bits that didn't fit. There is always a temptation in musical analysis to make everything conform to the model, and this earned a bad name for the traditional approach to musical form. At the same time this kind of approach did sometimes produce work in which the individual qualities of a given piece were examined more sensitively. An example is the long series of analytical essays Donald Tovey published during the first half of the century and which did much to establish the empirical climate of British musical analysis during that period. They began as programme notes to a regular series of concerts he conducted in Edinburgh, and – in contrast to the work of such continental contemporaries as Schenker – they were intended not for a professional readership but for the middlebrow, concert-going public. They lay somewhere between specialist analysis and journalism. Essentially Tovey wrote a prose commentary on the music (though sometimes he used a simple tabular format). He went through the composition in chronological order, briefly describing the effect of each section, quoting the principal themes as they occurred, and sometimes pointing out motivic similarities between them (or, as he put it, 'deriving' later themes from earlier ones); and he assigned each section to its place within the traditional formal plan. In this way he was constantly using traditional terms like theme and transition, exposition and recapitulation (although he preferred the term 'group' to 'theme' – first group, second group and so forth – on the grounds that a number of melodic ideas might have a single thematic role). However in using these terms he didn't mean to say that everything could be fitted into a preconceived plan; in fact he frequently ridiculed this tendency, and was himself much more interested in the differences between different composers' treatment of what was, analytically speaking, the 'same' form. Here to illustrate this is a comment he made about Schumann's Piano Quintet Op. 44 which is typical both of his prose style and of his tolerant, non-doctrinaire attitude:

> He is writing an altogether new type of sonata-work; a kind that stands to the classical sonata somewhat as a very beautiful and elaborate mosaic stands to a landscape-picture. In the mosaic the material and structure necessitate and render appropriate an otherwise unusual simplicity and hardness of outline and treatment, while at the same time making it desirable that the subjects should be such that this simple treatment may easily lend them subtlety of meaning – just as, on the other hand, the costly stones of which the mosaic is made have in themselves many an exquisite gradation of shade and tone, though the larger contrasts and colours of the work as a connected whole are far more simple and obvious than those of a painting.[1]

In other words, he is implying, a mechanical comparison of the way composers treat musical forms misses the point: what matters is the

[1] *Essays in Musical Analysis: Chamber Music*, p. 150.

11

aesthetic values, the approach to musical materials, that underlie the forms themselves. And he frequently relies on literary devices such as metaphor to explain what is at issue. Indeed it is a characteristic of Tovey's to point to peculiarities of style without making any attempt to explain them in theoretical terms of any sort. Speaking of the main *allegro* theme of Tchaikovsky's Fifth Symphony (Fig. 1) he observes that 'great harmonic distinction is given to this theme by its first note. Those who misremember it as B will learn a useful lesson in style when they come to notice that this note is C and not B'.[1] But just what is the lesson?

Fig. 1

What is Tovey getting at? Simply the rocking alternation of IV and I that underlies the tune? The fact that the tune arpeggiates a single C major triad, and that the avoidance of any dominant coloration means that there is only a weak cadential structure? Tovey doesn't say; he observes the phenomenon and leaves it at that; and his analyses fell into some disfavour after the middle of the century, in professional analytical circles at least, because of this lack of explicit theoretical content. What's the point, analysts began to ask, of describing the things that listeners can hear for themselves without attempting to explain them? More recently, however, people have been returning with renewed interest to Tovey and, in general, to straightforward, non-technical description of music. Simple but penetrating observations such as Tovey's make, if nothing more, an excellent starting point for a more technical analysis.

Returning to the earlier part of the century, and more particularly to continental Europe, there was a fairly general dissatisfaction with the fixed, normative models of the traditional forms. Increasingly analysts came to feel that the textbook forms that composition students were taught to imitate – 'the' sonata, 'the' rondo and the rest – had never actually existed in authentic classical music at all. As a matter of fact these compositional models weren't contemporaneous with the classical style; they had been invented around the 1840s, principally by the German analyst and aesthetician A. B. Marx. Marx was one of the main forces behind what became the widespread view that Beethoven's com-

[1] *Essays in Musical Analysis VI: Miscellaneous Notes*, p. 61.

positions represent the purest and most perfect models of musical form. At first sight Marx's view of Beethoven (who had died in 1827) contrasts oddly with that of Beethoven's contemporaries, who were more inclined to see Beethoven as the quintessentially romantic iconoclast. They felt that Beethoven had shattered traditional forms by subordinating everything to intensity and immediacy of emotional expression. But in fact this is not so different from what Marx himself thought. He believed that the form of a piece of music must derive from its expressive content; he described form as 'the externalization of content' and hence concluded that 'there are as many forms as works of art'.[1] However, he also acknowledged that forms have a tendency to become historically sedimented so that traditions of form arise – and it was in explaining this that he drew up his model for 'sonata form', a term which (as referring to a specific form) he had himself coined. What happened was that this model was taken out of context; people started using it as an analytical tool while ignoring Marx's broader conception of the nature of musical form.

The dissatisfaction with this misinterpretation of Marx that people felt in the early years of this century was on three main counts. First, as I said, that the normative forms were no more than pedagogical fictions. Second, that tonal relations (which, again, Marx had himself emphasized but which his successors neglected) were more important than thematic relations; the result of this criticism was a steady shift in the terminology for sonata form, away from melodic character and towards tonal function – the term 'first theme' being modified to 'first subject group', for instance, and then to 'first tonal area'. The third objection, however, was a more basic one: that the important thing about form in music was not how far it happened to fit or not fit with traditional patterns. Progressive analysts began to feel that it was the functional, and not the historical, aspects of musical form that mattered. They became increasingly interested in the harmonic or motivic content of music, because they felt that it was only by virtue of their relation to such things that musical forms had any meaning. They believed that the methodological division between the forms of music, on the one hand, and its content, on the other, was an artificial one and that the traditional formal moulds represented at best purely superficial aspects of the real formal process. In a roundabout way, therefore, they returned to something nearer Marx's original understanding of form.

---

[1] These translations of passages from Marx's *Die Lehre von der Musikalischen Komposition* are taken from Bent's article.

As a matter of fact these progressive analysts – whom we shall meet in subsequent chapters – were probably overreacting. Such things as the contrasts between thematic and transitional areas, the textural characteristics of different formal areas, and so on, have a great deal of importance for the listener. Composers take a great deal of care over them. And there are clear historical traditions within individual forms – so that for instance a composer, when writing a sonata, makes certain presuppositions about the form which derive from earlier composers. All these considerations were largely ignored in the analytical reaction against the traditional forms. And although historical studies of these matters continued, it is only quite recently, with the writings of Charles Rosen, that the traditional aspects of musical form have really become respectable again in analytical circles.

In his books *The Classical Style* and *Sonata Forms* Rosen attempts to explain the apparent diversity of forms found in classical music. He does this in terms of the aesthetic values that underlie them. Rosen is very emphatic that form was important to the classical composers and that their style was largely designed so as to delineate form clearly: 'sonata style', he says (and the definition of sonata as a 'style' is characteristic), 'is essentially a coherent set of methods of setting the contours of a range of forms into high relief and resolving them systematically' (*Sonata Forms*, Norton, 1980, p. 174). But the kind of form they wanted to delineate, as he explains, was not a pattern of themes or keys as such; rather it was a certain kind of structural coherence. The point about sonata form was not that there was anything special about it as a surface pattern, but that it presented a kind of tonal drama. This drama was based on the concept of one key, the tonic, being consonant and all the others being dissonant in relation to the tonic. And the thematic materials could be associated with key structure in two basic ways. They could be associated directly with one key or another so as to clarify these keys and make their formal function more readily perceptible. Or tonal and thematic plans could be staggered against each other so as to produce a more elaborate form – as in the recapitulation of a second thematic group in the tonic. But what is important is not the particular succession of themes and keys so much as the underlying concept of sections being consonant or dissonant, much in the manner of notes being consonant or dissonant in strict counterpoint. A section in a key other than the tonic is dissonant and requires formal resolution: it is this concept that Rosen regards as the common factor behind the variety of classical forms – indeed, he says 'the principle of re-capitulation as resolution may be considered the most fundamental and radical innovation of sonata style' (p. 272). As long as this principle is adhered to, any number of variations in surface form are possible. For instance, there may be only one thematic group which is used both in tonic and dominant (as Tovey observed, this is frequently the case in Haydn). Again, a theme may be recapitulated in the 'wrong' key, or new material introduced in the development; in either case the result will be an extension of the recapitulation or more probably a coda, in which the balance will be restored. The underlying rule is simply that all thematic material should appear for the final time in the tonic; and there is no limit to the number of surface 'forms' conforming to this underlying formal principle.

Rosen's account of sonata forms (the reason for the plural in his title should now be obvious) in terms of underlying concepts such as structural dissonance and formal balance is convincing and easy to follow, consisting as it does of verbal explanation and musical examples with a minimum of technical apparatus. At the same time it is important to point out that Rosen's approach is rather similar to the iconographical approach in art history, the aim of which is to recreate the artist's intentions by an exhaustive study of symbolical implications of his work – implications that would otherwise be overlooked today. In other words, Rosen is explaining form in terms of the composer's intentions rather than the modern listener's responses. Many listeners do not appear to be aware of the kind of large-scale relationships of tonal contrast that Rosen is concerned with – except, of course, for listeners with perfect pitch, who can follow these relationships almost as if they had the score in front of them. But, as Rosen says,

> no composer . . . has ever made his crucial effects depend on such perception: even if he expects his most subtle points to be appreciated only by connoisseurs, he does not write the entire work calculatedly above the head of the average listener. But there is at least one person who is sure to recognize the reappearance of a tonic even without thematic reference: the performer. It is for this reason that subtle effects based on tonal relations are much more likely to occur in a string quartet or a sonata, written as much for the performers as for the listeners, than in an opera or a symphony, more coarsely if more elaborately designed. (*The Classical Style*, Viking, New York/Faber, London, 1971; revised edn 1976, p. 299.)

What Rosen is saying here is that you can't fully understand classical music, especially classical chamber music, just in terms of how it is heard. You have also to understand it in terms of the musical thinking that gave rise to it, and of course it is the job of analysis to uncover what this musical thinking was. This means that music as it appears to the listener and music as it appears to the analyst may not necessarily be quite the same thing. The relationship between the two is one of the most problematic issues in the whole business of musical analysis and it will crop up repeatedly in this book.

III

So much for traditional ways of seeing form. What about traditional ways of seeing content? At the beginning of the century, as indeed nowadays, it was harmony that was regarded as the most crucial aspect of musical content – at least in the music of the eighteenth and nineteenth centuries. And as the traditional way of analyzing harmony was to rewrite it in terms of some kind of simplified notation, it is sensible to begin by briefly considering what a notation is and how it works.

Essentially there are two analytical acts: the act of *omission* and the act of *relation*. Conventional musical notation is analytical in both these respects. It omits things like the complex overtone structures of musical sounds, representing sounds by their fundamentals alone. Even in the way it represents these fundamentals it is schematic, because it reduces to a few symbols and a finite number of chromatic pitches the enormous variety of articulations and intonations that string players and singers, for instance, adopt. Similarly conventional notation does not show the fine detail of rhythmic performance; indeed it makes heavy weather of showing any rhythmic values which are not in the simplest arithmetical relationships. In all these respects, as in others, the ordinary performance score constitutes an informal and rather unsystematic analysis of musical sound, sacrificing detailed representation in the interests of clarity, simplicity and intelligibility. The various methods of representing harmonic formations in music which the rest of this chapter describes have the same aims of clarity, simplicity and intelligibility; but the pattern of omission and relation is different, since the purpose of the representation is not the same.

The first of these ways of representing harmonic relationships is the figured bass, which was of course a performance device in origin but continued in use after the demise of the baroque style as a means of analyzing harmony. It is reductive in that it assumes that register is of no significance, as Fig. 2 shows; consequently it says nothing about the

Fig. 2

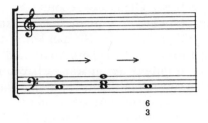

melodic relationships between one chord and the next. (Hence learning to realize a figured bass is not so much a matter of reading the notation as such, which is easy, as of supplying the correct voice-leading relationships in the upper parts: relationships which are implicit in the baroque bass line but about which the notation itself is silent.) Within these limitations, figured bass notation is very catholic in what it can notate; any combination of notes can in theory be represented by the use of a sufficient number of figures together with accidentals where necessary – although in practice the notation is not really legible in chords of any great complexity. Actually to talk about 'chords' in relation to the figured bass is something of a misnomer. This is because, though by convention you assume a triadic realization except when the figures specify something else, the notation simply shows aggregations of intervals. It does not, in other words, categorize chords as such at all. It does not distinguish chords from 'non-chords' – formations resulting, say, from passing notes. And it does not recognize that there is any special connection between, say, a root position triad and the same triad in first inversion. Figured bass is, in short, too literal-minded to be a powerful analytical tool: it does not give you any real criteria for deciding what is more important and what is less important, which is the basis of any analytical interpretation.

Roman-letter analysis is the second of the ways of representing harmonic relationships, and it overcomes many of these limitations. Unlike figured bass, it originated as an analytical device and not in performance practice.[1] Despite its apparent simplicity it is quite a

---

[1] For the early history of harmonic analysis, including the development of Roman letter notation, see David Beach, 'The Origins of Harmonic Analysis', *Journal of Music Theory*, 18 (1974), p. 274.

powerful analytical tool. Like the figured bass, it ignores register. But instead of relating the various notes of a chord to the actual bass – as does the figured bass, which in consequence only works in textures where there is a distinct bass line – it relates them to the root of the chord. (Figure 3 illustrates this.) Then, as a second stage, it relates this chordal root to the tonic, showing how many diatonic steps above the tonic the chordal root is: this is what the Roman letter itself indicates. The fact that harmonic formations are here translated into a single symbol, unlike the several numbers designating a harmonic formation in figured bass notation, means that Roman-letter analysis chops music up into a series of disjunct chords – in contrast again to the figured bass, where, as I said, there are no 'chords' as such but instead a series of intervallic values in relation to a bass, values which need not all change at once so that one harmonic formation can flow smoothly into another. The way in which it chops music up is both the strength and the weakness of Roman-letter analysis.

Fig. 3

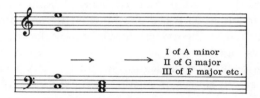

I of A minor
II of G major
III of F major etc.

Translating a series of chords into figured bass notation is an almost completely mechanical process that proceeds note by note and chord by chord. But assigning Roman letters involves a lot more in the way of analytical decisions. In order to assign a Roman letter you have to decide what key the music is in; you have to decide how many chords it should be chopped up into; and you have to decide what those chords are – which means deciding which notes in the music have a harmonic function and which are inessential, such as passing notes. Let us take these decisions in turn.

Suppose you are analyzing Beethoven's 'Waldstein' Sonata (Fig. 4 shows its first 38 bars). What key is this in? Since classical movements do not always begin in their tonic key, but invariably end in it, the easiest way to answer this question is to look at the end of the movement: it is in C major. But is the opening in C major? No: the first phrase spells out IV - V^7 - I of G. And the second phrase spells out the same chord series, only in F. What are we to make of this? Does it mean that there is a modulation between bars 4 and 5? If we say this, then as we continue we will find that the music is a patchwork of different keys and the piece will come out of the analysis looking a complete muddle. Then should we regard everything as really being in C, and so analyze the first eight bars as I – ̶I̶I̶^{7} – V – $^\flat$ VII – I$^{\flat\,7}$ – IV?[1] But this is not sensible, because the chord-symbols no longer demonstrate the similarity of harmonic pattern between the first two phrases. The best solution to this problem is to use the Roman letters in a hierarchical way, instead of relating every chord directly to the overall tonic. This means that we call the first phrase as a whole V, and the second phrase IV; and we relate the chords *within* each phrase to this overall harmonic function. We can write this as V (IV – V^7 – I), IV (IV – V^7 – I) – meaning that there is first a IV – V^7 – I of V and then a IV – V^7 – I of IV.[2] And if we analyze the whole of Fig. 4 this way, we will come up with the following chart:

Bar		
1	V	(IV – V^7 – I)
5	IV	(IV – V^7 – I)
9	V	
14	V	(IV – V^7 – I)
18	VI	(IV – V^7 – I)
22	̶I̶I̶I̶	(̶I̶V̶ – V^7 – I)

What does this tell us? The answer is, quite a lot. For instance, notice how chords on the same root (for instance the Cs at bars 1 and 6) appear on different occasions, but with a different analytical interpretation: the analysis is saying that a C chord will appear quite different depending whether it is functioning as a IV of V, as in bar 1, or a V of IV, as in bar 6. (As a I, of course, it would be different again.) In other words the analysis is saying that the way you experience the sound depends on the harmonic context, and because Roman-letter analysis does take account of context, in a way that figured bass notation does not, it is quite wrong to dismiss it as 'naive associationism'.[3] Associationism means making a mechanical link between an isolated stimulus and an isolated response (Pavlov's bell and his dog's

---

[1] The symbol ̶I̶I̶ means a II that is altered in some unspecified manner: here, because it is a D major chord when it 'should' have been D minor.

[2] Some people use an alternative notation for the same thing: $\frac{IV - V^7 - I}{V}$ instead of V (IV – V^7 – I).

[3] Eugene Narmour, *Beyond Schenkerism*, University of Chicago Press, 1977, p. 1.

Fig. 4 Beethoven, 'Waldstein' Sonata, I, bars 1–38

salivation), and this is just what is not characteristic of Roman-letter analysis, at least when it is done sensibly.

What else does this analysis tell us? It explains the otherwise puzzling relationship between the G chord in bar 4 and the B♭ chord in bar 5; or rather it says that there is not a direct relationship between the two (they are connected only indirectly, through the overall harmonies of the phrases to which they belong). Again, the analysis shows how Beethoven establishes his C major tonality without ever stating it directly at phrase level; that's an important observation on Beethoven's style. And it also reveals that there is a rather simple, and not immediately obvious, harmonic design behind this entire opening section. However, we need to be a bit careful here. The analysis says that the music starts with a V (IV – V⁷ – I). And so it does, looked at in terms of the overall design. But does it sound that way? Of course not, because the listener has no way of knowing that the first chord is a IV of V. In fact it is not till about the tenth bar, at the earliest, that any very definite sense of what overall key the music is in emerges at all. But this is something that Roman letters cannot express properly. To assign them you already need to have decided on the key, whereas the listener may have made no such decision. This is an example of one of the dangers of Roman letters, which is that they tempt you to say more about the music that you actually mean to.[1]

The other decisions I mentioned were how many chords the music should be segmented into and what they are. The opening of the

---

[1] When keys are not clear – at the beginning of a piece, in a transition or a development – you may want to segment the music into chords without assigning them a specific tonal function. In such cases you can simply call them D♭ chords, A♭ chords and so on – or better still, use pop music notation (in which D♭/F means a D♭ triad in first inversion, D♭/B♭ means a D♭ triad over a B♭ bass, and so on). If you begin by doing this, you can always add a Roman-letter interpretation at a later stage. It is better to say too little than too much about harmonic functions.

Fig. 5 Beethoven, *Pathétique* Sonata, I, bars 1–10

'Waldstein' presents no difficulties as regards these decisions, so we shall use the slow introduction of the *Pathétique* Sonata for illustration (Fig. 5). This time deciding on the key is easy (it is C minor), but which chords do we label? The thing not to do is to label every chord as it comes – for example, saying that the first bar consists of two I chords followed by a V_4^6,[1] followed by another I, followed by a . . . well, what is the next chord? It's a diminished seventh: how do we analyze that in relation to the tonic? The usual way would be to say that it is functioning as a kind of V^9 of V, that is to say as a variety of D chord. But try playing it as a D chord, replacing the $E^\flat$ with a D, and you'll find the effect of the music is quite spoilt. On the other hand if you replace the diminished chord with a I_4^6 (play a G in the left hand), you will find the music works much better. Why is this? It's because the diminished chord is not really a structural chord at all. It is a multiple-appoggiatura formation leading to the V with which the phrase ends; that is why it is perfectly all right to replace it with a I_4^6 (which is in essence just a double appoggiatura to V). However, if you change it to a V of V you get an extra chord that sounds structural and it is this that clogs the harmonic motion. And if you insist on applying some harmonic label to the diminished chord, then it will be this clogged version of the music you are talking about, not Beethoven's. This is the analytical equivalent of playing the music in rock piano style, placing an equal emphasis on each chord one after another: it shows the same lack of musical understanding.

Tangles like this inevitably arise if you try to go into too much detail using Roman letters. If you parse everything harmonically, you end up with an imposing series of labels but no clear idea of how the music works; and an analysis that does not simplify the music for you is really a complete waste of time. After all, there is no virtue in reduction as such: only in the kind of reduction that makes something intelligible to you that wasn't otherwise. But how can Roman letters be used to clarify the introduction to the *Pathétique*? The answer is that you have to step back from the music and take each phrase as a whole, rather than starting at the beginning and handing out labels one by one till you get

---

[1] People quite often combine Roman letters and figured bass numbers like this, either to indicate inversions (as here) or to notate chords containing dissonances (II^7, V^9). This is handy but you have to watch for confusions. For instance, in V_4^6 the 6 and 4 are being measured in relation to the *actual* bass, D; on the other hand people will refer to a dominant seventh G as V^7 even when it is in first inversion, so here the 7 is being measured against the *fundamental* bass (G).

to the end. Instead, ask yourself where each phrase goes from and to: in other words, look at the cadential structure. The first two phrases (bars 1–2) form a pair, going from I to V and back to I. The third phrase (bars 3–4) looks to be going to V but sidesteps and cadences with a II–V–I pattern onto III, the relative major. The music returns to the tonic minor, first with an interrupted cadence (bar 9) and then with a II⁷–V–I cadence whose final chord is the beginning of the Allegro (bar 11).

We do at least have an analysis now. We have said that certain chords are essential, and we have omitted everything else as being not so essential. For example, we have omitted the emphatic chords that straddle bars 6 and 7, and this is absolutely correct because these chords actually have no harmonic function at all. Play them and ask yourself where the music is going. You will find that they do not imply any definite cadential movement. They are enclosed within a sustained block of diminished seventh harmony lasting from the last beat of bar 5 to the second beat of bar 8; they don't form part of any larger progression. So omitting them in itself represents an analytical insight. But it is a negative one: can't we say anything more positive about these chords? The answer is no, not if we are going to stick to Roman-letter analysis. And the reason for this is that these chords have a linear rather than a harmonic function. Look at the bass in bars 5–7: the chords form part of a consistent stepwise fall (we can ignore the changes in register for now). Look at the top line: the chords form part of a line that rises, with a wave-like sequential motion, all the way from the F of bar 5 to the high F of bar 9. If you want to get a more detailed understanding of the music's harmonic structure, then you have to consider its linear patterns: and you can't do this if you reduce everything to harmonic symbols. What is required is some kind of analytical equivalent of a short score.

Now there was a final approach to the content of musical compositions which was not in itself an analytical method as such, but which greatly influenced the thinking of analysts round 1900 – and especially when they were dealing with the relationship between harmony and line. This was Fuxian (or species) counterpoint, a full explanation of which is outside the scope of this book. But it is worth making a few observations about it which are relevant to the way in which harmonic analysis developed in the twentieth century. It was a system of compositional training, and it took the form of a series of exercises. The simpler exercises consisted of purely consonant formations – two or more lines of music moving at the same speed and with only consonant intervals (such as the octave, perfect fifth and third) between them. In more advanced exercises the lines moved at different speeds and dissonances were allowed between them; but each dissonance had to be carefully 'prepared' by stating one of its notes as a consonance beforehand, and by resolving the dissonant note by step. From the analytical point of view, the implication of this was that dissonant formations could be seen as linear elaborations of underlying consonances, or, more generally, that complex harmonic formations could be seen as linear elaborations of simpler harmonic formations; Fig. 6 illustrates this. But Fuxian principles were only concerned with the handling of immediate successions from one note to the next. Large-scale harmonic and linear relationships could neither be taught nor understood in terms of strict counterpoint; traditionally, therefore, they were considered to be aspects of 'free composition', and governed solely by the composer's artistry and taste. This is why it was in a book of that otherwise curious title that Heinrich Schenker presented a means of combining harmonic analysis with the principles of strict counterpoint in such a way as to overcome the limitations of each, and so show that even artistry and taste were not wholly inaccessible to rational explanation.

Fig. 6

consonant basis:

CHAPTER TWO

SCHENKERIAN ANALYSIS

I

'Schenkerian analysis' is something of an umbrella term. In the first place it includes Schenker's own analytical techniques, notations and theories. These were developed in Germany in the years before the Second World War, and were in a state of constant evolution; so talking about 'Schenker analysis' does not mean too much unless you specify which stage of this evolution you mean. But in general when people speak not of 'Schenker analysis' but of 'Schenkerian analysis' they don't so much mean Schenker's own work as the application of his ideas in post-war America. This has become rather more standardized in its techniques and terminology than Schenker's own analyses ever were, and technically speaking it derives from the final stage of Schenker's work, and in particular from his last analytical book, *Free Composition*;[1] though it is worth adding that, apart from a few of Schenker's own pupils, the American exponents of Schenkerian analysis have chosen to ignore the psychological and metaphysical foundation for his theories which Schenker also presented in that book. The third and last body of work that might be referred to as 'Schenkerian analysis' is a further American development, in which the aim has been to develop a new theoretical foundation for Schenkerian analysis and to generalize his techniques on this basis; however this movement is generally known as 'neo-Schenkerism', and it will be considered briefly in Chapter 4. So it is the first two categories of Schenkerian analysis that we are concerned with in this chapter – the work of Schenker himself, of his pupils, such as Oswald Jonas and Ernst Oster, and of contemporary practitioners such as Allen Forte and John Rothgeb.

[1] English trans., Longman, 1979.

There are various ways in which Schenkerian analysis can be approached. Schenker himself, followed by Jonas, introduced it by first describing what he saw as the essential structures of music – the triad and its linear unfolding through arpeggiation, and through passing and auxiliary notes – in their most abstract form, and only then going on to discuss the forms which these structures might take in any actual musical context. In their *Introduction to Schenkerian Analysis*,[1] Allen Forte and Steven Gilbert did the opposite: they began by illustrating specific occurrences of arpeggiation, passing notes and so on at the note-to-note level, before going on to show how such formations can be used in more abstract ways to create large-scale musical forms. But one of the best ways to understand any analytical approach is in terms of what it aims to do – that is to say, by considering what kind of questions it sets out to answer. And this is a particularly appropriate approach to Schenkerian analysis since it is very easy to miss the point of it; for example, by producing graphs that look like Schenkerian analysis but do not, in fact, answer Schenkerian questions. What, then, are the aims of Schenkerian analysis? In a general way, of course, it aims to omit inessentials and to highlight important relationships; but then that is equally the aim of Roman-letter analysis. It is easiest to understand the particular way in which Schenkerian analysis sets about doing this if we compare it with an example where Roman-letter analalysis is clearly inadequate; this will let us see how Schenkerian analysis develops out of commonsense attempts to remedy these inadequacies.

Bach's C major Prelude from Book I of the *Well-Tempered Clavier* (Fig. 7) has no marked dynamics, no rhythmic change, no thematic, textural or timbral variation. Nor does it have a tune you could easily whistle. By a process of elimination, then, we can say that its structure as a piece of music must be principally harmonic. And since it merely consists of an arpeggiated series of chords, it is in a sense very easy to analyze harmonically. Fig. 8 shows two alternative notations for the first 19 bars: each accounts for every note in the music. And yet what do these harmonic labels actually tell us that we didn't know already? The second set of labels at least reveals something about the restricted range of functional relations between chords that wasn't obvious at first sight, as well as highlighting some harmonic sequences; but no Roman-letter analysis can adequately explain the sense one has in listening to the music that there's a continuous and measured harmonic evolution through the piece. By this I mean that each chord does not seem to

---

[1] Norton, 1982.

depend just on the previous chord (which is the maximum range of traditional contrapuntal theory), nor even on the previous group of chords (as in a hierarchical Roman-letter analysis); instead it is experienced as a part of a larger motion *towards* some future harmonic goal. It doesn't require any very special analytical techniques to show this; all we need do is ask 'how are the progressions directed towards a goal', and since the main goal is the end of the piece it is convenient to work backwards in looking for an answer. The piece ends, as it began, on a C major chord. Where does this final chord begin? If you looked just at the bass, you might say in bar 32; but though the final C pedal begins here and is clearly heard as tonic, the sense of harmonic resolution is deflected by the B♭ – a secondary dominant of F, which is only neutralized at bar 34. Furthermore there is obviously something cadential about the change of register at 34; it is at this point that there is a sense of formal finality, rather than merely of arrival on the tonic. So we already have the impression that something more than straightforward harmonic function is involved in creating the sense of an ending in this piece, so that the factors which bring about the sense of an ending can be staggered in relation to each other.

Fig. 7 J. S. Bach, C major Prelude

Fig. 8 Two Roman-letter analyses of the C major Prelude, bars 1–19

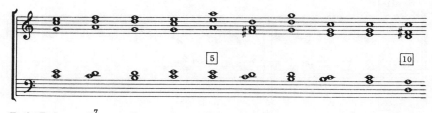

(Tonic) T: I — II⁷ — V — I — VI
         (Dominant) D: IV — II — V⁷ — I — IV⁷ — II⁷ — V —

I — II⁷ — V — I — V (II — V⁷) — IV (II — V⁷) — V (II⁷ — V⁷–

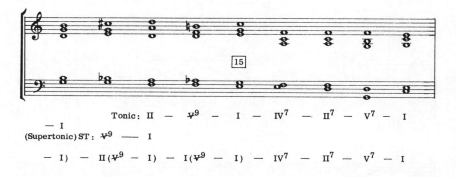

  — I
        Tonic: II — V⁹ — I — IV⁷ — II⁷ — V⁷ — I
(Supertonic) ST: V⁹ — I

  — I) — II (V⁹ — I) — I (V⁹ — I) — IV⁷ — II⁷ — V⁷ — I

What sort of cadence is there onto the final chord? Clearly the answer is a V-I – both immediately (at bar 34, superimposed on the C pedal) and in terms of the larger G pedal (bars 24–31) which resolves onto the C pedal. But is this G pedal felt to be a V (and hence a penultimate chord in terms of large scale harmonic relations) from its beginning? The answer to this is clearly yes: there is an expectation of the arrival of the final tonic from bar 24 onwards even though it does not actually arrive for another ten or so bars; if it were not for such an expectation, the pedal would seem unmotivated and the apparently rambling succession of Is and Vs superimposed on it even more so. All through this passage the tonic is implied but delayed: so you can say that it is at bar 24 that the piece begins to end.

If we have located the final V-I, in the sense of quite extended passages which are based on these harmonic functions, can we now work back further and decide where, in terms of large-scale harmonic structure, we quitted the initial I? In other words, can we say where the beginning of the piece ended? Working backwards, the first C chord we come to is at bar 19. First we need to ask whether this is a I of C or whether we are in some other key; the answer is, of course, that we are in C here, and this is clear because the added B♭ in the following bar is sensed as altering the harmonic function (in a way that the addition of a seventh to a V is not), as well as because of the strong II-V-I cadence that precedes it. Secondly, we need to ask whether this C chord is in effect continuous with the tonic chord with which the piece began, or whether it constitutes a *return* to it in contrast to intervening harmonies or keys. Here the important point to grasp is that no other harmony or key has been established in any structural manner during the preceding eighteen bars; there have been dominant and other colorations (mainly enclosed within harmonic sequences) but never has there been any sense of a structural, section-defining cadence. Even the II-V-I cadence in G at bar 11 – which rhymes with the one at bar 19 – is not a true modulation because it receives no support from the musical surface (nothing happens) or from the bars that follow it, which immediately go back to C-based harmonies. This is quite different from bars 19–20, where the retention of the C-based harmony for a second bar (it is the first time the same harmony has lasted for two bars) creates a kind of formal jolt – it feels as if one phase in the music has ended and another one is beginning. In an important sense, then, the influence of the opening tonic has been felt throughout this entire passage, so that the whole of bars 1–19 is like an expanded version of bars 1–4; or if you like you could simply say that bars 1–19 represent an expansion of the opening tonic itself. And this sense of there being a direct structural identity between bars 1 and 19 (such that the intervening bars can be discounted as an enclosed harmonic circuit) is greatly increased by the identity of the two bars apart from the octave transposition – just the sort of surface confirmation of a structural relationship that was absent at bar 11.

So far, then, we have reduced the essential harmonic content of the piece to the following:

Fig. 9

Bar 1   20   24   –   35
  I   ⟶   〰〰〰   V   –   I

Each of these sections has a single overall harmonic function, with the sole exception of bars 20–3. Harmonically, the entire evolution of the piece – from its beginning, which lasts up to bar 19, to its end which begins at bar 24 – lies in these four bars; and, as might be expected from this, they are the most intense bars of the piece, both polyphonically and harmonically. There is, for instance, the 'difficult' bass progression F# - A♭ of bars 22–3 ('difficult' because the notes are not related directly to each other but only indirectly through G),[1] and the abandonment for the first time at 23 of the arpeggio figuration, the result of which is an ambiguous harmonic formation. Furthermore bar 21 has a very emphatic effect, and this is not only because of the F/E discord (which is magnified by the F being in octaves and in a low register) but also because the F functions as a direct antecedent of the G at 24: bars 22–3 can in fact be literally 'bracketed out' without the harmonic continuity from 21 to 24 being affected (try playing directly from bar 21 to bar 24). Since the V[7] of F at bar 20 is simply a preparation for the F[7] chord at 21, we can rewrite Fig. 9 in the following way:

Fig. 10

```
Bar 1                          20      24      35
   I    ————————————→          IV⁷  –  V   –   I
```

And the effect of 'clinching' the harmonic progression of the piece which the IV at bar 21 creates can now be explained by its being the first structural departure from I in the course of the piece.

II

What I have said up to now is not a Schenkerian analysis: it is simply an attempt to answer the question 'how are the progressions directed towards a goal?' by describing the way in which they are experienced. It is this, and not the application of any analytical technique as such, that has allowed us to distinguish certain passages as moving towards a goal and others as tonally enclosed. Schenkerian analysis is a technique for

---

[1] Some players interpolate a bar of C minor$^6_4$ between bars 22 and 23. The effect is anodyne.

answering the same question in a much more specific and clearly demonstrable manner, and which is particularly designed to show the special importance that large-scale linear formations have in the creation of directed motion towards harmonic goals. At this point we can turn to Schenker's graphic analysis of this piece (Fig. 11),[1] which consists of three graphs aligned with each other so that the same point in each chart, working from left to right, represents the same point in the musical process (though the barlines are marked only in the bottom, and most detailed, graph). The middle graph shows the same structural chords that we reached by commonsense means (I–IV⁷–V–I) with the addition of a II – this chord, along with the IV, being omitted in the top graph which is intended to show only the most essential progression of the piece as a whole. In both the top two graphs the chords are written out in full as notes (note the difference in register between them, which I will come back to later) so that the Roman letters merely reduplicate the information for the sake of clarity. In marking these chords with Roman letters, and no others, Schenker is making an important negative point – that apart from these chords, everything in the piece is to be explained in terms of the motion of contrapuntal lines. These contrapuntal lines happen to create a series of disjunct chords in this particular piece, but Schenker is saying that these have no structural significance as harmonic units in the way the I–IV⁷–II–V–I do; structurally speaking, they might equally well have been staggered with each other to produce a more obviously contrapuntal surface.

If for the time being we think of the chord series I–IV⁷–II–V–I as being the central structural formation of the music, we can see the graph as showing the operation of linear processes in two areas on either side of this chord progression.

In the first place, we have the bottom graph. This is here marked 'comprehensive foreground graph' (*Urlinie Tafel*), but it is usually simply referred to as the 'foreground' (*Vordergrund*). It closely resembles the musical score, with the removal of only the arpeggio figuration;[2] and if we compare it with the middle graph (here marked 'structural

---

[1] From Schenker, *Five Graphic Analyses*, Dover, 1969. These graphs were actually the work of Schenker's students and were edited by Felix Salzer, but they were prepared under Schenker's close supervision and I am treating them as representative of Schenker's own work. I have translated the verbal annotations into English, in accordance with Salzer's glossary. I have also rescaled the graphs of *Ich bin's, ich sollte büssen* (Figure 15) so that the foreground graph is aligned with the others.

[2] The apparent discrepancy at bar 30, where the inner voice has a G in the score but an A in Schenker's analytical graph, is clearly a misprint; I have corrected it.

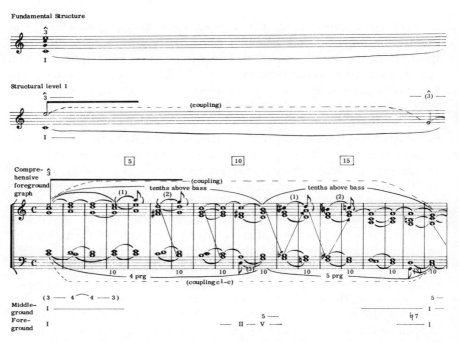

Fig. 11   Schenker, analysis of the C major Prelude

level 1' but generally known as the 'middleground') we can see how
the structural harmonies of the latter are elaborated in the foreground
by the motion of textural lines which either connect the notes of the
structural chords with one another or circle around them, and which
move in the mainly conjunct manner of Fuxian counterpoint. Thus in
bars 1–19 there is an overall descent in all parts, so that each mainly
consists of a continuous scalar motion though there are some minor
reversals of direction; in bars 24–32, however, there is an arch-like
shape in the upper lines over mainly static formations in the others.
Such basically conjunct motions connecting or encircling the notes of
the structural harmonies are rather similar to the sort of patterns that
baroque performers used to embellish a melody, and the arch-like
shape of 24–32 is not unlike a soloist's cadenza. Schenkerian analysis is
in fact a kind of metaphor according to which a composition is seen as
the large-scale embellishment of a simple underlying harmonic progression, or even as a massively-expanded cadence; a metaphor
according to which the same analytical principles that apply to
cadences in strict counterpoint can be applied, *mutatis mutandis*, to the
large-scale harmonic structures of complete pieces.

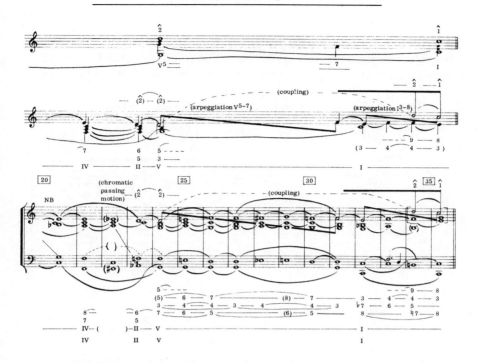

N. B. Bach's original notation of the bass in the autograph.

These linear motions are most coherent in the outer parts; there are some parallel octaves or intervallic non-sequiturs in the inner parts, indicating that they are at least partly functioning as harmonic filler (for example, where does the A in bar 16 come from?), and for this reason it is easier to see the important linear motions if we omit these inner parts and concentrate only on the outer ones. This is what Forte and Gilbert's graph of the same piece does (Fig. 12); it comes somewhere between Schenker's foreground and middleground graphs and makes a useful comparison with them. However, it is important to notice that the upper line of each graph – the top line of unfilled noteheads in Schenker's graph, and the top line of tailed notes in Forte and Gilbert's – is not identical with the top line of Bach's score. In particular, the top line of the score at bars 5, 7, and 12–15 is shown in both graphs as a subordinate formation to the main conjunct descent of the upper structural line – that is, it is being regarded as a purely local formation which fulfils a kind of motivic role within a series of sequences but has no larger significance (the same applies to the D and G in the bass at bars 10 and 18, which are seen as simply a harmonic support to the G and C that follow them).

Fig. 12   Forte and Gilbert, analysis of the C major Prelude

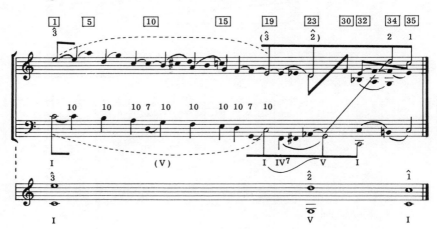

So much for the linear motion elaborating the structural harmonic progression I-IV⁷-II-V-I. At the other extreme, the background (marked 'fundamental structure' or *Ursatz* in Fig. 11) shows this harmonic progression to be itself linear in origin; it is contained within the conjunct descent of the upper line, which itself consists only of the harmonic functions I and V but which is elaborated to give the structural chord progression shown in the middleground. As in the foreground graph, it is the outer lines which are regarded as the most important (hence both Schenker and Forte mark them by unfilled noteheads); and the elaboration again follows the principles of Fuxian voice-leading, which Schenker considered to be even more important in the background than they are in the foreground. Because the structural chord progression is itself the outcome of a linear process, it is important to realize that it is not simply a succession of harmonic functions or (what comes to the same thing) a series of chordal roots that is being elaborated at foreground level; it is a series of *notes*, at specific registers and in specific linear relations with each other, that constitutes the structural harmonic progression. Schenker's use of the term 'fundamental structure' for the background progression avoids viewing it as either simply linear or simply harmonic: instead it is a conjunction of the two. For this reason any linear motion in a Schenkerian analysis that doesn't form part of a harmonic aggregate cannot be considered as of genuinely structural significance.

III

This much is comprehensible simply from examining Schenker's graphs, without calling for any special technical knowledge of Schenkerian analysis. However at this point questions arise which can not be answered without some consideration of the theory behind what Schenker is doing. For instance, why is the first note of the upper line in the background and middleground graphs an E? Simply because it is the highest note of the first bar of the piece, falls on a relatively accented beat in the arpeggiation pattern, and is equally prominent at bar 4? The answer is no, and the reason is that there is an essential difference between the lines of the musical surface and the structural voices which are shown in a Schenkerian analysis.[1] As I said, the basis of a Schenkerian analysis is seeing music as directed motion in time, and for Schenker this was tied up with an almost metaphysical conception of music being a temporal unfolding of the overtone series which exists as a simultaneity in all natural sounds. More specifically, Schenker saw music as the temporal unfolding, or *prolongation*, of the major triad – the 'chord of nature', as he called it, since it exists as the first five partials of the overtone series, and which Schenker therefore saw as a specially privileged formation and indeed at the point of junction between what exists in nature as a simultaneity and what exists in art as a temporal process.[2] Any analysis by Schenker is intended to show how the music

[1] 'Voice' and 'line' are not technical terms here: but I shall distinguish them in this way for the next few pages for the sake of clarity. However there are many technical terms in Schenkerian analysis – that is, terms which have a non-obvious but generally accepted meaning – and these are italicized whenever they occur. The German terms and their English (or rather, American) equivalents are not always used in quite the same way, and this can create minor confusions.

[2] Actually this metaphysics is highly questionable (why only the first five partials? What is the relevance of the overtone series anyhow?) and few people today take it seriously, or the problems it poses and which greatly exercised Schenker's and his contemporaries' minds: problems such as how to explain the minor triad which is not found in the overtone series and hence has to be seen as an artificial 'copy' of it. But I don't think one can understand why Schenker did what he did without taking this metaphysics into consideration; in particular, it explains otherwise arbitrary prejudices and restrictions in his analytical techniques.

in question is derived by means of elaboration from its tonic triad, which is its ultimate Schenkerian background.

However the major triad is in itself static; and as the art of music is essentially temporal, the most background formation from which any composition can be directly derived is the triad in motion. And for Schenker the triad in motion meant an upper voice which fell in a conjunct diatonic progression from any note of the triad to the tonic, coupled with a progression in the lower voice which would support the upper voice through the creation of root position triadic harmonies[1] and specifically a V coinciding with the $\hat{2}$ in the upper voice (the notation $\hat{2}$, $\hat{1}$ and so on refers to linear scale degrees in the upper voice, in contrast to Roman letters which indicate harmonic functions supported by the lower voice). This meant that the *fundamental structure* of any tonal piece could be categorized as one of three possible patterns, in which the descent of the upper line begins on $\hat{8}$, $\hat{5}$ and $\hat{3}$ respectively (Fig. 13)[2]; note that in each case the descent of the upper line takes place within a single octave. Any other progression, such as the I-IV[7]-II-V-I of the C major Prelude, is not properly speaking a background structure but lies somewhere in between the background and the foreground; it is primarily the result of a linear elaboration of the lower voice of the fundamental structure. Such an elaboration often takes the form of an arpeggiation in which III is inserted between I and V (in this case the lower voice is termed a *bass arpeggiation*), but it may also take the form of other linear motions enclosed within a single octave; of these the I-IV-V-I outlined by the bass of the C major Prelude is the most common.[3] Although I have been referring to the middleground harmonic formation of the C major Prelude as a 'structural progression', there is not anything absolute about this: I simply mean that it is more structural than other formations. The only absolute is the fundamental structure shown in its three possible forms in Fig. 13, and for this reason it is worth observing

[1] 'Triadic' is to be taken literally here: Schenker would not admit of other formations, such as seventh or ninth chords, being part of the fundamental structure. He regarded them as always linear derivatives of the fundamental structure – as in the IV[7] of the Bach C major Prelude, which is to be found in the middleground but not the background graph.

[2] *Free Composition*, figs. 9, 10(a) and 11(a).

[3] Schenker published an exhaustive list of the possible forms of middleground bass arpeggiations, and of the possible results of these in conjunction with fundamental lines beginning on $\hat{3}$, $\hat{5}$ and $\hat{8}$: *Free Composition* figs. 14, 15, 16 and 18 respectively. Confusingly, the term 'bass arpeggiation' is also sometimes used for the lower voice of the fundamental structure proper – the I-V-I of the background being regarded as an incomplete arpeggiation.

Schenker's terminology for it carefully – *fundamental structure* or *Ursatz* for the structure as a whole, and *fundamental line* or *Urlinie* for the descending upper voice.

Fig. 13   The three forms of the fundamental structure

Now, it is obvious that the fundamental structure is an abstraction far removed from the listener's experience of any given piece – especially since each form of the fundamental structure is shared between many thousands of different tonal pieces. In fact the fundamental structure is analytically meaningless in itself and to do Schenkerian analysis does not mean claiming that people actually hear fundamental structures when they listen to music; rather the aim is to show *how* people listen to music. Hence the fundamental structure becomes meaningful only in its relationship to a specific composition: it reveals the pattern of elaboration in which the music's unique qualities lie. Accordingly the analysis proper takes place in the middleground, or series of middlegrounds, that show the relationship between foreground and background; for this reason there is little value in presenting a background graph on its own, without the middleground graphs that give it content and make its interpretation convincing or unconvincing. In other words Schenkerian analysis consists of inter-relating the actual foreground lines of the music – which may be continuous or discontinuous, directed or meandering, chromatic or diatonic, and which may shift between registers – with the imaginary voices of the background, which are by definition continuous, directed, diatonic, and do not shift registers. All the symbols used in Schenkerian graphs serve to distinguish between structural and non-structural formations, and to show how surface discontinuities of pitch, register or texture elaborate the continuous, directed motions of the fundamental structure. Almost all the mistakes that can be made in Schenkerian analysis arise out of confusing foreground lines and structural voices with each other.

IV

As illustration of this requires detailed examination of Schenker's graphs, it is necessary at this point to explain the special conventions Schenker uses in them. I have already commented on the most obvious fact about a Schenkerian analysis, which is that it consists of a number of graphs aligned with each other (though, for reasons of economy, background graphs, being much less dense, are sometimes presented separately): the background graph, which in theory consists only of the fundamental structure, but sometimes includes the most important middleground elements too; the foreground graph, which approaches the musical score, though the exact extent of this approximation varies according to the nature of the individual piece and the comprehensiveness of the analysis; and between these extremes one or more middleground graphs, their number again varying from case to case. The use of the horizontal format is helpful in making large-scale connections easy to see at a glance; most analysts stick sheets of manuscript paper together.

The other immediately obvious feature of a Schenkerian graph is the use of the symbols that conventionally distinguish rhythmic values to distinguish degrees of structural importance instead. (This is possible because Schenkerian graphs do not show rhythmic values – though, as will become clear later, they do not ignore them either.) *Unfilled noteheads* are normally reserved for the fundamental progression, which may be made clearer through the addition of tails and beams – though registral shifts, which do not properly belong to the fundamental progression at all, may sometimes be shown, as in Schenker's middleground graph of the C major Prelude or Forte's more detailed graph of it.[1] *Filled noteheads with tails*, like crotchets, indicate middleground structures, and connections between them can be seen by following the line of the tails. (This is different from the way in which single quaver tails are used: they are merely there to bring a particular note into prominence for any reason, and Schenker also used exclamation marks and 'NB' signs for the same purpose.) *Filled noteheads without tails* indicate foreground formations, and connections between them are shown by the use of slurs or phrase-marks, which may be dotted when the connection is an indirect one (such as returning to a

---

[1] The liberal use of unfilled noteheads in Schenker's foreground graph is unusual. Forte and Gilbert's analysis is more typical. For convenience I shall simply refer to it as Forte's.

note previously quitted). There is a rather subtle difference between the conventional use of phrase marks and the Schenkerian one, in that whereas conventionally they show what goes *to* what (for instance a V resolving to I) in Schenkerian analysis they invariably show what goes *with* what[1] – which generally means the linear elaboration of a single harmonic unit. Such a slurred elaboration is frequently subdivided into smaller slurred units, normally corresponding to consistent moves in one direction; these consistent linear motions are termed *linear progressions*.[2] The combination of these different rhythmic symbols in a single graph means that, apart from the occasional discrepancies between levels that result from registral change and temporal displacement, it would in theory be possible for one graph to show everything from foreground to background. But this would be too cluttered for easy reading, which is why several aligned graphs are generally used. And this means that it is not necessary to distinguish all levels on a foreground graph where doing so would result in excessive complexity.

Three further symbols are used to indicate connections between notes. The first is a straight diagonal line, which is used to indicate any kind of relationship between notes which are separated in time but which are to be understood as belonging to the same harmonic unit. An example is bars 6–9 of the C major Prelude; here the diagonal lines show parts moving in parallel motion elaborated by a suspension (where Schenker merely wishes to indicate parallel motion he uses figures, such as the 10s at bars 4, 7, 9 and 11). The other two arise from discrepancies between foreground lines and structural voices. Of these one is the straight diagonal line with an arrowhead; this indicates that a structural

[1] Instructor's Manual to Forte and Gilbert, p. 10.

[2] The use of this concept is unfortunately complicated by the differences between a linear progression in the bass and one in the upper parts. In either case the linear progression is linearly motivated – thus it rises or falls continuously, without changing direction – but whereas when it occurs in the upper parts it connects two notes which both belong to the harmony on which it ends (so that it can be thought of as an anticipatory prolongation of that harmony), when it occurs in the bass the final harmony is often incompatible with the first note of the linear progression. Bars 1–11 of the C major Prelude illustrate the normal way this occurs – the bass falling a fourth from I to V. Where they are extended, as here, or of some motivic significance linear progressions may be marked '4 prg', '5 prg' and so on (4-zug, 5-zug in German). The whole issue of linear progressions, as also of unfoldings which they sometimes resemble (see below) is intricate; Forte and Gilbert attempt a rationale in Chapters 19–20 of their book. But the most instructive course is to examine Schenker's phrase-marks in detail, as for instance in *Ich bin's, ich sollte büssen* (Fig. 15).

voice is passing from one foreground line to another, usually in association with a change of register as at bars 11–15. A special case of this is where two structural voices exchange positions; this is shown by a crossed pair of arrows and known as *voice exchange*. The other is the diagonal beam that connects the tails of two notes from different directions, as at bars 24–31 and 32–5 of both Schenker's and Forte's graphs of the C major Prelude; this indicates that a single foreground line is connecting two structural voices and is known as an *unfolding*. Thus in bars 24–32 of the C major Prelude Schenker is deriving the arch shape of the upper line from two sources: the D at bar 24 is a transference of the upper structural line (see the background graph), and the G and F at 29–31 come from an inner structural line, while the rising E, F and F♯ are purely foreground phenomena.[1]

What has been described up to here – notehead, tail, beam, slur with or without arrowhead, and diagonal line – is a nearly comprehensive list of the symbols used to show connectedness in Schenkerian graphs,[2] and once the conventions governing their use are understood it is possible to understand a Schenkerian analysis without any textual explanation. Nevertheless there is a permissible range of variance in Schenkerian graphs; this is shown by the comparison between Schenker's and Forte's graphs of the C major Prelude, which represent virtually identical analytical interpretations.[3] Forte's graph is more typical of Schenkerian practice as a whole, in that no notes are shown unless some symbol makes an explicit connection between that note and one or more others; after all, it could be argued, what's the point of showing a note but not its function in an analytical graph? This is a good principle in the presentation of a completed analysis. However when one is actually making an analysis it is often useful to put notes in without immediately committing oneself to a definite analytical inter-

---

[1] Some simpler examples of unfolding can be seen in Schenker's graph of *Ich bin's, ich sollte büssen*, where a comparison of the second and third structural levels shows how the unfoldings are a linear statement of notes which belong to a single harmonic formation; this is part of the definition of an unfolding, and unfoldings generally occur in groups between which consistent voice-leading relationships hold, rather in the manner of chains of suspensions.

[2] A few more will be encountered later in this chapter. There is a convenient glossary of Schenkerian graphic symbols in *The Music Forum*, Vol. 1, 1967, while *Five Graphic Analyses* contains a glossary of the German terms Schenker used in his graphs together with English translations.

[3] For a rather different graphic presentation of what is essentially the same analysis, see p. 263 of *A Generative Theory of Tonal Music* by Fred Lerdahl and Ray Jackendoff (MIT, 1983).

pretation, or simply to add tails, slurs and other markings to a performance score or a straight harmonic reduction; so that Schenker's graph, while not perhaps ideal as a completed analysis, is a good model for the analytical process.

V

We can now complete our examination of Schenker's analysis of the C major Prelude. Three points remain outstanding; all of them refer in different ways to the relationship between foreground and background. The first is the question posed some way back but not yet answered: how do we know that the first note of the fundamental line (this is referred to as the *primary tone*) is an E, and not (as it might equally have been) a G or a C? As we now know, structural voices and foreground lines are quite different things; the facts that the E is at the top of the texture and that it continues in prominence through bar 4 are facts about the foreground lines and, while they lend some weight to the interpretation of the E as the primary tone, they are by no means conclusive.[1] There is in fact no way in which an examination of the first bar by itself, or even of the first four bars by themselves, can prove what the primary tone is. The reason is that it is the fundamental line as a whole that defines the primary tone as such. Therefore the best procedure, both in making a Schenkerian analysis and in reading one, is to work backwards from the final note of the fundamental line – which must by definition be the tonic – and establish the successive stages in the descent of the fundamental line in accordance with the bass arpeggiation: in other words, in accordance with the structural harmonic progression of the music. As I said before, fundamental lines and structural harmonic progressions are mutually definitive: a structural harmony coincides with a fall in the fundamental line and a fall in the fundamental line must be supported by a consistent harmonic foundation.

The second point that remains outstanding concerns bar 22, where the bracket in the slurs and the absence of any harmonic notation

---

[1] See Forte and Gilbert, p. 178 ff, where the authors discuss problems in identifying primary tones in chorale-based textures. In practice $\hat{3}$ is a much more common primary tone that $\hat{5}$ or $\hat{8}$. But for this reason it is too easy to start in all instances from the presupposition that the primary tone will be $\hat{3}$; it is almost better to try the others first and be forced to the conclusion that it must be $\hat{3}$.

indicate that Schenker regards the F♯ in the bass as an interpolation, rather than as being part of the middleground, semi-structural voice which the bass otherwise represents. His argument is that the E♭ in the upper voice is merely a chromatic passing tone (as he indicates), and that the F♯ in the bass is no more than a harmonic support for this passing tone. The real progression, as his brackets indicate, goes directly from bars 21 to 23. (Compare this with our intuitive conclusions about it!) Actually the little diagram marked 'NB' tells us the real reason for this fuss. Schenker was uncomfortably aware of the lack of documentary evidence that the composers of the past were in any way familiar with the principles of fundamental structure and prolongation. He was therefore always looking for corroboration of his theories in composers' manuscripts. The direction in which Bach tailed his bass notes at this point happens to be consistent with Schenker's argument about the F♯ being a structural interpolation, and this leads Schenker to call Bach's tailing 'an unusually bold notation' which 'very successfully indicates the true meaning of the voice leading'.[1] I imagine it is this consideration which leads Schenker to emphasize the continuity between bars 21 and 23 by adding the II chord in the middleground, a harmony which is both unnecessary (because the progression IV^7-V-I is by itself strongly directed) and problematical (because a chromatic seventh chord is an unlikely formation to find in the middleground). Forte and Gilbert wisely omit the II chord altogether in their graph.

The final point that remains outstanding has to do with register. Intuitively it is obvious – in fact we commented upon it – that the unexpected rise of register in the final two bars contributes greatly to the finality of the ending by establishing a close link with the register of the opening. Schenker marks the fall of the upper part from E to E in bars 1–19, and its corresponding rise from D to D in bars 24–34, by a dotted slur and the word '*coupling*' – which is a technical term meaning the registral transfer of a note of the fundamental line or bass arpeggiation. Schenker's purpose in doing this is not, as might appear, simply descriptive. You may remember that the motion of both the fundamental line and the bass arpeggiation took place within the maximum range of an octave. This 'rule' of Schenkerian analysis – which is probably to be explained by the analogy with the overtone series – means that the fundamental motion must take place at a single register throughout the piece: this is called the principle of *obligatory register*. But of course it frequently happens, as here, that the notes of the fundamental line do not all appear at the same register in the actual music. Therefore such deviations have to be explained as registral transfers. Since

---

[1] *Five Graphic Analyses*, p. 9.

the Prelude begins and ends at the higher register this is assumed to be the structural register and the lower octave at which the $\hat{2}$ appears is assumed to be the displacement; this is what Schenker's 'couplings' are intended to indicate. In fact this Prelude is frequently quoted by Schenkerians as the classic instance of obligatory register; Schenker's pupil Ernst Oster described the way it returns to the upper octave at the end as a 'magnificent confirmation' of the principle. But if the Prelude had ended at the lower octave, then the beginning would have been regarded as registral displacement and the E at bar 19 as the primary tone proper; so the principle would still hold (and in fact there is an earlier version of this Prelude in which it finishes at the lower octave[1]). It is difficult to see quite what evidence would suffice to refute the principle of obligatory register; evidently not the fact that the bass line actually descends through two octaves, which seems to me to contribute to the effect of finality just as much as does the ascent of the upper line to its original register. In fact the registration of bass arpeggiations seems to be a matter of much greater indifference to Schenkerian analysts than that of fundamental lines; I do not know what theoretical justification might be offered for this.

VI

In Bach's C major Prelude there is a fairly direct link between the foreground lines and the structural voices. This is in part because of the texture, which is essentially that of a chorale with figuration; but it is also because the music is absolutely through-composed, without any surface articulation into semi-independent sections. For this reason the main function of a Schenkerian analysis of the C major Prelude is to

[1] See Oster's 'Register and the large-scale connection', in Maury Yeston (ed.), *Readings in Schenker Analysis and other approaches*, Yale University Press, 1977, pp. 55–6. Oster argues that the validity of obligatory register is shown by Bach's revising the earlier version (from the Friedemann *Klavierbüchlein*) in accordance with it: implying that the final version of a work is the most significant, because it is the most highly developed from an aesthetic point of view. On the other hand you might equally argue that the initial versions of a work, or sketches, are more significant because they most closely represent the composer's creative idea of the piece – and in fact there are several respects in which Schenker's interpretation of this Prelude corresponds better to the earlier than the later version (for instance his middleground II appears literally in it). For a discussion of the analytical significance of sketch studies, with further references, see Joseph Kerman's 'Sketch Studies' in Holoman and Palisca (eds.), *Musicology in the 1980s*, Da Capo Press 1982, pp. 53–65.

show how this through-composed surface is experienced as articulated into a series of sections coinciding with the structural harmonies. In other cases it may be the sectional articulation of the music that is obvious at surface level, so that the analytical task becomes one of showing the underlying continuity and directedness that binds the sections into a coherent whole. This is important because it brings up the whole issue of the relationship between Schenkerian analysis and the surface aspects of traditional (and non-traditional) forms we discussed in Chapter 1. What is involved can be seen in miniature in another analysis from *Five Graphic Analyses*: the chorale *Ich bin's, ich sollte büssen* from the Saint Matthew Passion (Figs. 14–15).[1]

There are a number of immediately obvious features of this graph as against that of the C major Prelude. First, the inner parts are omitted even in the foreground graph, except at the main cadences. Second, at the foreground level the primary tone is not at the beginning but half way through the second bar, at the first cadence; the initial C anticipates it, but Schenker sees the first two bars as a directed ascent towards the primary tone proper (achieved through an unfolding). This is known as an *initial ascent* and is quite commonly met in Schenkerian analysis, sometimes on a much larger scale; it should be viewed as an anticipatory prolongation of the primary tone, which is why the primary tone appears from the beginning of the piece in the background charts. Third, there are no less than three middlegrounds (quite apart from the little charts clarifying the progression from bars 8–10). This is unusual in so short a piece but is explained, on the one hand, by the unfoldings (the only difference between the second and third structural levels is that the latter shows the unfoldings and the former does not), and, on the other, by the *interruption* that distinguishes the background graph from the first structural level. This interruption is indicated by the sign ‖ at bar 6 in all the graphs except the background, and it is Schenker's way of correlating the single directed motion from $\hat{3}$ to $\hat{1}$ in the background with the binary design of the musical surface – that is to say, as two sets of three cadential phrases, which match each other melodically (except that the final phrase is, of course, altered to end with a perfect cadence instead of the imperfect one at bar 6). Schenker is saying that while the perfect cadence at the end is heard as part of the structural motion of the piece as a whole, the matching imperfect cadence is not; so that the

---

[1] Again Lerdahl and Jackendoff have published an analysis of this work using 'tree' notation, together with a comparison between their version and Schenker's: 'An overview of hierarchical structure in music', *Music Perception*, I, 1983/4, pp. 229–252.

Fig. 14 J. S. Bach, chorale *Ich bin's, ich sollte büssen*

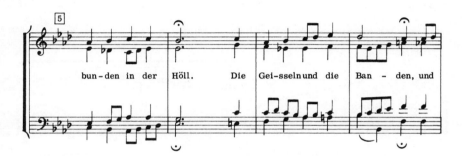

formal repetition of the piece is a middleground, and not a background, event. At the same time the half-way cadence is an event of crucial importance because all the middleground and foreground voice-leading of the first half is related to it in the same way as that of the second half relates to the final, and this time structural, cadence. The graph of the first structural level, then, indicates that at every level except background, the $\hat{2}$ of bar 6 functions as a resolution of the primary tone; but it marks an interruption between this $\hat{2}$ and the resumption of the primary tone at bar 8 (following another initial ascent).

Fig. 15   Schenker, analysis of *Ich bin's, ich sollte büssen*

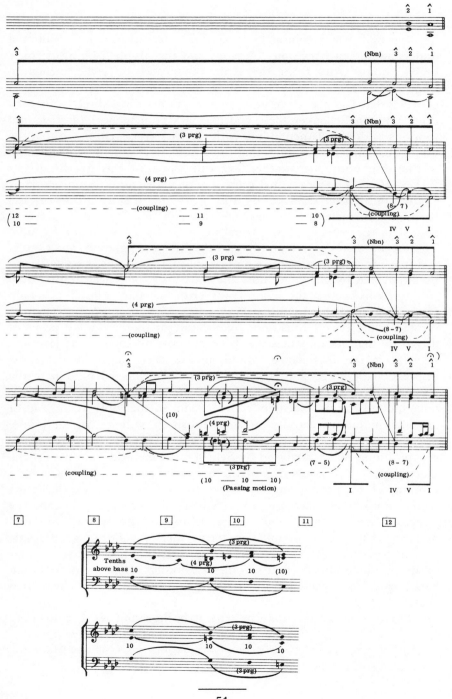

51

To realize exactly what the interruption mark means we have to bear in mind that there is an essential difference between the traditional understanding of harmonic functions and that implied by a Schenker graph, quite apart from the issue of greater or lesser structural importance. Traditionally something like I-IV-V-I means a series of chords related concentrically to a tonic, rather than directly to each other. But in Schenker these chords mark coincidences of structural motions in the fundamental line with the bass arpeggiation, so that the use of Roman letters implies that the chords have a definite, sequential relationship with one another: we can represent this graphically as I→IV→V→I. The idea is that each tone of a structural motion remains 'active' until it is resolved by the next, and that it influences the harmonic character of the passage throughout which it is active – almost in the manner of the pedal notes of Bach's C major Prelude. These pedal notes, corresponding to the bass arpeggiation, are a literal and overt statement of what is in general merely implied and so has to be discovered by analyzing how the music is experienced, rather than simply by inspecting the score. Another of Schenker's pupils, Oswald Jonas, described this by an analogy with strict counterpoint when he wrote of 'the covert retention, by the ear, of the consonant point of departure that accompanies the dissonant passing tone on its journey. It is as if the dissonance would always carry along with it the impression of its consonant origin'.[1] Since the directed motion of the background does not repeat itself, this means that a structural note, once quitted, cannot become 'active' again; so that only at the end of its final period of activity in a composition will a structural note resolve and be succeeded by the next. That is why so many compositions, when analyzed by Schenkerian methods, consist for the main part of a prolongation of the primary tone, with the structural motion all happening rapidly towards the end; one of the most common mistakes in learning to do Schenkerian analysis is locating the structural descent too soon – that is, mistaking for the structural descent what are in Schenkerian terms merely subordinate descents (and in particular the 'reflections' of the structural line that sometimes occur in the middleground[2]). This is another reason why working backwards from the end is so useful a procedure in Schenkerian analysis.

Now while all this may be true at background level, a strongly

[1] *Introduction to the Theory of Heinrich Schenker*, English trans. Longman, 1982, p. 64.

[2] See Forte and Gilbert, pp. 235–7.

articulated surface form can significantly alter the way in which one tone of a fundamental line is experienced in relation to another. A formal (thematic, textural) return to the primary tone is much more likely to be heard as a return to 'the same' tone, and a formal cadence half way through a piece as a resolution of it, than would be the case in the absence of such foreground articulation. By 'the same' I mean that a direct connection is being established between two temporally remote points, a connection which goes over the top of whatever linear motions there may be in between. It is just such a connection that creates Schenker's 'interruption'. The $\hat{3}$ after the fermata is a direct reference back to the primary tone, over the top of the $\hat{2}$ that precedes it. Consequently, there is no directed continuity between the $\hat{2}$ and the $\hat{3}$; the situation can be represented as in Fig. 16. And this example of interruption represents in miniature the Schenkerian conception of form, which is a dialectic between the irreversible, goal-directed continuity of the fundamental line and the articulated surface of the composition with its disjunctions and repetitions. In Schenkerian terms, for instance, determining whether a form is tripartite, bipartite or consists of only one part is not a matter of assimilating it into traditional formal models of some sort, but a matter of determining whether its middleground involves two, one or no interruptions of the fundamental line. According to Schenker, 'only the prolongation of a division (interruption) gives rise to sonata form' (*Free Composition*, p. 134), and in fact the interrupted $\hat{3}$-$\hat{2}$-$\hat{1}$, as shown in Fig. 16, is the basic Schenkerian pattern for sonata form and for any form which involves a structural cadence in the dominant.

Fig. 16

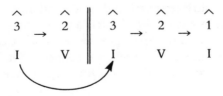

VII

I don't think people have sufficiently realized that Schenker analysis is in this way a theory of musical form. But then you have to admit that Schenker's own attempts to develop a theory of the traditional forms on this basis were fairly rudimentary, and in any case misunderstandings have arisen from his rather reckless remarks to the effect that traditional forms (along with themes, motifs and modulations) were no more than analytical illusions.[1] What Schenker meant, I think, is that traditional forms make no sense viewed purely as surface configurations, as 'things to hear'; the important thing is to view them in the context of the fundamental structure, which shows *how* they are heard – how for instance there can be surface repetitions within a work which is experienced as a continuously directed evolution from beginning to end. In other words, Schenker saw form as psychological (he used this word frequently to characterize his theories, particularly in his earlier book *Harmony*), in the sense that it has to do with how things are experienced in particular musical contexts, and not with the physical or formal properties of those things considered in isolation. In fact this applies to Schenkerian analysis at all levels from the smallest to the largest. On the smallest scale, the analysis of the C major Prelude shows how, for example, bars 18 and 27, though physically identical, are experienced quite differently (the first as a prolongation of $\hat{3}$ and hence of I, the second as a prolongation of $\hat{2}$ and hence of V). On the largest scale, Carl Schachter's Schenkerian analysis of Schubert's *Moment Musical* Op. 94/1 suggests that the first and last formal sections of this piece – an extended ABA – have quite different harmonic and linear functions, even though the one is the exact repetition of the other.[2] Some critics of Schenkerian analysis have been worried by such discrepancies between surface form and analytical interpretation; for instance Eugene Narmour says that 'when a given Schenkerian pitch transformation shows no direct correspondence to what are manifestly clear formal events on the same level, we suspect that something is wrong' (*Beyond Schenkerism*, p. 107), and Joseph Kerman, speaking of

---

[1] *Free Composition*, pp. 131–2, 27, 112 respectively. For Schenker's theory of the traditional forms see Part III Chapter 5 of *Free Composition*; but the treatment of these forms in Forte and Gilbert's *Introduction to Schenkerian Analysis* is much more comprehensive.

[2] In Yeston, *Readings in Schenkerian Analysis and other approaches*, p. 183 (example 10.13).

the 'Ode to Joy' from Beethoven's Ninth Symphony, makes the same point when he asks 'why, when [the second] couplet makes its cadence at "Heiligtum", must we interpret this as structurally different from the identical cadence at "Flügel weilt"?' (*Musicology*, p. 82). By contrast it seems to me that the ability of Schenkerian analysis to demonstrate graphically what is one of the most intuitively striking features of musical form, namely that the same things are experienced differently in different contexts, is the best possible demonstration of its power and sensitivity as an analytical technique. However it is undeniable that this lack of direct correlation between score and analysis does create certain difficulties in judging or verifying Schenkerian interpretations, and these difficulties need to be considered.

By way of illustration we can return to the Bach chorale. As we saw, at background level Schenker sees the piece as through-composed, but from his first structural level onwards this through-composition disappears and is replaced by the interruption. Couldn't the through-composition be regarded as permeating the middleground too? And is Schenker right to suppress the E♭ which is the highest note of the piece and recurs in bars 1, 3, 7 and 9 but which plays no part in Schenker's middleground? And what about the stressed B♭ minor inflection at bar 8, which is approached by the longest scalar movement in the bass of the entire piece but which again disappears in Schenker's middleground? Here is an alternative analysis which remedies all these features, and in consequence does away with the interruption altogether (Fig. 17). It should not by now require verbal explanation.

This graph is Schenkerian enough in most of its details but a number of its major features are less so. The most important question is whether the entire passage from bars 8–11 can be convincingly regarded as a prolongation of a B♭ minor formation and in particular a D♭ in the upper voice. Of course the note of the fundamental line that 'actively' dominates a particular passage cannot possibly be a harmony note of every foreground chord – that would make analysis impossible – but its influence should be felt covertly as the 'consonant point of departure' Jonas spoke of. Isn't the D♭ markedly foreign to this passage with its D♮s? Yes, but then doesn't its dissonant relation to this passage serve to underline its 'active' character as the first move away from the primary tone? Doesn't it generate an impulse towards resolution which was absent in the first half of this chorale? Isn't it picked up by the D♭'s of bar 11, which is when this resolution is achieved? Can it then be shrugged off as nothing more than a neighbour note, as in Schenker's graph?

Fig. 17 Alternative analysis of *Ich bin's, ich sollte büssen*

These are psychological questions: that is, they have to be answered by deciding what one hears in the music and not by staring hard at the score. But the whole idea of deciding 'what one hears' is problematical. After all, I can 'hear' the most preposterous analytical relationships if I choose to; it is a question of deciding what I want to hear. Certainly I *do* hear the music as directed – it sounds quite different played backwards! – but I *can* hear bars 8–11 as either prolonging a $\hat{4}$ or a $\hat{3}$; I can even alternate between the two. Hence the claim Schenkerian analysts tend to make that their analyses explain in detail just how listeners do, in fact, hear music is really rather dubious. There are two points here. First, if Schenkerian analysis explained how people normally hear music, why would it be necessary to learn a new way of hearing music in order to do Schenkerian analysis? (Ever since the publication of Felix Salzer's *Structural Hearing*[1] there has been a lot of emphasis on Schenkerian analysis being a 'way of hearing', a type of analysis that can be done directly from musical sound, given sufficient training). Second, there are a number of difficulties which Eugene Narmour has emphasized and which have to do with the perceptibility of the fundamental structure. I said earlier that you cannot determine what the primary tone is at the beginning of a piece (or even if there is a primary tone at the beginning of it) by considering the beginning in isolation: it is a matter of its relation to the piece as a whole and particularly to the end – that is why I recommended working backwards. But listeners do not work backwards. They cannot know the answer to this question except in retrospect; and the same applies to obligatory register too. In these ways, and more generally in its tendency to ignore ambiguities whereby a given foreground event might be interpreted in different structural ways, Schenkerian analysis is not a truly credible model of the way listeners normally experience music.

Now Schenker was an out-and-out elitist and would probably have retorted that this was because his account of musical structure corresponds to the way the inner meaning of masterpieces (not run-of-the-mill compositions) is apprehended by those few listeners capable of appreciating them: if most people don't hear the music like that, then so much the worse for them. Schenker, in fact, regarded his theories as constituting a touchstone of excellence – music which did not work according to his principles was primitive, degenerate or plain bad – and he justified this on the grounds that his theories of musical structure were directly based on human psychology or even physiology, so that they were equally applicable to the musical productions of all times and places. Now it is an undeniable fact that Schenkerian analysis works very well for some music and hardly at all for

[1] Dover,

other music. It works well in eighteenth and nineteeth century music, and within this period it is best for through- composed forms and German music in general (with the exception of the nineteenth-century 'progressives' like Wagner); but it is not so good for highly sectional forms and for French, Italian or Russian music. Basically this coincides with Schenker's own tastes and he was perfectly prepared to conclude that other music must be aesthetically worthless (in fact the development of his analytical theories seems to have gone along with a certain narrowing of his tastes: at any rate, there are six examples from the 'progressive' composers Berlioz, Liszt and Wagner in Schenker's *Harmony*, published in 1906, but none at all in *Free Composition* which came out some twenty years later!). Indeed such an aesthetic conclusion is quite inevitable if one accepts the premise that Schenkerian analysis is based directly on the psychological principles that govern musical listening.

Such views, which condemn a large proportion of the musical repertoire and indeed have undisguisedly racialist overtones, are no longer acceptable and form no part of present-day Schenkerian analysis. (They will mainly be found in an appendix to the English edition of *Free Composition* consisting of passages which Jonas and Oster suppressed in their editions of Schenker's text.) But if you are not willing to accept such conclusions then you should not accept the premise either. You cannot, that is to say, go on maintaining that a Schenkerian interpretation is in accordance with the facts of human biology or psychology whereas other types of interpretation are not. So what are you to say? Perhaps all you can say is that it is a matter of taste: I choose to see the piece one way, you another, and that's an end to it. But even if it is ultimately a matter of taste, there is still a considerable value in the standardization of Schenkerian practice, especially if comparisons between analyses of different works are to be made so that, for instance, the common feature of a whole repertoire of pieces can be established – a procedure which turns Schenkerian analysis into a valuable historical and style-analytical tool. And such standardization can only be achieved on the basis of shared conventions not only regarding the application of graphic symbols but also the kind of interpretational issues raised in the two possible analyses of *Ich bin's, ich sollte büssen*. My analysis is wrong, and Schenker's right, not so much because mine is less true to experience, factually incorrect, or internally inconsistent, but simply because it is non-standard in treating as part of the fundamental line a note which is clearly dissonant in relation to the passage that prolongs it. And there are many postulates of the Schenkerian system – that is, things which are taken for granted by the very act of doing a

Schenkerian analysis – which strike me as being purely conventional, rather than expressing necessary truths, the contradiction of which would be inherently absurd. Why shouldn't structural dissonances be prolonged as well as, or rather than, structural consonances? Why should triads be assigned a privileged role as against sevenths or ninths, or indeed non-triadic functions altogether, especially in music where such formations make up the prevailing sonority? Why should structural lines necessarily descend and why do they have to be contained within a single octave? Why should a piece be derived from a single tonal formation rather than evolving from one to another? Why should the voice-leading rules of strict counterpoint necessarily apply, and especially at middleground or background levels where there is surely no auditory correlate to the effect that things like parallel fifths make in the foreground? The only safe answer to these questions, I think, is that in the absence of such shared conventions and expectations nobody would understand anybody else's analyses properly.

VIII

It follows that there is no reason why the normal conventions of Schenkerian analysis should not be replaced by others where this has some practical advantage, provided that the analyst makes it clear what conventions he is adopting or inventing – that is to say, that he makes it clear what he sees as being prolonged and by what means. Doing this can result in useful analytical results with music which is more or less a closed book for traditional Schenkerian analysis. However it is important to realize that the results of such an analysis may mean something different from the results of a traditional Schenkerian analysis, even when they *look* the same. People don't always appreciate this, and therefore it is a good idea to look at an analysis whose procedures seem at first sight orthodox enough but in fact are not entirely so – and necessarily, because they are dealing with a composer whom Schenker himself regarded as a 'surface composer' and therefore intrinsically unanalyzable. The work is Wagner's *Tristan* Prelude and the analysis is by William Mitchell.[1]

---

[1] 'The *Tristan* Prelude: Techniques and Structure', in *The Music Forum*, Vol. I, 1967, pp. 162–203.

Tristan is obviously a much more complex work texturally than either of the Bach examples we have discussed, and this means that the relationship between the structural voices and the musical surface is considerably less direct. In works with a figurated chorale texture, like the C major Prelude, it is possible to do a Schenkerian analysis more or less on the basis of a harmonic reduction — and consequently Schenkerian analysis is sometimes described (though I think misleadingly) as a process of harmonic reduction followed by subsequent relinearization. But this cannot be the case in textures which are essentially contrapuntal in the first place, such as *Tristan*, where problems of chordal segmentation and of distinguishing harmonically essential from inessential notes make a harmonic reduction at best a drastically impoverished model of the music. One might think that it would help to work at least from a piano reduction; but Mitchell specifically warns against this, on the grounds that register, which is inevitably mangled in piano reductions, is a crucial guide in deciding what the structural lines, and therefore the harmonies, are (p. 168). Now, there is a logical difficulty here of a rather similar nature to the one we encountered in the case of obligatory register (p. 47 above). It is a basic principle of Schenkerian analysis that the top line need not present the highest structural voice, nor need a downbeat or dynamic accent denote a structural tone, nor will essential motions of the fundamental structure necessarily coincide with breaks in the surface articulation of the form; in fact the issue of form, which we discussed in relation to *Ich bin's, ich sollte büssen*, is merely one instance of the general issue of the relationship between fundamental structure and musical surface. Schenker repeatedly says that all these things are meaningless except as interpreted in the light of the fundamental structure. On the other hand, here is Mitchell advocating a consideration of register in determining what the fundamental structure is; John Rothgeb, in an article on the topic, states that in general 'changes in surface design usually coincide with crucial structural points, and accordingly such changes must be given the most thoughtful attention in deriving or verifying an analysis'.[1] In fact it is clear that in practice Schenkerian analysts take a great deal of notice of features like register, modulation, dynamics, rhythm, orchestration and thematic structure; almost all tonal music is so rich in connections, considered purely as an abstract pattern of notes, that any number of quasi-Schenkerian patterns can be

---

[1] 'Design as a Key to Structure in Tonal Music', in Yeston, *Readings in Schenkerian Analysis and other approaches*, p. 73.

found if such features are ignored. The way *not* to do a Schenkerian analysis is to look by eye for ribbons of descending scales, in the way a computer might; good analysis comes from self-interrogation about the nature of the music as it is experienced, and register, rhythm and the other surface features have a decisive influence over how patterns of notes are experienced. Therefore no good Schenkerian analysis ignores such things (though this is often claimed, especially in respect of rhythm[1]); instead it presents the *results* of a careful consideration of these features, though it does so silently.

Fig. 18 Mitchell, analysis of Wagner's *Tristan* Prelude

---

[1] Schenker's conceptual approach to rhythm was the same as for form (and for that matter the other aspects of surface design I have mentioned) – as a foreground formation which only makes sense viewed in relation to the background. However his treatment of rhythm (*Free Composition*, Part III, Chapter 4) was again rudimentary. Maury Yeston has tried to refine it (*The Stratification of Musical Rhythm*, Yale University Press, 1976) but the most practical application is Carl Schachter's 'Rhythm and Linear Analysis: Durational Reduction', *The Music Forum*, Vol. V, 1980, p. 197. Schenkerians have recently been becoming increasingly interested in the whole question of exactly how surface features relate to underlying structure; a number of essays in *Aspects of Schenkerian Theory*, edited by David Beach, are devoted to this (Yale, 1983).

Where such aspects of design do successfully clarify the structural voice-leading, it may be possible to analyze a work section by section before proceeding to synthesize these into a whole; though I doubt that any Schenkerian analyst ever begins to analyze a section in detail without at least a tentative glimpse at the structural development of the whole. But in the case of the *Tristan* Prelude the profusion of motivic working and modulation is such that one inevitably has to approach the section-by-section details with rather fixed expectations and use these as a basis for categorizing the details one finds. Not surprisingly, then, Mitchell's large-scale graph of the Prelude (Fig. 18) is based on the same 3̂-2̂-1̂ fundamental structure that will by now be familiar, except that it is elaborated by means of a 44-bar initial ascent and the interpolation of harmonies on VI and ♭II⁹.[1] I suggest that you now compare this graph directly with Wagner's score, without for the moment referring to the section-by-section graphs which Mitchell gives to substantiate his interpretation (and which are not reproduced here). The structural changes of harmony that Mitchell picks out do, on the whole, coincide with the textural and/or thematic changes in the score, and in fact the first and last notes of Mitchell's fundamental line are both preceded by the striking ♯4–3 figure at bars 44 and 94. At the same time, this fundamental structure is curiously out of kilter with the actual experience of the music. I cannot really hear the opening as an introduction (which is what the initial ascent implies), whereas the section beginning with the primary tone at bar 45 sounds more like an episode than the main body of the movement. Again, bar 84 sounds to me much more like a structural resolution than bar 95 (the numbers refer to the concert version of the Prelude), which contradicts Mitchell's graph. And some of the notes of Mitchell's fundamental line are remarkably hard to find in the score. The C♯ in the oboe at bar 45, which is the seventh of a secondary seventh chord, is extraordinarily unprominent for a primary tone (or should this be read as an octave transference of the lower C♯ in the strings, which is however itself merely part of a sequential figure?). The D which Mitchell marks at the top in bar 53 is no more than a melodic appoggiatura, while the one at the bottom again

---

[1] This in itself marks Mitchell's graph as very much a middleground, not background, formation in traditional Schenkerian terms: first because ninths cannot be structural harmonies, and second because a fundamental structure is necessarily diatonic – modulations of any sort being viewed as purely middleground prolongations. (This is Schenker's radical solution to the problem of proliferating tonics which I raised in Chapter 1 in relation to Roman-letter analysis: see pp. 18–19 above.) A further eccentricity from the orthodox Schenkerian viewpoint is the barely disguised parallel fifths between the VI and V chords.

involves a registral transference. The top C at bar 74 is not actually there but has to be explained either through yet another registral transference or as an anticipation of the C that Mitchell's more detailed graph shows at 77 – which is in the violin melody, and merely part of a sequential rise through F to A♭.

Such deviations between analysis and score are found within Schenker's own analyses; they can be recognized by notes marked in brackets. Generally this means a registral transfer but sometimes a note is added in the graph which is not actually in the score at all, and this is called an *implied note* – meaning that it is so strongly implied by what is there that it is in some sense experienced as functioning even though not literally present. Obviously this is a potentially dangerous concept, because it can be used to 'justify' any *a priori* interpretation the analyst likes; and if this were a piece of classical music, such a high proportion of discrepancies between the analysis and the score would suggest that Mitchell's analysis was a bad one – bad in proceeding too rapidly from foreground to background, and in its failure to make the kind of judgments about the nature of the musical experience that I have described. But in truth such judgments are hard to make in the *Tristan* Prelude. Do I really hear the C at bars 74–7 as directly connected with the D at 53? I don't know! I can imagine the connection, but only in a rather abstract way; the answer doesn't present itself as readily as it did in the Bach examples. And I think that this is not so much a fact about Mitchell's analysis as one about the *Tristan* Prelude. What is happening here – as in much of the 'progressive' nineteenth-century repertoire when it is analyzed by Schenkerian means – is that the foreground and the background are tending to drift apart. In classical Schenkerian analysis it is the middleground that is all-important; the analytical importance of the background is really only that it clarifies the middleground, which is why in general a Schenkerian analysis that is all detailed foreground and remote background with nothing much in between is not a good one. But it is this middleground which disappears in Wagner. On the one hand there are the rather static pillars of Mitchell's fundamental structure – the chordal blocks which he marks with Roman letters and which do at least constitute a workable framework for 'seeing' the Prelude as a whole despite its proliferation of detail; if nothing more, they make it easier to remember exactly what order things come in, and perhaps they correspond to some extent with the way Wagner planned the music out. On the other hand, the effect of the music derives from all the things Mitchell leaves out – the orchestral colours, the huge changes of tension, the harmonic reinterpretation of the 'Tristan chord' at the climax,[1] the constant sense of modulating towards goals which are all the time changing before they are reached. Perhaps it is this characteristic of the harmonic goals in Wagner that particularly explains the difficulties in making a satisfactory Schenkerian analysis of his music. Instead of there being in any real sense an overall harmonic goal which is determined at the level of form, there is an endless chain of purely local goals, each deriving from the previous few bars of music and usually deflected before a cadence is reached. How can one expect to analyze the Prelude as a prolonged triad when its opening is so purposely vague (I have never really succeeded in hearing it as in A minor) and when it can finish in either of two keys – A minor for the concert piece and C minor (the key of the Sailor's Song) for the opera?

IX

Schenker's own analyses assume that music has form because the part acquires its aesthetic meaning from its relation with the whole, and that the main sphere in which this happens is that of directed tonal motion. That is what Schenker analysis is about. But Debussy was just as interested in harmonic progressions that have no sense of directed motion, as a well-known snippet of conversation between him and an academic musician shows. Debussy had played a progression on the piano.

> GUIRAUD: It's all very meandering.
>
> DEBUSSY: Certainly not! . . . Counterpoint is not given to us for nothing. As the parts go forward we come across some splendid chords.[2]

When, therefore, Schenkerian, or quasi-Schenkerian, techniques are applied to Debussy's music the result is not a demonstration of organic coherence through directed motion. Instead either or both of two things happen. The first is that there are little fragments of coherent voice-leading where there is a temporary harmonic goal, but these do not link up into larger-scale structures. Here, then, we have directed motion but

[1] For the 'Tristan chord' see below, p. 218.

[2] Lockspeiser, *Debussy: his Life and Mind*, Vol. 1, Cambridge University Press, 1979, p. 208.

not organic coherence; and it is worth remembering that this only differs from the situation in classical Schenkerian analysis as a matter of degree – virtually never does Schenkerian analysis have anything to say about the relationships between movements of multi-movement works, and even the different sections of a single movement can sometimes be analyzed as so many subordinate 'pieces'. The second thing that may happen when Debussy's music is analyzed is the reverse of the first. One finds consistent lines, sometimes, though not always, at a consistent register, which do persist over long stretches of a composition or even the whole of it, and which serve to lend it some coherence; but they are not directed. They may be static; they may meander around a central point; they may even fall or rise consistently, but there is no sense of successive notes resolving on to one another, or of long-range harmonic goals. As illustration, Fig. 19 is an analysis of *Puck's Dance* from Book One of the Preludes.

Fig. 19

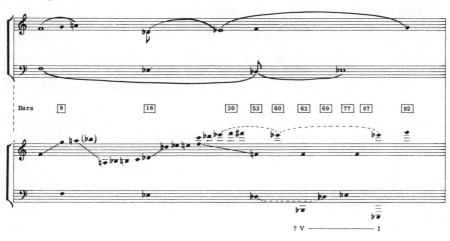

The foreground of this analysis corresponds quite well to the secondary-feature emphasis of the music; I do not think it is simply the arbitrary selection of notes to fit a preconceived scheme that quasi-Schenkerian analysis of twentieth-century music can so easily become. And if this is true, then shouldn't we see this piece as the background chart indicates, that is as the triadic prolongation of a non-triadic fundamental structure – specifically, of a whole-tone one? Certainly this is a *logical* possibility, and there have been a number of attempts to show

how the scope of Schenkerian analysis can be extended by regarding non-triadic formations as capable of prolongation. In an article called 'Towards a New Concept of Tonality?', for instance, Roy Travis defined tonality independently of the triad. 'Music is tonal', he said, 'when its motion unfolds through time a particular tone, interval or chord':[1] so, for example, he suggested that the opening six bars of *The Rite of Spring*, in which the bassoon and clarinets begin on a non-triadic chord and descend at varying rates until they reach the same chord an octave lower, should be regarded as a 'prolongation' of that chord (in just the same sense as the first nineteen bars of the C Major Prelude are a prolongation of its opening triad). But is this actually sensible? The important question is not whether it is a logical but a *psychological* possibility: that is to say, whether one experiences this motion as harmonically directed in the way Travis describes. I don't think I do; it seems to me that this passage is not like a Schenkerian prolongation but rather like the chromatically falling lines you find in the bass or inner parts of music by composers like Berlioz, Tchaikovsky and Delius – notes which have nothing to do with large-scale harmonic direction but instead bind the texture together and lend local colour to what is usually rather a static harmonic framework. They are not experienced as prolonging chords; instead chords are pegged onto them, like clothes to a washing line. The conjunct lines of *Puck's Dance*, while buried a bit deeper under the musical surface, fulfil essentially the same function. They are not experienced as interacting contrapuntally to create a sense of cadential extension or direction, and consequently they do not create form – at least not form as Schenker conceived it.

[1] *Journal of Music Theory*, iii, 1959, p. 261. A characteristic rebuttal by Oster, based on the traditional Schenkerian view of 'the triad as given by nature', appeared in the following year's issue (p. 85 ff). For a general discussion of this whole topic see James Baker, 'Schenkerian Analysis and Post-Tonal Music' in David Beach (ed.), *Aspects of Schenkerian Theory*, Yale University Press, 1983; and for a particularly good example of the application to twentieth-century music of techniques loosely derived from Schenker, see Edward T. Cone's analysis of Stravinsky's *Symphonies of Wind Instruments* ('Stravinsky: the Progress of a Method', in Boretz and Cone (eds.), *Perspectives on Schoenberg and Stravinsky*, Norton 1972, pp. 155–64).

CHAPTER THREE

PSYCHOLOGICAL APPROACHES
TO ANALYSIS

I *What is meant by a 'psychological approach'?*

Schenker's approach to analysis was 'psychological' in the sense that he was interested in how musical sounds are experienced, rather than in the sounds themselves; so that he interprets one C major chord one way and another differently because the context is different and consequently the chord is experienced in a different way. However to say this is to use the word 'psychological' in rather a loose manner. A lot of Schenker's thinking could actually be better described as 'phenomenological', and it is worth understanding what the difference is since two rather distinct approaches to music are involved here. Schenker believed that the most fundamental stratum of musical experience is that of directed motion towards an ending-point, and that at this background level almost all music exhibits more or less the same structure. He is not saying: this is how music composed in Europe during the period 1750–1900 happened to work. Rather he is saying: this is what music is, regarded as a class of human experience. Now the term 'phenomenology' refers to the study of the essential qualities of human experience. To study an experience phenomenologically means to gain an immediate awareness of that experience by stripping away everything that is not essential to it – things like conventional associations, purely contingent circumstances, and so forth. This process is known as a 'phenomenological reduction' and it has some similarities to the way in which Schenker tried to reveal the fundamental structure of music by stripping away such inessentials as surface 'form'. However, phenomenologists of music such as Thomas Clifton have attacked Schenker for not doing the job properly. Schenker's conceptions of things such as 'background' or 'prolongation', they argue, are tied to a particular historical and geographical style, that of tonality. Schenker was being absurdly chauvinistic in thinking that tonal music is the only real sort of music. Instead he should have carried the reductive process a stage further, in order to arrive at broader conceptions of 'background' and 'prolongation' that would be applicable to all types of music. Indeed if a genuinely phenomenological conception of prolongation were developed, that is to say one that simply embodies what it is to experience prolongation, then there is no particular reason why the term should be a specifically musical one at all. In his book *Music as Heard: a Study in Applied Phenomenology*,[1] Clifton describes the unfolding and prolongation of harmonies in Bach's C major Prelude. He then adds: '"Prolongation" need not be exclusively construed as a specifically musical technique. It also aligns itself with the persistence of a single color, or of the enduring of a single quality or affect, regardless of its appearance in a particular medium' (p. 176). Similarly, space and time are essential dimensions of human experience, presented equally in music, painting, dance or whatever. When he analyzes music, then, Clifton is trying to show how the piece in question presents space or time. For instance, he discusses space in the C major Prelude by showing how the music is experienced in terms of surface and relief. He argues that there are a number of patterns built into this Prelude that serve to connect distant passages with each other, creating the sense of high points and low points that constitutes relief. Fig. 20 shows some of these patterns.

Fig. 20   Thomas Clifton, analysis of Bach's C Major Prelude, bars 5–19.

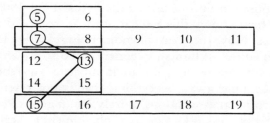

The figures refer to bar numbers and the boxes indicate that the bars within the box are experienced as a single unit in some way. Bars

[1] Yale University Press, 1983.

5–8 and 12–15 are each made up of two-bar sequences (that is why they are arranged in a two-by-two format). Bars 7–11 and 15–19 have no such internal organization (that is why they are shown as one-dimensional) but they are related to each other by sequence. Cutting across this organization is another pattern shown by the numbers that are ringed and connected with one another (bars 5, 7, 13 and 15): here the link is that they are all six-three chords. And Clifton comments that 'the presence of these patterns tends to make the surface "breathe", that is, to create a suprametrical rhythm of arsis and thesis, a quality of movement which accounts for relief on a level other than that of the diminution' (p. 177).

Analysis of this sort is inclined to make professional 'music analysts' uneasy and impatient; the findings seem so obvious, so laboured, and so pretentiously expressed in comparison to the precision and economy of something like a Schenkerian analysis. The reason for this is not that phenomenologists analyze music badly (though some do, of course) but that they are analyzing music with a different purpose in mind. The phenomenologist is using individual pieces of music as a means of discovering the general properties of musical experience *per se*.[1] On the other hand the music analyst studies music with the aim of finding out more about the particular composition in question. And he values general theories about the nature of musical experience simply to the extent that they help him understand individual pieces. If I have a high opinion of Schenker, it is not because of his concept of the fundamental structure being the irreducible basis of musical experience – the phenomenological component of his thinking, that is to say. It is because of the particular insights that this approach yields in particular cases, and here it is perfectly correct to talk of the analysis being 'psychological' in that it attempts to isolate the specific factors that determine people's musical responses in given contexts. However, it is unlikely that any psychologist would easily recognize a Schenkerian analysis as being 'psychological'. The reason is again that the psychological principles in terms of which Schenker explains musical response are all muddled up with the particular stylistic formations and even the notation of tonal music. Analysts who have based their work on explicit psychological principles – usually drawn from Gestalt psychology or from Freud – have done so with the aim of distinguishing psychological

---

[1] However, for a more practical application of phenomenological techniques (to Varèse's *Poème Electronique*) see Lawrence Ferrara, 'Phenomenology as a Tool for Musical Analysis', *Musical Quarterly*, LXX, 1984, pp. 355–73.

function from stylistic realization, in the hope that this will both allow a refinement of the kind of analytical interpretation offered by Schenker and extend the range of musical styles that can be interpreted. Of the two psychological approaches to analysis to be discussed in this chapter, Leonard Meyer's has the more obvious affinities with Schenkerian analysis and so considering this first will make it clear just what a specifically psychological approach can contribute to musical analysis.

II *Leonard Meyer*

Meyer sees music primarily as pattern. By this I do not mean that he is unconcerned with its emotion or meaning – in fact his first book was called *Emotion and Meaning in Music*,[1] and though its emphasis was more theoretical than analytical it set out the basic principles on which all his analysis has been based. Meyer drew upon various psychological theories that were current in the 1950s, when he wrote this book, and which explained emotion as resulting from the frustration of expectations – or, as the psychologists put it, the inhibition of a tendency to respond. In accordance with this, Meyer tried to explain the emotions to which music gives rise by analyzing just what it is that a listener expects to happen at any given point in a piece of music, and comparing this to what in fact does happen. And he saw these expectations as being determined by two things. The first of these is a set of norms by means of which a 'competent listener', as Meyer puts it, interprets what he hears; this is more or less like knowing a language, in that a listener who is not familiar with a given style simply won't understand the music because he will not know what to expect (at least, this is what Meyer believes). The second is the patterns the music makes when interpreted by means of such norms. For example, in tonal music a progression which begins and ends on the tonic is closed; meaning that the listener does not expect the pattern to continue (provided, of course, that he is familiar with the tonal style). On the other hand, a progression which does not end on the tonic is open: it implies some kind of continuation. In his more recent writings Meyer has tended to talk about what the music 'implies' rather than what the listener 'expects', but in either case the same thing is being talked about – the way in which a competent listener responds to the music.

[1] University of Chicago Press, 1956.

Whereas Schenker's concepts of prolongation, directed motion and so forth were tied up with tonality – they were expressed in terms of a particular historical style – concepts such as openness and closure are not tied to a single style. They take different forms in different styles, but the implication is the same: that the music will continue in some manner, or that it will not. So in theory an analytical method based on general psychological principles involving things like openness and closure will be applicable to any kind of music. However, this assumes a wholly adequate understanding of the particular norms by means of which these general principles are realized in a specific style. Meyer uses the term 'style analysis' for the study of such norms, and is constantly complaining about the inadequacy of our understanding of them. Only when we know much more about stylistic norms, says Meyer, will we really be able to explain the emotional content of a given piece of music in terms of its technical structure. This has two consequences for the analyses that Meyer offers. The first is that instead of attempting to deal with the full emotional content of music, Meyer more or less restricts himself to the experience of unity and coherence in music: why, he asks, do the various parts of this piece belong together as a meaningful whole? And the second is that he more or less restricts himself to the analysis of tonal music, on the grounds that we do have an extensive if unsystematic understanding of its stylistic norms: for example, as he puts it, 'there is agreement about which pro-gressions are strongly implicative and which are less so, which triads are relatively stable and which tend to be mobile and on-going, and so on'.[1] Both these restrictions mean that in practice his analyses are closely comparable with Schenker's, so it will be useful to consider a couple of Meyer's analyses side by side with Schenkerian ones in order to see what the differences actually amount to.

Fig. 21 shows a simplified score of *Das Wandern* (from Schubert's song-cycle *Die schöne Müllerin*) together with two analyses of it. There are some obvious similarities between Meyer's analysis (which is shown above) and the Schenkerian one.[2] Each consists of a reduction which uses musical notation and is aligned with the original so as to show which notes have a structural role. Each also uses beams to group structural notes into patterns. But the beams mean slightly different things. When the Schenkerian chart uses beams to link the D, C and B♭ it means that these constitute a single structural motion. When Meyer

[1] *Explaining Music*, University of California Press, 1973, p. 27.

[2] The Meyer analysis collates Ex. 79 and 81 of *Explaining Music*, with some minor corrections and additions.

Fig. 21   Two analyses of Schubert's *Das Wandern*

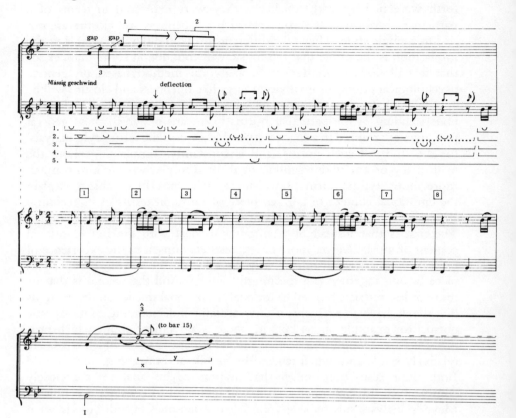

links together the E♭ – D – C – B♭ corresponding to bars 1–3 he means the same, plus a bit more. Meyer's beam is divided into two halves, with arrowheads marking the division. The significance of this is that the first two notes (E♭ and D) act as a unit which implies the second two (the C and B♭) as a continuation. Why is this? Because it is a general principle of implication that 'patterns tend to be continued until they become as complete and stable as possible' (p. 130). And how does this principle apply here? In the first place, because the E♭ – D initiates a scalar fall. Second, and more specifically, because the E♭ is preceded by an A and this leap initiates what Meyer calls a *gap-fill motion*. The principle of this is that 'a disjunct interval may be understood as a kind

Fig. 22

of incompleteness – a gap – which implies that the note or notes skipped over will be presented in what follows' (p. 144). This is what is meant by the word 'gap' in Meyer's reduction, and this particular gap is an especially implicative one because of the unstable nature of the diminished fifth within the tonal system. The result of all this is that the A –E♭ – D functions as what Meyer calls a *generative event* forcefully implying the C – B♭ as continuation. But why just C – B♭? Why shouldn't the motion continue through A and beyond? This is a question of stylistic norms; being the tonic, B♭ is a stable note and this makes it the logical, or psychological, goal of the pattern.

The pattern we have been analyzing is not stated literally in the music, of course; it is prolonged by means of surface elaboration in a manner which is perfectly familiar from Schenkerian analysis. But in this instance the implied motion did follow directly upon the generative event, which is not always the case. In the group marked '3' in Meyer's graph, the implied motion is delayed. This is another gap-fill motion, the F – B♭ – A of bar 1 implying the G – F of bars 10–12; it actually encloses the whole of the E♭ – D – C – B♭ pattern we discussed before. And cutting across this is yet another pattern, which Meyer marks '2'. This is another case where the implied motion is delayed, but this time the nature of the implication is different. It is rather more complicated than what we have discussed so far, because it involves not just a pattern of pitches but rather the relationship between pitch patterns and rhythmic patterns. The symbols underneath the music represent Meyer's analysis of its rhythm, but we will not consider this in detail just yet. For now all that matters is that Meyer sees a contradiction between what the pitches imply and what the rhythms imply in bars 1–4. The rhythm implies something like Fig. 22; that is, it suggests a closed group ending with bar 2 and leading to a contrasted consequent of some sort. The pitch on the other hand delays closure (that is to say, the expected tonic) until the third bar; the result of this discrepancy between pitch and rhythmic implications is the curious emptiness of bar 4. Now, in Meyer's view this discrepancy sets up a tension that demands resolution; it acts as a generative event implying 'a patterning in which the motion from E♭ down to B♭ occurs without a deflection or break' (p. 155); and, as the arrows show, this is precisely what happens in bars 13–14. The ending of the song, then, functions as a high-level resolution, and this is one reason why it makes a satisfactory conclusion; others which Meyer mentions include the way in which the final phrase as a whole summarizes the melodic motion of the first three bars, and the echo-like repetition in the last two bars which act as 'a sign of relaxation and hence of closure' (p. 155) and correspond to the repetition of the opening at bars 5–8.

Now the sort of explanation that Meyer is attempting here is quite similar to what Schenkerian analysis provides. In both cases the analysis is saying why it is appropriate for the music to end where and how it does, and in both cases it does so by separating the different structural levels at which meaningful patterns occur. So now let us make a direct comparison between Meyer's analysis and the Schenkerian one also shown in Fig. 21. Some features are common to both reductions, such as the way that bars 13–14 summarize the pitch pattern of the first three bars. Some of the features to which Meyer draws attention disappear in the Schenkerian analysis: for instance the B♭ – A – G – F pattern which Meyer marks '3', and the tension betwen pitch and rhythm at bars 1–4. On the other hand the Schenkerian chart yields insights that Meyer's does not. The most important of these concern the fundamental line $\hat{3}$ – $\hat{2}$ – $\hat{1}$, which is reflected near the surface at bars 2–3 and 13–14. The notes of the fundamental line do appear as important notes in Meyer's chart, though the motion from D is shown as beginning at bar 9 rather than bar 2 (Meyer does not connect the Ds in these two bars, which is a pity because doing so explains the static quality of the first eight bars as against the dynamic quality of the ninth). But Meyer's chart does not explain *why* these notes are important – for instance, why the important C is the one in bar 11 and not the one in bar 14 (which Schubert has actually marked with a stress). It is possible to guess how Meyer would justify this: he might say that the sequential organization of bars 9–12, in which both D and C are supported by triads, means that these notes are of an equivalent importance. But then it is simple to invent an alternative version of the music which does not have the sequence but in which the C at bar 11 still plays a decisive structural role; Fig. 23 shows it. What would Meyer say now? I don't know; whereas the Schenkerian analysis provides an answer that holds for both cases. This is that the C

Fig. 23

at bar 11 is supported by the structural V harmony which leads directly to the final tonic; for this reason a Schenkerian analysis that showed the structural $\hat{2}$ at bar 14 would be simply incorrect.

So far we have ignored an important aspect of Meyer's analysis, and one which does yield detailed insights absent in a Schenkerian analysis. This is rhythm. Meyer's approach to rhythm[1] is complementary to his approach to pitch; that is, it is based on precisely the same principles of patterning (this is where formulating the analytical approach in terms of general psychological principles pays off). Rhythms are seen as patterns whose basic units consist of a downbeat plus one or two upbeats associated with it. The different ways in which upbeats can be associated with a downbeat give rise to five different types of rhythmic group and these five types of group are the basis of all Meyer's rhythmic analysis. He adopts names for them which are derived from Greek prosody, and uses − to indicate a downbeat and ∪ for an upbeat. Here are the five types of rhythmic group:

iamb	∪	−	
anapest	∪	∪	−
trochee	−	∪	
dactyl	−	∪	∪
amphibrach	∪	−	∪

Each of these functions analogously to the groups into which Meyer analyzes pitches. An incomplete rhythmic group implies continuation, a complete group implies closure at a given level; and in most music rhythmic groups are organized hierarchically – into groups of groups, groups of groups of groups and so on. The analysis under the music in Fig. 21 shows how it falls into rhythmic groups from the largest to the smallest scale. On the largest scale, which is marked '5', the whole piece constitutes a single group (an iamb); on the smallest scale, which is marked '1', the groups vary from half a bar to a little over a bar's duration. What determines just how small the groups are to be at the smallest scale? Why are the larger groups at this level not further subdivided? The reason is that by level '1' (or the *primary rhythmic level*) Meyer means the smallest level at which the music divides into a continuous series of rhythmic groups; some of these groups can be

---

[1] I should really say Meyer and Cooper's, since they were co-authors of *The Rhythmic Structure of Music* (University of Chicago Press, 1960) in which this kind of rhythmic analysis was developed. But for convenience I shall continue to omit Cooper's name.

further broken down but others cannot, so that the result would not be a continuous series of groups. Sometimes it is useful to break down the music beyond the primary rhythmic level, and Meyer uses the letters i, ii and so on to refer to these fragmentary rhythmic levels (an example will be found at the beginning of Fig. 25).

The whole system, then, is based on the rhythmic group; and the rhythmic group in turn is based on the distinction between downbeat and upbeat. To make a rhythmic analysis you first need to determine where the downbeats are, and then decide how the upbeats are associated with them to form groups on successive levels. But what actually distinguishes a downbeat from an upbeat? An accent, replies Meyer. And what is an accent? It is 'a basic, axiomatic concept which is understandable as an experience but undefined in terms of causes' (*The Rhythmic Structure of Music*, p. 7). This sounds like an evasion but, in fact, is not. Meyer's point is that unlike a dynamic stress (which simply means a louder noise), a rhythmic accent has a psychological significance. An accented beat is one that is 'marked for consciousness in some way' (p. 8), and there are all sorts of ways in which a particular beat can become marked for consciousness. Dynamic stress is one. Duration is another (particularly at higher levels). And these are not the only factors. If you play Bach's C major Prelude with absolutely even tempo and dynamics, and even if you don't sustain any of the notes longer than others, you will still find that the notes group themselves into upbeats and downbeats; so that these must be determined by such things as harmony and repetition. In fact all aspects of musical structure can be significant for rhythmic accentuation. It is important to realize that when Meyer analyzes rhythm he is not simply considering one aspect of music and ignoring the others. Instead he is using rhythmic accentuation as a means of clarifying and notating his response to the music as a whole; as he puts it, 'the effects of melody, harmony and form can all be made subject to the summarizing influence of rhythmic analysis' (p. 153). You may remember that we have met a similar situation once before, only the other way round: in the last chapter I said that a Schenkerian analysis does not ignore rhythm but presents conclusions about it in terms of pitch structures. Schenker's analysis of the C major Prelude is, by implication, a rhythmic analysis because it shows how accents emerge where they do at the various structural levels. Meyer, by contrast, analyzes rhythms explicitly.

Let us return to *Das Wandern* at this point and see just what criteria Meyer is using in deciding where accents fall and how they are grouped. At level 1, the first accent is on the beginning of bar 1. Why? Because of the metre; notice that at level 1 all first beats and some third beats are accented, but never second or fourth beats. But how can metre be established at the very beginning of the piece? The answer is that this is not the beginning of the piece; there are in fact four bars of piano introduction, which Meyer omits. These four bars are more than sufficient to establish the metrical pattern, and where such things as melody, harmony and repetition are not active then rhythmic accentuation will tend to coincide with metre. If, then, it is metre that makes the F, A and D of bars 1–2 accented at the first rhythmic level, what is it that determines the grouping? Here the answer is melodic structure. Proximity of pitch joins the B♭ and A together, and separates them from what comes before and after. This also explains the association of the E♭ and D. But why are these two notes shown as part of an amphibrach lasting four beats instead of as a two–beat iamb like the B♭ and A? Because the D is prolonged by means of a tonic arpeggio completed by the F; all four beats are fused into a single rhythmic impulse. Imagine how unmusical it would be to breathe before the F, or to give it a dynamic stress! Here, then, melodic pattern takes precedence over metre.

Now let us turn to the second rhythmic level. The analysis of the first level has a few obligatory consequences for the second. Each group at the first level will correspond to a beat at the second, and this means that each group at the second level must start and end coincidentally with some group at the first level rather than half way through them.[1] Beyond this, there are no strict rules about deducing one level from the next. The same criteria that were used to determine accents and grouping at the primary level are used at the second and subsequent levels. However, we encounter something new as soon as we look at the first beat at the second rhythmic level: the symbol ⌣̄. By this Meyer means a beat that at first seems to be accented, but turns out in retrospect to have been unaccented (the symbol for the converse, which is rarer, is ⌣).[2] To grasp what Meyer is driving at, suppose that the song had begun as in Fig. 24. This is a simpler rhythmic pattern than the one Schubert wrote, and in it the first two beats at the second rhythmic level make up an iamb. Now, it is a

---

[1] The only exception is when, as sometimes, there are superimposed groups staggered against each other at one rhythmic level (see Fig. 25). Where this happens, either one of the groups is non-structural – it plays no part in higher-level organization – or else the music is ambiguous.

[2] For a complete list of the symbols used in Meyer's rhythmic analysis, see *The Rhythmic Structure of Music*, p. 204.

principle of Gestalt psychology (which is where most of Meyer's psychological principles come from) that the mind will interpret things in the simplest possible way, and Meyer is saying that the simple iambic pattern of Fig. 24 is what the listener expects to happen as he listens to the beginning of Schubert's song. But in the event the melody continues up to E♭ and D, the result of which is a more complicated group with D as its downbeat: that is why the initial beat turns out to have been unaccented after all. But how do we know that the D is accented at the second rhythmic level? Obviously this is so; Meyer is right. But he does not explain it. The Schenkerian analysis does, though. The D is the primary note, the beginning of the piece's structural motion; naturally then it is 'marked for consciousness', whereas the preceding bar (which constitutes an anticipatory prolongation) functions as an upbeat.

Fig. 24

Let us continue with the second rhythmic level. The dotted-line notation for bars 3–4 refers to their peculiar emptiness, mentioned earlier; these are, as Meyer puts it, 'felt but unperformed beats' (p. 204), and this is also why Meyer puts the upbeats here in brackets. In bars 9–10, and again in bars 11–12 which are a sequence, Meyer indicates trochees. Why trochees rather than iambs? Possibly Meyer's reason is that on the primary rhythmic level the first group, which corresponds to the first beat at the second level, lasts longer than the second; and as I mentioned, where other things are equal, duration tends to create accents.[1] But other things are not equal on this occasion. The harmonic structure implies iambs; though all the harmonies at this point are part of a cycle of fifths, their distribution

---

[1] I don't know if this interpretation is correct, for two reasons. First, I have added the primary level in bars 9–12 since Meyer does not give it. Second, there is a mistake in the notation of the second and higher levels in his Ex. 81, where the groups are shown as starting on the barlines. This contradicts both the sense of the music and Meyer's own analysis in Ex. 79, so I have corrected it to what I think is intended.

is such that they behave as V—Is, first of VI (in bars 9–10) and then of V (bars 11–12). And continuing with the second rhythmic level, why do we again have trochees rather than iambs in bars 13–16? Isn't the weight of each phrase on the tonic rather than the dominant?

When you don't at first agree with a Schenkerian analysis, you can usually work out why the analyst is saying what he is by looking at his interpretation of adjacent levels; and as often as not, by the time you have done this you have decided he was right after all. But this often is not possible with one of Meyer's rhythmic analyses. The correlation between rhythmic levels just isn't that significant. Both Meyer's first and third rhythmic levels at bars 9–16 would be compatible with a second rhythmic level consisting of iambs instead of trochees. And this means that Meyer's method of analyzing rhythm is not very successful as a means of *explaining* music. However it is quite successful as a means of *observing* music and notating these observations. Trying to write down your responses to music by means of Meyer's symbols involves constantly asking yourself 'where do I feel there to be downbeats, and relative to what?' and this is an excellent way of clarifying a problematic passage; once you have decided just what it is that you are trying to analyze, you may find that some other technique – such as Schenkerian analysis – will allow you to explain it.

However it seems to me that rhythmic analysis is less useful as a means of observing large-scale structure than it is at a more detailed level. The reason for this is that the nature of accentuation changes as between foreground and background levels. To illustrate this, let's jump to the fifth rhythmic level of *Das Wandern*, where the whole song appears as a single iambic group. Why is it an iamb? Because the weight of the music's motion is towards its final cadence; in this sense calling the whole song an iamb means precisely the same as the Schenkerian graph showing how the fundamental structure is directed towards the final tonic. In other words there is nothing specially rhythmic about the music's structure at this level, or at least about Meyer's presentation of it. Calling the whole song an iamb doesn't say anything the Schenkerian graph doesn't say; whereas the Schenkerian graph says a lot which the rhythmic notation does not, since it shows precisely how this final goal has been implied by what came before. And there is a further point. At this background level, you more or less know in advance what the rhythmic structure is going to be, at least if the music is in some conventional form. For instance, because of its tonal structure, any sonata is likely to come out as

Exp.	Exp. (rpt)	Devpt	Recap	Coda

and this means that the analytical emphasis has to be not on *what* the large-scale rhythmic structure is but on *how* it is realized in a given instance. The situation is exactly the same with Schenkerian analysis; the Schenkerian prototype for sonata form was given in Fig. 16. Both in a sense come to the same thing. But because it is better at showing *how* this form comes about, Schenkerian analysis can refine your initial response to the music in a way that I don't think rhythmic analysis does, or not so well. When it is not immediately obvious whether something is an upbeat or a downbeat, choosing between the two can seem pretty arbitrary – you feel that the analysis is forcing you to make judgements that are not demanded by the music itself. All these are reasons for restricting this kind of rhythmic analysis to relatively foreground levels, at least when Schenkerian analysis is available as an alternative. But of course, this does not apply with music Schenkerian methods cannot interpret, such as atonal music; there it can be worth attempting large-scale rhythmic notation.[1]

We have now covered the basic methods by which Meyer shows patterns of implication and realization to occur in musical pitch and rhythm; so let us conclude by looking at a more complex example of Meyer's analysis, which is the first twenty-one bars of Beethoven's Sonata 'Les Adieux' (Op. 81a). Fig. 25 is a collation of various charts from Meyer's *Explaining Music*, while Fig. 26 again offers a Schenkerian analysis for purposes of comparison. By now the charts should speak for themselves, so instead of working through them in detail I shall jump to the conclusion they support.

At the largest scale, Meyer considers the whole of this passage as 'a single event: more specifically, as an extended prolongation of tonic harmony with the third in the soprano voice' (p. 265). Actually his main

---

[1] See the analyses of Webern's Piano Variations and Stockhausen's *Klavierstuck III* in Chapters 9 and 10 below; also Cone's discussion of rhythmic analysis of atonal music in 'Analysis Today': P.H. Lang (ed.), *Problems of Modern Music*, Norton, 1962. For further refinements and criticisms of Meyer's techniques of rhythmic analysis see Cone's *Musical Form and Musical Performance* (Norton, 1968) and *A Generative Theory of Tonal Music* by Fred Lerdahl and Ray Jackendoff (MIT, 1983).

Fig. 25 Meyer, analysis of Beethoven's *Les Adieux* Sonata, I, bars 1–21

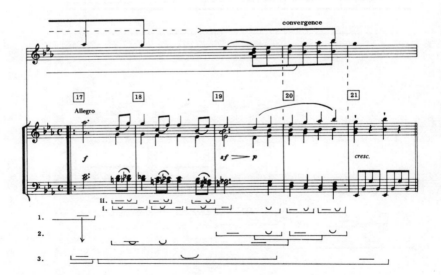

analytical graphs do not show this at all, so he adds another which shows a neighbour-note motion identical to the one that appears in the Schenkerian graph (Fig. 27). At this level, then, the two analytical approaches are in agreement, but the Schenkerian one is much more successful in showing how the continuity of this large neighbour-note motion is tied in with successive patterns of continuity at different levels of hierarchy. For instance, level 'C' of Fig. 26 shows how the neighbour-note motion is part of a larger prolongation pattern C – B♭ – A♭ – G which composes out the VI harmony of bar 2. And level 'B' shows how this larger pattern is echoed on a smaller scale within the first seven bars, at the lower octave. Because this pattern ends on 3̂ it all constitutes an anticipatory prolongation of the primary note of the movement as a whole, which is the G at bar 21 (this is the first G to have proper tonic harmony support); everything that has come before is in this sense inessential, simply an introduction. But the introduction is itself structured as a complete piece, made up of a descent from the initial 3̂ through 2̂ (bar 12) to 1̂ (bar 21: the bar numbers refer to level 'C' of Fig. 26, where the notes of this descent are shown in their implied rather than their literal positions). This descending motion is at the same time an expansion of the opening motif and a diminution of the motion of the movement as a whole; one of the interesting things about this movement is the way in which the obsessive repetition of the opening motif creates an identity of foreground and background structure towards its end. Finally the G♭ passing note within the 3̂ – 2̂ – 1̂ motion of the introduction both anticipates the alternations of G and G♭ in the exposition and gives a linear continuity to the remote harmonic regions of the intoduction; that is to say, these regions are harmonic expansion of the G – G♭ – F – E♭ motion that appears at level 'C'. In all, then, Schenkerian analysis shows this introduction to be powerfully unified both within itself and in terms of its implications for the rest of the movement.

But does the success of this analysis in showing the harmonic continuity of these twenty-one bars necessarily make it a good analysis? Isn't it the discontinuities which are more characteristic of the music – such things as the opening interrupted cadence (which is a kind of conceptual dissonance since, as Meyer says, the horn call implies, but at the same time withholds, a resolution in E♭), the even remoter interruption at bar 8, and the silences and elliptical changes of mode in bars 14–16? Meyer stresses the 'quasi fantasia' quality of this introduction, and sees this as 'the result of a lack of strongly processive relationships between successive foreground events . . . Though there is hierarchic structuring within low-level patternings, there is little between them' (p. 256). To explain. Apart from a very distant implication of a D (see Fig. 25, graph 6), the G – F – E♭ motto in bars 1–2 doesn't create any particular expectations as to what will follow; as Meyer puts it, 'the prolongation follows the motto but is not implied by and does not follow *from* the motto' (p. 257). Hence the absence of further connections in Meyer's graphs of either pitch or rhythm. By contrast his analysis shows that bars 2:2–4:2 are tightly integrated. The graphs of pitch show a number of gap-fill and arpeggio patterns (the latter also appear on the Schenkerian chart). Consequently the rhythmic analysis shows a single anapest at level 1, its strong beat coinciding with the half-cadence on VI. On the other hand Meyer does not think there is any strong sense of continuity between these bars and what follows. The repetition at bar 5 becomes an 'afterbeat' creating an overlapped trochee at level 1, while there is a lacuna at level 1 in bar 6. What Meyer is saying here is that neither the repetition at bar 5 nor the progression

Fig. 26 Schenkerian analysis of *Les Adieux*, bars 1–21

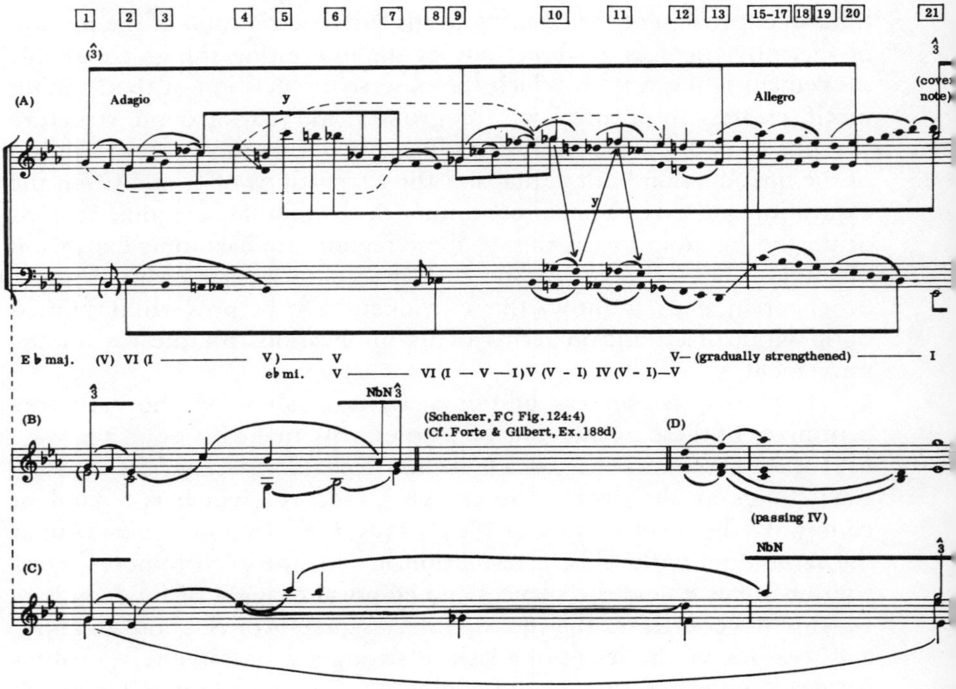

from B♮ to B♭ form part of any continuously evolving process, so that the music just stumbles onto the repeat of the opening motif at bar 7. As Meyer puts it, 'there is a feeling that the "Lebewohl" motto returns not because it is implied by the prolongation that precedes it, but because the previous statement of the motto was deflected from its goal . . . The repetition in measures 7 and 8 is, so to speak, a second "try" at reaching a cadence in E♭; and it too is abortive' (p. 261). Now Meyer may feel that there is no harmonic continuity leading to the return of the motto, but I don't. On the contrary, the B♭ at the end of bar 5 strikes me as a very telling note not just because it effectively opens up the higher register (it will lead to the A♭ – G of bars 15–21) but also because it immediately implies a cadence in E♭; bars 6 and 7 are fused with it in a single dominant upbeat. And if we understand bar 7 to be part of the preceding phrase, then the whole periodic pattern of these bars becomes quite straightforward. Bars 2–5 form a four-bar phrase (constructed as 3 + 1); bars 6–7 are a two-bar cadence. And this pattern persists into the second main phrase (from bar 8 on), the only difference being that this time the cadence is extended.

Fig. 27

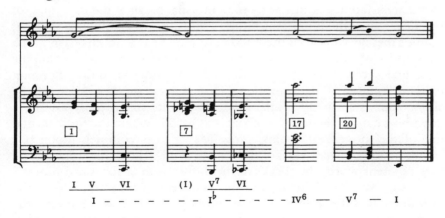

In this case it seems to me that harmonic structure is the key to accurate observation of the music, which is why it results in a much simpler analysis of the passage than Meyer's more abstract interpretation of linear and rhythmic patterns. Let us look at two more places where the same applies. These are both points where the surface texture changes dramatically – at bar 12 (where the repeated-note pattern starts) and bar 17, the beginning of the *allegro*. Meyer regards the D at bar 12 as a strong downbeat, and gives a complicated – but probably correct – explanation of this: the E♭ that precedes it breaks the previous sequential pattern (it 'should' have come at the beginning of bar 12 itself) and this makes the E♭ a particularly emphatic upbeat. This in turn makes the D a particularly strong downbeat. Where I do not agree with Meyer is in seeing this D as strongly implied by the previous pitch patterns. For example he shows it as the goal of gap-fill motions initiated at bars 3 and 9 (graphs 5 and 4 of Fig. 25). But for me the characteristic thing about this D, and the V harmony that supports it, is the way the music blunders onto it. It is particularly the anticipation of both the D and the harmony in bar 10 that creates this effect. When the music settles onto the V chord in bar 12 it does not sound convincing as a dominant at all; the music could just as well resolve as VI (V – I) – II – V – I of G♭. And it is this that makes sense of bars 12–20, the purpose of which is to transform this blurted-out harmony into a real dominant. Essentially bars 12–20 consist of a single V chord supporting a middleground cadenza that rises, like most cadenzas, to the seventh of the V chord and falls to the tonic. And this is why I disagree with Meyer's interpretation of bar 17 as a structural downbeat (see his rhythmic level 3) coinciding with a structural IV chord, as shown in Fig. 27. Of course there is an A♭ chord at surface level, just as there is a formal break at the beginning of the *allegro*. But the important thing – which is not so obvious – is that both of these disappear in the middleground. As my Schenkerian graph shows, the A♭ chord is simply the result of a passing motion within the structural V chord, which spans the end of the *adagio* and the beginning of the *allegro* in a single motion. That is why the beginning of the *allegro* sounds so oddly insubstantial despite its superficially assertive, downbeat nature; the real downbeat is at bar 21, where the fundamental line of the movement begins. Now Meyer does comment upon this contradiction between surface and background structure, except that he uses different words: he speaks of the 'bifurcation of form and process' (p. 266). By 'form' he means the surface organization into *adagio* introduction and *allegro* movement proper; by 'process' he means the structures created at underlying levels by relationships of implication and closure. So he is really saying the same thing as the Schenkerian chart. But again the Schenkerian approach refines, strengthens and explains Meyer's observations.

What I want to emphasize is not so much the superiority of Schenkerian techniques over Meyer's as the complementarity of the two approaches. A Schenkerian reduction tends to clarify the long-range harmonic continuity of music but suppress foreground contrasts. On the other hand, Meyer's techniques are useful for observing surface features, and in particular rhythmic contrasts. Both approaches tend to distort the music we experience; so, as I said in the Introduction, the important question is not 'which approach is the more true?' but, 'what are the circumstances in which each approach is more useful?'. As we have seen, the analytical techniques introduced by Meyer are useful for observation but tend to be less useful for generalization and explanation. They clarify the obvious things about music, and this is an excellent starting point for analysis. But in analysis the aim is to advance from the obvious to the non-obvious, and here Schenkerian analysis has the advantage because in most instances – as in 'Les Adieux' – it is the discontinuities that are obvious and the reasons why the music is none the less coherent that are not. Suppose that you were going to perform this sonata: which analysis would be more helpful in refining your interpretation, Meyer's or the Schenkerian one? Surely the Schenkerian one: because the difficulty lies not in projecting the fantastic constrasts of the foreground, but in achieving some kind of background continuity. It is rather like playing Chopin, where you need a very secure grasp of the underlying rhythm in order to make the surface rhythm as free and improvisatory as possible. Schenkerian analysis can provide the same kind of secure grasp when it comes to long-range harmonic structure. More is said about this in Chapter 10.

III *Rudolph Reti*

The problem with Meyer's brand of musical analysis is that neither he nor anybody else really knows how to formulate the harmonic structures of tonal music in terms of general psychological principles; that is why Meyer and his followers tend to neglect harmonic organization in favour of melodic and rhythmic patterns. The second main analytical approach I am going to talk about in this chapter also tends to neglect harmonic organization, concentrating instead on motivic patterns. This time the reason is quite different, however. To understand what the reason is, and what it has to do with psychology, we need to go back to Schoenberg, who was closely associated with this approach.

Schoenberg's atonal music is densely motivic; that is, it is made up of recurring intervallic cells. Fig. 28 is taken from George Perle's *Serial*

Fig. 28 Motivic patterns in Schoenberg's Op. 11, I, bars 1–3

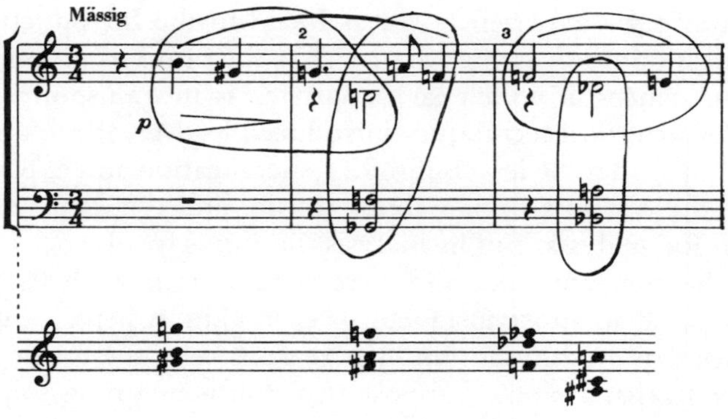

Perle's *Serial Composition and Atonality*,[1] and it shows how motivic cells explain not just melodic but also harmonic patterns in the first of Schoenberg's Three Piano Pieces Op. 11. Not all Schoenberg's music can be divided up into motivic cells quite so neatly, of course. But even when the style is more free in this respect than it is in Op. 11, it is the motivic aspect that Schoenberg himself stressed when analyzing his own music (which is a characteristically twentieth-century thing to do, by the way). Take for instance the Four Songs Op. 22, which Schoenberg analyzed for a radio talk in 1932.[2] This is texturally an extremely dense composition involving a gigantic orchestra – hence the rarity of performances – but it begins with a lightly accompanied melody for clarinets (Fig. 29). This initial idea (note that this is in itself a psychological term) is the basis of Schoenberg's analysis. What he does is to show how much of what follows is prefigured in this initial motif. Sometimes it is the contour that recurs (Fig. 30); that is obvious enough. But what is the connection between the initial idea and Fig. 31? Schoenberg's answer is that both are made up of patterns of minor seconds and minor thirds; each can be derived from a basic cell of three notes combining those intervals within the overall compass of a major third. (That is what the brackets beneath Figs. 29 and 31 are showing.) But then what about Fig. 32? The basic shape is still there, says Schoenberg, only it has been transformed – so that the minor second has become a major second and the minor third a major third. (I have

---

[1] 5th edition (1981), Ex. 7.

[2] A translation of Schoenberg's talk can be found in Boretz and Cone (eds), *Perspectives on Schoenberg and Stravinsky*, Princeton, 1968, pp. 25–45.

labelled the original cell as 'x' and the transformed one as 'z'; 'y', reasonably enough, is a halfway stage.) In this way passages that seem at first sight to be unrelated turn out to be variants of a single motivic cell.

Fig. 29

Fig. 30

Now the motivic technique of Schoenberg's atonal music, which prefigures Schoenberg's serial technique, is the culmination of a historical process going back through Wagner and Liszt to Beethoven. All these composers relied heavily on brief, recurrent motifs; this is one of the most obvious things about their music – particularly Wagner's, the point of whose leitmotifs is that they must be immediately recognizable even when half buried in a complex texture. Just because it is so obvious, no special technique of analysis is necessary in order to discover this; indeed commentators had been talking about such things since the days of E.T.A. Hoffmann. But following Schoenberg's lead a number of analysts developed quite sophisticated techniques whose purpose was to show that motivic patterns played just as important a role when they were not immediately visible (or audible) on the surface of the music. In fact, these analysts tended to assume that hidden patterns of motivic recurrence and transformation played a crucial role in all music – though it was particularly the music of the classical period that they concentrated on. In Britain, though not elsewhere, this became for a time the most influential technique of advanced analytical enquiry, and its principal practitioners were Rudolph Reti (who had been a pupil of Schoenberg's and actually gave the first performance of the Op. 11 piano pieces) and Hans Keller. Keller coined the term 'functional analysis' to describe his method, and published a few examples of it in the form of diagrams with

Fig. 31

a verbal commentary; but he subsequently decided that musical analysis ought to be presented musically rather than graphically, so he began to produce his analyses in the form of scores written for the same forces as the original work. These alternated passages of the work being analyzed with demonstrations of the motivic links between them, and the idea was that the whole thing should be presented as a performance rather

Fig. 32

than simply read.[1] Some of these analytical performances were broadcast in Britain in the late 1950s. However, they have not been repeated and until recently only one of the scores was available in print;[2] the result is that Keller's work has been less influential than might otherwise have been the case. By contrast Reti's analyses have long been available in book form, so it is his work that I shall discuss.

One of the pieces Reti analyzed in his first book, *The Thematic Process in Music*,[3] was Beethoven's last quartet, Op. 135; Fig. 33 shows its first sixteen bars. What Reti sees as its basic motifs are not on the surface; you cannot simply ring them as in Schoenberg's Op. 11. Instead Reti takes the opening two bars and compares them with what follows, looking for literal or altered recurrences. It is these alterations that are crucial. One of the most important is when other notes are *interpolated* betwen those of the motif. Fig. 34(a) is an example of this. It suggests

[1] See Hans Keller, 'Functional Analysis: its pure application', *The Music Review*, 18:3, pp. 202–6.

[2] 'FA No. 1: Mozart, K.421', *The Score*, 22 (February 1958), pp. 56–64. Another has recently appeared in print: 'Functional Analysis of Mozart's G minor Quintet', *Music Analysis*, 4 (1985), pp. 73–94.

[3] New York, 1951. Rufer's analysis of Op. 135 builds on hints thrown out by Schoenberg in 'Composition with Twelve Notes (1)' in *Style and Idea*, Berkeley, 1984, p. 220 ff.

Fig. 33   Beethoven, Op. 135, I, bars 1–16

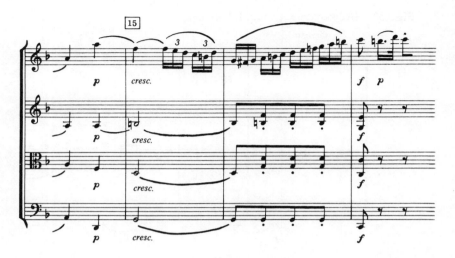

that the viola's and violins' entries in bars 4–5 spell out a variant of the opening three notes of the work; Reti puts all three instruments onto a single stave (in fact his analysis is based on a two–stave reduction of Beethoven's unusually fragmentary score), transposes the viola part up an octave, and prints the 'interpolated' notes in light type so that the underlying motif stands out. It is recurrences like this, says Reti, that justify our calling the first three notes a motif; in other words, when you call something a motif you are not talking about how it looks (or sounds) in itself but about what it is doing in the piece. However these three notes are only a secondary motif (that is why Reti labels it 'II'); the third to sixth notes in the viola, $B\flat - F - G - E$, are

Fig. 34

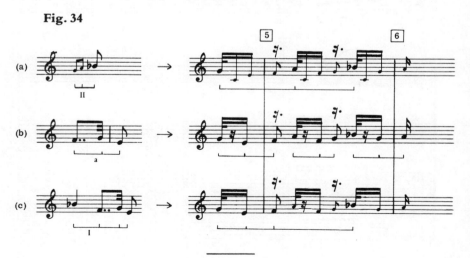

the primary motif, recurring more frequently and in more widely altered forms. In fact the same passage we just derived from motif II can also be derived from the primary motif. Fig. 34(b) shows that if we omit the C pedals, the first three notes are G–E–F; and these are the same as three of the notes of the primary motif, only they appear in *interversion*, that is to say in a regrouped sequence. And Fig. 34(c), which picks out the G – E – F – B♭ of bars 4–5, is intended to show its derivation from the primary motif as a whole; this time the notes appear more or less in *reversion*, that is to say

Fig. 35

Fig. 36

in reversed order. The primary motif appears in other places, too. In bars 6 – 7, for instance, it can be found in the first violin and viola; the only alterations are octave transposition and interpolation. Fig. 35 shows this, and in addition shows how it is preceded by another occurrence of the pattern – but this time at a different transposition within the F major set. Reti also finds the same transposition of the motif (F – C – D –B$\flat$) in the top notes of the first violin's part in bars 10–13, and another in bar 15 – except that this time the transposition is literal rather than tonal (that is, it has a B$\natural$ instead of a B$\flat$). Fig. 36 shows all this and more, and it represents Reti's conception of the entire passage as essentially a single melodic line in which the two underlying motifs appear in a variety of guises.

Now all this certainly provides some measure of the motivic homogeneity of the music. However for Reti it was merely the starting point for analysis. Two things primarily interested him: the way in which motivic formations of this sort had significance at the level of large-scale form, and the psychological significance of motifs in terms of the composer's creation of the music. As regards the first, his analytical method was intended to demonstrate and rectify the shortcomings of the traditional conception of form. What was the point, Reti asked, of describing how movements were built up of thematic sections, or compositions from movements, if you couldn't explain why this particular theme belongs in this work, or this movement in this symphony? As far as traditional concepts of form were concerned, Reti argued, you could substitute any theme, or movement, for any other which happened to be in the right key and tempo; which showed that there must be factors governing musical form which the traditional approach to form altogether ignored. And this is where he saw motifs as playing an essential role. He believed that in any coherent piece of music not only the various themes but the different movements will, on inspection, turn out to be made up of the same set of motifs. He is committed, therefore, to finding the primary motif of Op. 135 in the two middle movements. Fig. 37 shows how he manages this. Effectively he splits the primary motif into two component parts, which he now labels separately as 'I' and 'II'; these consist respectively of a perfect fourth and some combination of seconds and/or thirds. All this is rather tenuous, so Reti hurries on to the final movement, where there is a much better case to be made. This movement is highly unusual in that it has a title (*Der Schwergfasste Entschluss*, the grave decision) together with a musical inscription (Fig. 38). These phrases recur in the course of the movement itself, and Reti argues – reasonably enough – that for Beethoven to have picked them out in this way and assigned words to them suggests that they had some special allegorical or expressive significance to him, as well as a purely musical one. Now in strictly musical terms, Reti points out, these phrases are closely linked to the opening of the first movement; this is obvious in the second 'it must be!' (Fig. 39), and the first two phrases are simple derivatives of the third (by inversion and transposition respectively). And the final theme of the work (Fig. 40) embodies the opening motif of the work yet again, and in such a manner – as Reti puts it – that 'the phrase that originally was, in all its brevity, an expression of somber woe has now become an utterance of light and almost dance like cheer. In the transformation of the somber opening *motif* to the serene *theme* of the Finale, the thematic resolution and the innermost content of the quartet come to fulfilment' (p. 217). Musically, then, the opening motif of the work not only has a dominating role in the entire work – so assuring its homogeneity – but also begins a process which the final theme terminates; while at the same time the title and inscription prove how this purely musical process was bound up with some kind of extra-musical meaning in Beethoven's own conception of the music. For these reasons Op. 135 had a double significance for Reti. First, it proved that his analytical method could decipher the symbolical meaning embodied in music as well as its technical structure. And second, it could make sense of music which was unintelligible in traditional terms – in the case of Op. 135, because of the absence of anything resembling what was normally meant by a 'theme' in the first movement. The basic coherence of a piece of music, Reti argued, lay in its motivic patterns; whether or not these were bundled into easily recognizable themes was a matter of compositional style and not of the music's essential structure. This is rather similar to Schenker's distinction between surface form and background structure, and the

Fig. 37

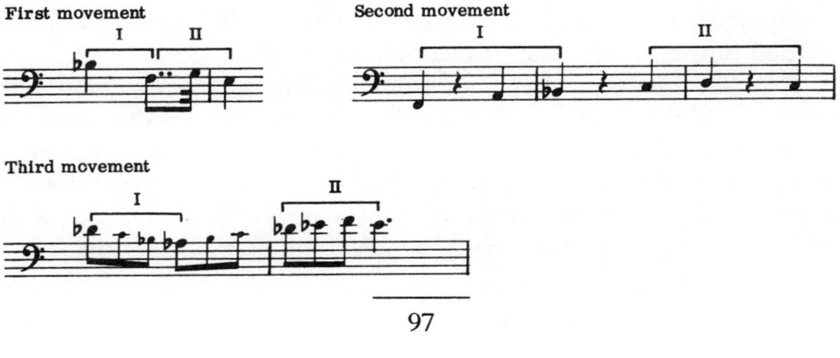

First movement

Second movement

Third movement

Fig. 38

Grave

Must it be?

Allegro

It must be! It must be!

Fig. 39

Opening shape

It must be!

Fig. 40

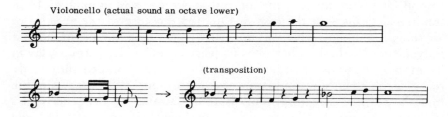

Violoncello (actual sound an octave lower)

(transposition)

similarity is the result of a basic conception shared by both analysts: each saw musical composition as the organic elaboration of some kind of underlying idea. It is in this particular sense that both Schenker and Reti regarded music as essentially psychological.

Reti has a habit, as here, of suddenly leaping from a minute examination of the opening of a work to broad conclusions about its large-scale structure. These transitions tend to be the most problematical part of his analyses, so we ought to look at an analysis where the intervening stages are spelt out in some detail. Reti's analysis of the *Pathétique* Sonata is exceptionally detailed and it was published posthumously in a book called *Thematic Patterns in Sonatas of Beethoven*.[1] The concept of a thematic pattern, which hardly appears in the analysis of Op. 135, plays an important role in Reti's method, but before it can be illustrated we need to identify the basic motivic constituents of the Sonata. There are six in all, and all but two of them can be found in the opening *Grave* section (for the music, turn back to Fig. 5 on p. 23 above). The other two are the 'melodic' motif, which is a rising minor seventh as at bar 56; and the 'Rondo' motif, made up of a falling plus a rising semitone (for instance C – B♮ – C in the first bar of the Rondo). Though Reti gives the motifs names rather than numbers on this occasion, he explains that this is merely a matter of convenience, and sets out a table listing each motif in the *Grave* together with its inversion. Fig. 41 shows this, while Fig. 42 shows his detailed analysis of the *Grave*. Why are bars 1–4 and 5–10 in different formats? Because Reti regards each of the inner parts of bars 1–4 as a separate melodic line rather than as harmonic filler, so that there are four structural parts in bars 1–4 as against three in bars 5–10. And what does this analysis tell us? It gives an explanation for things like the otherwise odd bass leap

Fig. 41

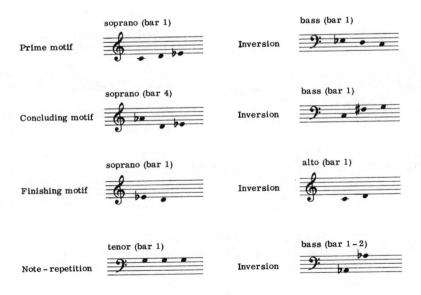

[1] Faber, 1967.

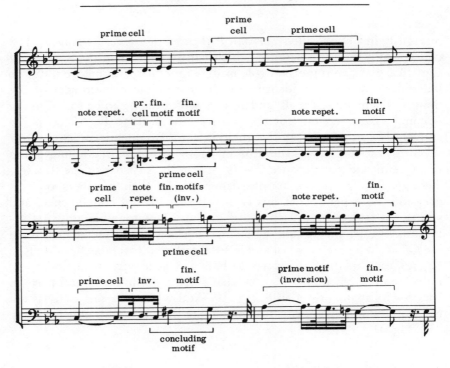

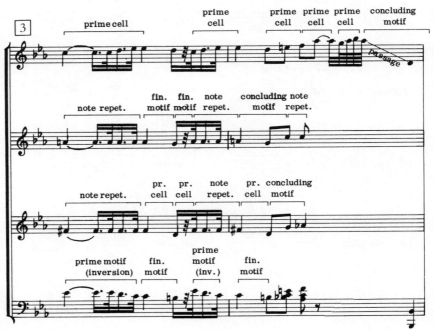

Fig. 42 Reti, analysis of the *Pathétique* Sonata, I, bars 1–10

from C to F♯ in the first bar (it is part of the concluding motif), the choice of the transposition between bars 1 and 2 (the D–F spells out the prime cell), and the larger transposition from the opening C minor to its relative major at bar 5 (the C and E♭ again spelling out the prime cell). But the point of this analysis is not so much to explain the *Grave* section in itself, as to enable Reti to explain the rest of the Sonata in relation to it. The basic principle of Reti's analysis is that 'the *Grave* was formed as a model for the entire work. To function as an outline for the structural source of the first movement specifically, and as a structural source for the whole sonata in general, is its innermost architectural idea' (pp.29–30). In other words, Reti sees the *Grave* as functioning in the same way as the initial melody from which Schoenberg derived what followed in his *Four Songs*. In effect Reti's method assumes that all music works this way.

The real findings, then, begin when the remainder of the Sonata is compared to the *Grave*. Again and again Reti discovers not only that the *Grave's* motifs recur in succeeding themes and movements, but that they recur in the same, or at least a similar, order. Fig. 43 shows his detailed analysis of the first *allegro* theme, on the basis of which he compares it with the *Grave* as follows (p. 35):

Bar 1, *Grave* and *Allegro*: Prime motif in C.

Bar 2, *Grave* and *Allegro*: Prime motif in F.[1]

Bars 3 and 4, *Grave* and *Allegro*: Repetition of the first two bars an octave higher.

End of bar 4, *Grave*; bars 5–8, *Allegro*: Descending passage, expressing the concluding motif.

Fig. 44 shows how more or less similar *thematic patterns* occur in the other themes and bridging groups of the *Allegro*, as well as in the themes of the remaining two movements. Furthermore such similarities are not restricted to a single level, one theme being shaped like another; they occur hierarchically too. Fig. 45 sets each of the *themes* of the *Allegro* against the corresponding *phrase* of the *Grave*. And all these structural similarities mean that for Reti the sonata possesses not only *motivic unity* – the homogeneity resulting from motivic recurrence – but *thematic consistency* too: each theme is a variant of the same underlying pattern.

[1] When Reti says 'in C' or 'in F' he is talking about the note that dominates the motif, not about the key (the two may or may not coincide).

Fig. 43 Reti, analysis of the *Pathétique* Sonata, I, bars 11–18

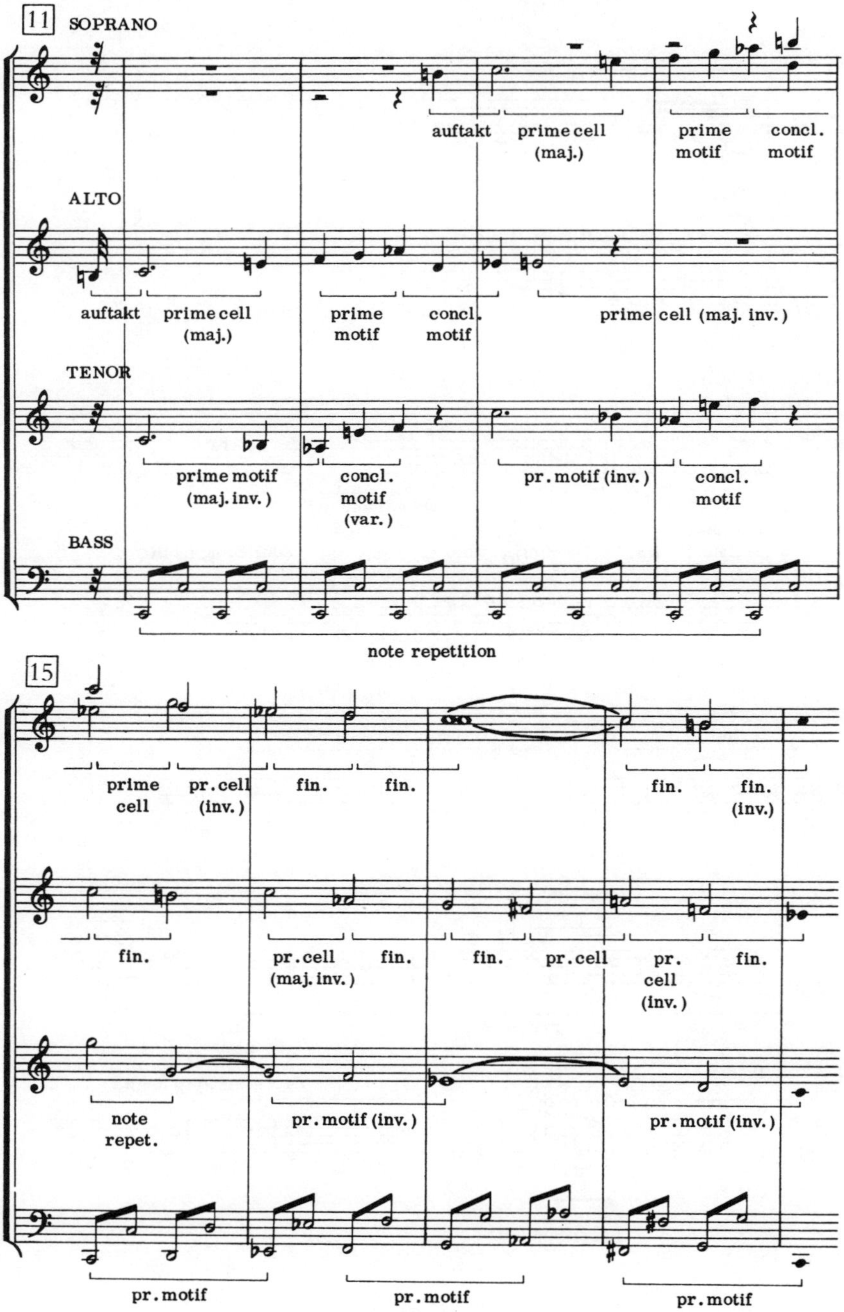

Fig. 44 Reti, thematic patterns in the *Pathétique* Sonata

Second *Adagio* theme:

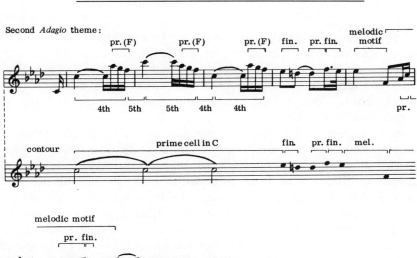

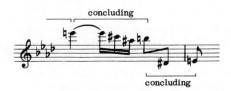

Third *Adagio* theme:

As Reti puts it, 'if the cells and motifs can be regarded as bricks of a work's structure, then the "patterns" are its larger units. Or, more specifically, the patterns are the motivic ideas of the themes' (p. 46). The themes *seem* different – it is a necessary condition of the classical style that they should – but at the deeper level they are the same: and that is why they belong together.[1]

Motivic unity and thematic consistency are hierarchically related: thematic consistency assumes motivic unity and adds something else to it. (Reti disliked the term 'motivic analysis' and instead referred to his technique as 'thematic analysis' in order to stress its significance for large-scale form.) However, there is also a third stage in this hierarchy, which Reti called *architectural planning*. He defined it as 'the method of shaping the motifs and themes from the beginning in such a way that, by transforming them in an appropriate manner as the work progresses, and finally leading them to a resolution, a kind of story or "architectural plot" is evolved which makes all the shapes of a composition a part and expression of one higher unity' (p. 141). Reti uncovers such a structural process in the *Pathétique* when he compares the tonal plans of the three movements. Tonal shifts are predominantly by thirds in the first two movements, he points out; indeed he adds that 'the pivotal keys of the *Allegro* are C, E flat, E natural, C, while the main keys of the *Adagio* are A flat, F natural, F flat, A flat. Or in other words the key pattern of the *Adagio* is the exact contrary motion of the key pattern of the *Allegro*' (p. 69). But in the Rondo almost all the structural key-relationships are by fourths or fifths. How, then, can it even belong within the same composition, let alone function as a satisfactory resolution of it? Reti's answer is that the thirds so characteristic of the first movement represent 'shapes of tension' which, from the very beginning, have a tendency to resolve into fourths and fifths – the 'shapes of resolution', as he calls them (p. 80). But in the first movement this tendency is repeatedly blocked: hence the tension of the movement as a whole, a tension that receives its structural resolution only in the last movement. More specifically, he points out the association of the prime motif, the minor

---

[1] Keller lays even more stress on the essentially monothematic nature of music or at least of great music, as he considers this the principal criterion for distinguishing the great from the merely good. This kind of monothematicism, where the thematic pattern is buried deep under the surface, is quite different from nineteenth-century cyclic thematicism. Composers like Liszt and Franck simply transformed themes, not their underlying patterns, and the transformations are very simple – they have to be, since the identity of the theme is intended to be immediately obvious to the listener.

Fig. 45 Reti, comparision of *Allegro* themes with *Grave* phrases

third, with diminished seventh harmonies (the *Grave* particularly illustrates this), and with the unusual modulation in the *Allegro* from C minor to E♭ minor – a modulation that constitutes a harmonic dead-end and which leads, at bars 289–94, to what Reti calls the 'dramatic outcry . . . when the prime cell C to E flat, with the F sharp as bass, finally flows into nothing – a rest' (p. 74). Only in the final seven bars of the *Allegro* is this shape given a tonal resolution (Fig. 46) – but, Reti explains, a fully structural resolution cannot be attained simply by means of a single final cadence. So the structural tension remains unresolved, and the opening of the *Rondo*, which arpeggiates a C minor triad, repeats the shape of resolution with which the *Allegro* ended. In fact the whole *Rondo*, in Reti's view, constitutes a formal resolution of the previous movements, and the way in which fourths and fifths constitute a resolution of the earlier thirds is underlined by the second and third rondo themes – themes which are wholly based on fourths and fifths, and which betray no motivic affinity with any of the previous themes of the entire sonata. Anywhere else in the composition they would have been out of place, but here they embody the thematic resolution of the work as a whole. And to dispel any lingering doubts, Reti points to the two chords in the third and fourth bars from the end of the sonata (Fig. 47): each states the prime cell in its original transposition (C to E♭), but whereas the first couples it with an F♯, and so with the unresolved tensions of the first movement, the second couples it with a G and so with resolution. 'The whole story of the structural drama of the *Pathétique*', Reti concludes, 'is compressed in these two *pianissimo* chords' (p. 84).

Fig. 46

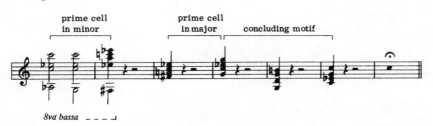

Reti's method is very ambitious in its aims, but it has come in for a great deal of criticism. One major criticism is that he picks out the evidence that fits his interpretations and ignores what does not. Consider his demonstration of the inversional relations between the keys of

Fig. 47

the first and second movements of the *Pathétique* sonata (p. 106 above). To be sure, the C and E♭ of the first movement are structural keys, but why pick out the E minor from the development when it is preceded by G minor and followed by the same passage transposed to D major? Why pick out the F minor of the second movement when it lasts only three bars, initiating a cycle of fifths that returns to A♭? The answer is all too obvious: to fit the plan. The problem is not simply one of Reti's analytical scrupulousness, but of the nature of the motifs and transformations on which he based his analyses. Suppose we were to regard the second (major or minor) as a basic motif. And suppose that we said that statements of this motif could be coupled together to give thirds, fourths and so on. We can now demonstrate all Western art music to be derived from this motif. But obviously this demonstration is totally meaningless. Now this is of course a gross exaggeration of what Reti did. But he did sometimes regard single intervals as motifs (the 'finishing' motif of the *Pathétique* was a second, the prime cell a third). He defended himself against the criticism that this led to indiscriminate and empty 'explanations' by saying that 'the individual form of a composition is not built by the use of so many and such-and-such intervals as bricks, but by the specific and always different way in which these elements are introduced, developed and finally combined into higher units' (p. 98). This sounds all right in principle, but do we see these 'specific and always different' characteristics in his actual analyses? Look again at Reti's charts of the inner lines of the first four bars of the *Pathétique* sonata (Fig. 42). He labels every relationship of a third as the 'prime cell', whether it is a skip or filled stepwise, whether it is major or minor, whether it is rising or falling. Similarly the 'finishing motif' occurs as a rising or falling interval, and as a major or minor second, so that any scalar pattern whatever can be derived from it. And sometimes, like our all-explaining motif of a second, Reti's motifs do not vary just in the size of their scale steps (major or minor second) but in the number of them too. Consider the following instances of the 'concluding motif', all of which are drawn from Reti's charts (Fig. 48): just what is the common factor? Is it anything more than the combination of one small and one large interval? And when you consider that Reti sometimes regards features like note-repetition or arpeggiation as themselves constituting motifs, it becomes clear that the technique is capable of indiscriminate explanation. It becomes impossible to imagine anything that couldn't logically be shown to be thematic in more or less any context.

Fig. 48   Variants of Reti's 'concluding motif' in the *Pathétique*

Now all this shows that the way Reti analyzes music is not very objective, but that does not necessarily mean it is bad analysis. After all, the same kind of objections can be made to Schenkerian analysis. You can always derive any music from any fundamental structure simply by picking out notes. The point, however, is not what you *can* derive but what you *choose* to derive. Good Schenkerian analysis is good not because it is more objective than bad Schenkerian analysis but because it is more musical: that is, because it takes proper account of harmonic and rhythmic implications, because it respects or even clarifies dynamics, phrasing and articulation in general. By contrast Reti frequently ignores all of these.[1] He justifies this as follows:

> 'The conscious phrasing and grouping of a work's shapes, as they finally appear in the score, need not necessarily conform in every detail with the mold in which these shapes first grew in the composer's mind from his motivic ideas. . . . The frequent discrepancy between the

[1] In his book *Beyond Orpheus* (MIT, 1979) David Epstein presents a number of Beethoven analyses which are essentially Reti-like, but in which the identifications of motifs are based on more-or-less Schenkerian criteria.

manner in which shapes seem to be divided if one follows the phrasing marks given by the composer, or if one traces the motivic elements, is the reason that the phrasing marks are often omitted in the musical examples quoted in this study' (*Thematic Process*, p. 204).

In other words, he is saying, when you analyze music in terms of motifs you are not primarily talking about the music as it is heard, but about the compositional process that gave rise to it. You are reconstructing the logical or psychological structure of that process – which is likely to correspond more or less to its outward chronology, though it need not necessarily do so.[1]

Fig. 49

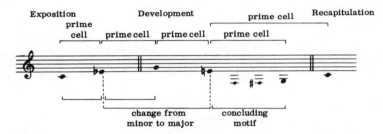

But discovering things about a piece of music and discovering things about the process of its composition are quite different things. And what Reti regarded as the most decisive confirmations of his interpretations occur when motivic links are either irrelevant from the point of view of musical sense, or when they actually run counter to it. An example of when motivic links are more or less irrelevant is when the same shape appears on a tiny scale, say as an ornament, and on the largest scale, for instance in a pattern of keys. Fig. 49 shows how the motifs of the *Pathétique* are reflected in the tonal plan of the first movement as a whole. Now nobody is likely to hear such a link: it is not in that sense musically significant. But, argues Reti, it is just this that proves its psychological reality: Beethoven must have had the shape in mind, so that it was naturally reflected at quite different levels of the musical structure, for otherwise why should the link be there at all? And an example of when motivic links actually run counter to the musical sense is provided by the beginning of the third movement of Beethoven's Quartet Op. 130 (Fig. 50). Why those odd rests in the

[1] See Reti's discussion of the genesis of the *Pathétique* sonata in *Thematic Patterns*, p. 97.

Fig. 50   Beethoven, Op. 130, III, bars 1–4

second violin part during the last bar, when they could so easily and naturally have been filled by passing notes? The reason, says Reti, is that this is a quotation from the quartet's opening theme which is shown underneath. The omission of the passing notes renders it a literal, note-for-note repetition (apart only from the changed accidentals). And the musical oddness of the result is the proof – 'a proof of almost mathematical conclusiveness', Reti called it – that this hidden thematic reference is not a chance occurrence but must be the result of a conscious compositional decision on Beethoven's part. Reti in fact believed that the techniques of thematic transformation he described had been adopted quite consciously by the classical composers, and that they had planned their works out in elaborate detail – more or less in the same way as he analyzed them. Few people accept this conclusion, and it is odd, to say the least, that there is no documentary evidence for the existence of so subtle and complex a compositional technique – especially when you compare it to the amount of fuss that Romantic composers made about their much more crude and obvious technique of thematic transformation. But the question whether classical composers were conscious of what they were doing actually is not so important. It would be perfectly possible to think that everything Reti describes was in fact done unconsciously. Either way Reti's analytical technique would be equally significant. In the one case it would be telling us about the history of compositional technique, and in the other about the psychology of the compositional process. And in either case the correctness or incorrectness of a given analytical interpretation would be as much a matter of fact as that of any other historical or psychological interpretation. Questions of how 'musical' the interpretation was simply wouldn't enter into it.

At the same time Reti also believed that his method did have something to say about the way in which listeners perceive music, and it is here – in what I see as the central area of musical analysis – that the essentially unmusical, or even anti-musical, nature of thematic analysis becomes a real problem. As I mentioned, Reti denigrated traditional analysis of form for its failure to answer what he considered the basic analytical question, 'why in music one group can be followed only by certain other groups and not by random groups which happen to fit in key, rhythm and the like' (*Thematic Process*, p. 349). In other words a given theme will be experienced as being satisfactory in one context and unsatisfactory in another. And how does the context influence the way the theme is experienced? Because, says Reti, of the listener's subconscious recollection of the motifs and pattern of earlier themes, to which he refers the new theme as he hears it. His recollection is obviously subconscious, because until Reti people didn't realize what it was that made the theme appropriate. Consequently for a motivic relationship to be musically significant it is not necessary 'that it must be heard and understood as a motivic utterance by the listener. The unnoticeable influence that it may exert on the listener as a passing subconscious recollection – in fact, *its theoretical existence in the piece* – suffices' (*Thematic Process*, p. 47). But if he is not to refer to his own experience as a listener, how is the analyst to decide what motivic relationships are important and what are not? Is he simply to label everything he can see, regardless of how it is experienced? Motivic analysis easily degenerates into a purely mechanical exercise in which the score is analyzed without ever really being read properly, and this tendency is exacerbated by the special importance Reti attached to what he called 'identical pitch'. By this he meant a motif recurring in its original notes, except that the accidentals may be quite different (the recurrence of the opening theme in the *Andante* of Op. 130 was an example of this). And frequently the harmonic context will be quite different, or the motif will appear in the same notes but in a different key.[1] In other words it will *sound* quite different, but it will *look* the same. The whole tendency of motivic analysis is to suggest that music is some kind of complicated cipher, and that the way to break the code is to stare at the score for long enough. It does not encourage sensitive listening.

I do not mean to say that Reti did not have good musical insights about the way that pieces are experienced. And to be fair to Reti we have to remember that he was just about the first analyst in the English-speaking world seriously to tackle the problem of large-scale coherence in music: in 1950 hardly anybody in Britain or the USA knew of Schenker's work. But nowadays the shortcomings of Reti's method are very apparent. The point of an analytical method is that it should guide you towards a clear and compelling account of the music as you experience it. And the Schenkerian method provides such guidance by suggesting initial questions, such as how the music is experienced as directed motion, and by means of a graphic technique that poses these questions in an increasingly refined and searching form. A Schenkerian graph not only expresses an analytical interpretation: it also constitutes a way of arriving at the interpretation, and an argument for its validity. It constantly refers you to the score, so as to check a particular motion against your experience of the passage or to see how it is confirmed by rhythm, phrasing and other means of articulation. But Reti's method rules out all these things; and instead of referring you to the score, it encourages you to pick out the themes and ignore everything else. (It is extraordinary just how much of the *Pathétique* sonata Reti leaves completely unexplored at the end of 78 pages of analysis.) His method also tends to blunt your sensitivity to the individual qualities of each piece. It

---

[1] For examples see Reti's analysis of Schumann's *Kinderscenen* in *Thematic Process*.

applies the same procedure to everything – a detailed examination of the opening so as to find the motifs, followed by a rapid comparison with successive themes. To be sure, Schenkerian analyses also begin in a standardized manner – that, after all, is what having an analytical method means. But the way a Schenkerian analysis develops depends on the individual piece, and the result is an insight into that piece. By contrast, each of Reti's analyses ends up with more or less the same insight, and this insight (if it really is an insight) concerns the nature of the compositional process in general rather than the particular quality of the music being analyzed.

CHAPTER FOUR

FORMAL APPROACHES
TO ANALYSIS

I *What is meant by a 'formal approach'?*

As its simplest 'formal analysis' means any kind of analysis that involves coding music into symbols and deducing the musical structure from the pattern these symbols make. Traditional analysis of form, which codes one thematic block as 'A' and another as 'B', is therefore an example of formal analysis, but the methods to be described in this chapter code music into symbols at a much more detailed level; they are not therefore simply concerned with 'form' in the traditional sense.[1]

Fig. 51   Schubert, *Heidenröslein*

---

[1] In this book I make a distinction of terminology between 'formal analysis' and 'analysis of form', but elsewhere 'formal analysis' can have either meaning. Or sometimes people use the term 'formalistic' for the kind of analysis this chapter is about.

But the most important thing that groups together various methods of musical analysis as 'formal' is not the specific techniques that they share so much as a basic attitude to musical structure. In order to understand the point of the techniques of formal analysis it is important to be clear what this attitude is, so we shall look at an analysis which is not formal in any technical sense (that is, it doesn't use symbolic coding) but which nevertheless betrays a formalistic conception of music. The analysis is of Schubert's *Heidenröslein* (Fig. 51) and it comes from Jeffrey Kresky's book *Tonal Music*.[1] This book systematically develops a more or less Schenkerian method of analysis from the simplest logical and perceptual observations of music; it altogether ignores the theory and jargon of Schenkerian analysis and in fact does not even mention Schenker's name. Kresky's analysis of *Heidenröslein*, as might be expected, discovers a fundamental line (though he does not use the term) which begins with B, moves through A, and terminates with the G in the lower vocal register at bar 14; this motion being recapitulated in the singer's last three notes. And, like any Schenkerian, Kresky sees the move from G major through B minor to D major (bars 5–10), which coincides with the voice's excursus away from the register of the fundamental line, as a prolongation of the initial triadic sonority. But neither the procedure nor the tone of Kresky's analysis is conventionally Schenkerian. He begins by 'slicing' the music into two-bar units, which he then associates into larger units, on the basis of surface features such as recurrences, changes of texture and fermata (Fig. 52). He then analyzes each of the intermediate-level 'slices' (or segments, as most people would call them) in order to show that each 'expresses' a given triad. Thus in bars 1–4 the vocal line is an arpeggiation of the tonic triad while, he argues, each of the four lines in the piano part 'expresses' a single member of that triad, elaborated by means of neighbour notes or other linear motions. Bars 5–10 also 'express' the G major triad, but at a higher level since the arpeggiation here forms the bass of a series of root position chords – so that, unlike the first segment, the second is tonally open (its I-V circuit, of course, being reversed in the third and final segment). And at this point Kresky makes a typically formalistic observation: 'just as the first phrase grows out of the G-major triad expressed by the first measure, the entire piece grows out of the G-major triad expressed by the first phrase. Note that the first measure is one-fourth of the first phrase, and the first phrase is just one-fourth of the composition' (p. 74). What motivates this statement is a belief that

[1] University of Indiana Press, 1978.

any musical form is the expansion of a kernel structure of some kind, an expansion that works hierarchically according to more or less strict rules – so that the analyst's job becomes one of working out just what these rules are in any given case.

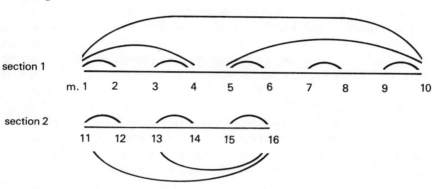

Is this really so different from the Schenkerian conception of music prolonging a fundamental structure? It is and it isn't. The essential difference is that Kresky, with his boxes-within-boxes approach, stresses the static aspects of musical structure; he sees it synoptically, as a pattern. He does not see it psychologically, as a process taking place through time – which is how a normal Schenkerian would approach this piece, asking 'how is the music experienced as being directed towards an ending?' This difference of approach is evident even in Kresky's use of the term 'express' where a Schenkerian would say 'prolong'. To see the primary tone of *Heidenröslein* (the B) as 'prolonged' means that its resolution (through A to G) is implied but postponed: it stresses the psychological experiences of anticipation and delay. But to see it as 'expressing' the G major triad stresses the formal structure the music presents rather than the effect the music has on a listener, and in fact other formal analysts use the term 'present' in exactly the way Kresky uses 'express'.

But does this difference of approach actually matter in practical terms? The answer is yes, and two examples will illustrate this. Kresky describes the B minor of bar 8 as 'the major link between the former and new tonalities' (p. 75) – that is between G major and D major. Looking at the pattern G–B–D nothing is more obvious than the fact that B links G and D (as successive diatonic thirds, and as members of the G major triad). But psychologically the B does not in fact function as a link at all. To verify this, all you have to do is play through the song to the end of bar 8, harmonizing the last note with a D major chord instead of B minor. The cadence on the dominant is perfectly coherent without the mediant, so the B minor cannot be functioning as a link. In fact it is just the opposite: it is an interrupted cadence and, as the name implies, it serves to postpone the expected resolution – that is, it has a psychological function involving the experiencing of musical time. The second example is Kresky's description of the A♯ of bar 9 as 'mysterious', on the grounds that it does not belong to the diatonic set of the current harmony. Consequently he explains it as a reference back to the B minor of the previous bar. This explanation seems quite unconvincing in view of the B minor inflection having been 'cancelled' by the A♮ of the D major chord at the beginning of bar 9. But what is more important is the very fact that Kresky feels the A♯ needs explaining at all – that is, that he finds what is after all a routine chromatic neighbour note analytically 'mysterious', when it obviously presents no mysteries to the listener. The reason is that if you explain music in terms of the formal structures it presents and not in terms of psychological factors like listeners' expectations, then the fact that chromatic neighbour notes are normal in Schubert's style becomes irrelevant. Instead it becomes necessary to find an explanation for everything in terms of the structure of the individual piece under analysis. That is why Kresky analyzes *Heidenröslein* rather as if some cataclysm had resulted in the loss of all other tonal music; he takes nothing for granted.

Where did this formalistic concept of music 'expressing' or 'presenting' structures come from? In the USA at least (where formal techniques of analysis are strongest) the most direct source was the theory of serial music developed by Milton Babbitt and George Perle. Both emphasized the extent to which serial music was determined by structural relationships formed by the complete complex of a series in its various transformations (inversion, retrogression and transposition – but it is not necessary to understand the details at this point). Now, such a complex is a purely abstract structure, existing quite independently of musical time. Perle used the term 'precompositional' to denote these formal properties of the series, thereby distinguishing them from the 'compositional' aspects of the music – that is, the manner in which the composer chooses to present the formal structure in time by means of actual musical sounds. You can see how this way of thinking can be applied to Schenkerian analysis: the fundamental structure is seen as the abstract precompositional aspect of the music which can be presented compositionally in all sorts of different ways – by means of different prolongations, interruptions or whatever. And it is this distinction between the logical structure of a piece of music and its presentation through sound that is at the heart of the formalistic approach. It has been most forcibly stated by Benjamin Boretz (a colleague of Babbitt's at Princeton University, which became a stronghold of formalism under Babbitt's influence). According to Boretz 'we need not *ever* construct sounds to construct music, regardless of their indispensability in its transmission, for once we have extracted their full burden of significant relational information . . . we have no further *musical* use to put them to'.[1] Naturally, there are general conditions regarding what sounds are capable of transmitting such relational content: they must not be excessively quiet, high and so on. But such general conditions are not the analyst's concern: as Babbitt puts it, 'the discovery and formulation of these constraints fall in the province of the psycho–acoustician'.[2]

One of the results of this separation between the logical structure of music on the one hand and its expression in sound on the other has been a reinterpretation of Schenker's analytical method. Conventional Schenkerian analysis is expressed in terms of a single historical style, that of Western tonality. But people like Boretz believed that if the Schenkerian method could be restated in terms of purely logical relationships between musical structures, then the basic principle of the method – its conception of music as a series of structural levels – would become just as applicable to styles other than those of Western tonality. There is a comparison here to be made with physics. Newtonian physics is expressed in terms of certain physical conditions that apply to the universe as it was known in the seventeenth century. Relativity is expressed in much more abstract terms, and it includes Newtonian physics in the sense that it provides a theory of what happens under those same physical conditions. But equally it also provides a theory of what happens under any other conceivable conditions, so that relativity is of a much more general application than Newtonian physics. In just the same way, what Boretz and other neo–Schenkerians were aiming to do was to generalize the Schenkerian method, so that while it would explain what happens under the particular stylistic conditions of tonal music, it would equally explain what would happen under any other conceivable stylistic conditions. Boretz set out a very comprehensive

---

[1] 'Metavariations (II)', *Perspectives of New Music*, Spring/Summer 1970, p. 63.

[2] 'Past and Present Concepts of the Nature and Limits of Music', in Boretz and Cone (eds.), *Perspectives on Contemporary Music Theory*, Norton, 1972, p.9.

theory along these lines in a widely known (though possibly not so widely read) series of articles called 'Metavariations', which set out a hierarchical model applicable to all music. It began with simple discriminations of identity or non-identity in terms of pitch and time: this was the most elementary level of musical structure as he saw it, and one shared by all musical cultures. It then structured these elementary discriminations by means of various logical rules or operations (which were expressed in terms of symbolic logic), and these generated higher levels of musical structure. Not all these rules applied to all music. For example, higher levels of musical structure could be generated by rules determining either the order of events or their content: the first corresponded to serial, and the second to tonal, music. So at these intermediate levels different types of musical organization were being distinguished. At the highest level it was individual pieces that were being distinguished from one another. Accordingly analyzing music, for Boretz as for other formalists, meant devising a series of formal rules showing how the structure of the individual piece (or at least the best possible approximation of it) could be reconstructed from the elementary discriminations of pitch and time common to all music.

How far is Schenkerian analysis recognizable in its new guise?[1] The logical structure of Schenkerian analysis is still there: that is, the series of structural levels from the most to the least determinate (although there is a change of emphasis, in that Schenkerian analysis is mainly concerned with working from the foreground to the background, whereas neo-Schenkerian analysis concentrates on the way in which the background generates the foreground). But what is not still there is the psychological structure of Schenkerian analysis. The Schenkerian question – 'how is the music experienced as directed motion?' – is replaced by a new one: 'how can the score be shown to be logically structured?' or perhaps more accurately 'how should we recode the score so that its formal unity will become self-evident?' One aspect of this we commented on apropos of Kresky: where the Schenkerian analyst is interested in the psychological experience of time, the formal analyst conceives structure statically, in terms of logical patterns. But an equally important aspect is that whereas Schenkerian analysis uses the *experience* of music as its raw material, formal analysis quite literally analyzes the

---

[1] If you would like to make a detailed comparison between a Schenkerian and a neo-Schenkerian analysis, you might contrast Schenker's and Boretz's analyses of the first theme of Brahms's Fourth Symphony. Schenker's analysis is in *Free Composition*, Fig. 81 (2); Boretz's is in 'Metavariations (IV)', *Perspectives of New Music*, Spring/Summer 1973, p. 160.

score. It does so for what formal analysts consider a very good reason, which is that we can make precise and objective statements about musical scores whereas we can only talk about our experience of music in an imprecise and subjective manner. (Boretz makes fun of analytical methods based on concepts such as expectation or surprise by asking what reason we have for considering these reactions more significant than those of another listener who goes to sleep.) To appreciate this you have to realise that the formal approach did not arise for purely musical reasons. It also reflected a general reaction at the time against loose and impressionistic thinking, a reaction associated with logical positivism and in particular with Carnap, Goodman and Quine – philosophers who repeatedly crop up in essays by Boretz and other formalists. Babbitt put this viewpoint very clearly when he wrote: 'There is but one kind of language, one kind of method for the verbal formulation of "concepts" and the verbal analysis of such formulations: "scientific" language and "scientific" method . . . Statements about music must conform to those verbal and methodological requirements which attend the possibility of meaningful discourse in any domain'.[1] There are two possible views on this. One is that to talk in 'scientific' terms about the patterns of symbols in musical scores makes it altogether impossible to say anything worthwhile about music as a humane artefact; the point being that musical scores are not texts, they are merely a convenient though rather inaccurate way of representing musical sounds for purposes of performance. (More on this in Chapter 6.) The other view is that however little formal techniques of analysis may tell us about music, they at least tell us it in precise and explicit terms. Both views are defensible. Which you hold really depends on what sort of person you are.

On the whole formal methods of analysis have not made a lot of impact as regards the tonal repertoire. (If people read Boretz on the first eighteen bars of Brahms's Fourth Symphony, they do so to find out about Boretz rather than Brahms – which is a way of saying that Boretz counts for more as a theorist than as an analyst.) Where formal methods have had more of an impact is in dealing with early music, twentieth-century music, and non-Western music – repertoires to which Schenker's method (or for that matter Meyer's or Reti's) cannot be applied very successfully. And in the USA the main example of a formal approach is set-theoretical analysis.

---

[1] *Past and Present Concepts of the Nature and Limits of Music*, p. 3.

II *Set-theoretical analysis*

Fig. 53 shows the last of Schoenberg's *Six Little Piano Pieces* Op. 19. You cannot analyze this piece in terms of traditional tonal structure, in the way Kresky analyzed *Heidenröslein*; there is no tonic (at least, how could you decide what the tonic is?), and there is not the same kind of triadic elaboration you find in Schubert. What people usually do when faced with atonal music like this is to pick out certain things they regard as significant and ignore the rest. For example, you might pick out such familiar formations as the superimposed fourths in bars 1 and 5, or the whole-tones that become increasingly prominent in bars 5–6. Or you might pick out motifs that recur within this piece, for instance the way in which the prominent E – D$^{\#}$ of bars 3 – 4 is echoed in the middle of the texture in bar 8. But picking out things and ignoring the rest in this way is like picking out triads in a tonal piece and ignoring the underlying structure which they prolong – which is precisely what Schenkerian analysis teaches us not to do. The aim of set-theoretical analysis, which was evolved by Allen Forte (the same Allen Forte we met in Chapter 2), is to provide the same kind of insight into the underlying structure of atonal music that Schenkerian analysis provides into tonal music: as Forte himself puts it, it 'establishes a framework for the description, interpretation and explanation of any atonal composition'.[1]

Let us begin in the same way as Kresky began with *Heidenröslein* and slice Op. 19/6 into sections. Fig. 53 shows how it falls into six sections labelled from A to F, which are distinguished from each other on the basis of surface features like texture, rhythm and dynamics. Now what we want to do is establish a network of relations between these various sections comparable to the Kresky diagram reproduced in Fig. 52, but without using the same kind of reductive techniques that are appropriate for tonal music. For example, we do not want to say that the D$^{\#}$ in the left hand at bar 3 is an inessential note and the E that follows it an essential one, or the other way round, because we do not know what would make one note essential and another one inessential in an atonal piece. So rather than risk making inappropriate selections from the notes in each section, we shall try and see what structural relations exist between the entire content of each section considered as a harmonic unit. All we will assume is that register makes no difference to

---

[1] *The Structure of Atonal Music*, Yale University Press, 1973, p. 93. For a recent re-evaluation of set-theoretical analysis, see Forte's 'Pitch–class set analysis today', in *Musical Analysis*, 4 (1985), pp. 29–58.

Fig. 53   Schoenberg, Op. 19/6, with segmentation

the harmonic function of a note – in other words that, as in tonal harmony, a C functions the same way regardless of what octave it appears in. (In jargon, what we are interested in is *pitch classes* – Cs in general – and not pitches, such as this high C, that low C.) What this means is that our analysis will be based on what is shown in Fig. 54: we are using this as a working model of the music, hoping that the most important aspects of the original piece's structure are retained in this simplified version.[1]

Fig. 54

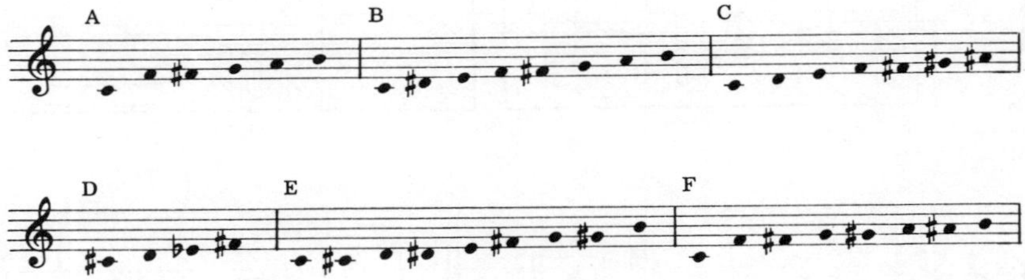

Fig. 55

Certain relations between the harmonic content of the various sections are immediately obvious. For example, the content of section B includes the content of section A, and similarly the content of section F includes that of section A. Actually you do not need Fig. 54 to tell you that! But without it you might not notice that the content of section E includes the content of section D – you can see this in the score, to be sure, but Fig. 54 makes it easier to see, while Fig. 55 spells out the relationship in two different ways. So far we have looked only for literal inclusion relationships – that is, where the pitch classes of one section include the pitch classes of another. (This is like saying a dominant seventh on G includes the G triad.) But one section might include the content of another, only at some transposition (in the way that the dominant seventh on G includes the E major triad when transposed by

[1] Is this sense? See the discussion of Op. 19/3 in Chapter 10.

a third). This is the relation between sections B and D of
Schoenberg's piece, and Fig. 56 spells out how it works. However, we
do not have to limit ourselves to the inclusion and transposition
relationships you get in tonal harmony: we can look for other relationships too. For instance, the content of one section might include
the content of another section only when it is inverted: and in fact this
is the relationship between sections A and E. You can see that this is so
from the music notation in Fig. 57. However, as the relationships we
are dealing with become more complicated, so they become increasingly difficult to handle by means of conventional notation. So
you may find it easier to see this kind of relationship if we use
numerals instead. We shall call the lowest note of each group '0' and
represent the other notes in it by the number of semitones by which
they are higher than the lowest note. The lowest note of section E is
C, so this becomes 0, C♯ becomes 1, and so on. This means that
we can write the harmonic content of section E as [0, 1, 2, 3, 4, 6, 7, 8,
11] and that of section A as [0, 1, 2, 4, 6, 7]. So the numerals in Fig. 57
mean exactly the same as the music notation, and they make it a little
easier to pick out the notes from each section that correspond to each
other under inversion: you simply look for pairs of numbers that give
the same value when added together (here the value happens to be 8,
but this depends on the transpositional relationship between the two
sets of notes). Some people find this kind of mathematical notation
off-putting: it looks so abstract, like an arithmetic primer. But really it
is no more abstract than the usual note-letter notation; it is just
different. You may find it useful to practise sight-singing from these
numbers. It is quite easy to pick up, and you can sing the notes as you
scan the numerals, looking for patterns.

What have we done so far? We have found three ways in which
the pitch content of the various sections in Op. 19/6 can relate to each

Fig. 56

Fig. 57

other: by literal inclusion, by inclusion under transposition, and by inclusion under inversion. Now there is a further type of relationship that is important in this piece, and it is based on complementation. What is complementation? Take the pitch content of section F. It includes all the notes of the chromatic scale, except C#, D, D# and E. And that means that these four notes are the *complement* of the eight notes in section F. In other words the complement of any given set of notes is simply all the other notes that together make up the chromatic scale. And we shall discover a whole lot more relations between the sections of Op. 19/6 if we take complementation into account. For example, there is not any direct relationship between the content of section F and that of section E – neither includes the notes of the other, whether literally, under transposition or under inversion. But section E does include the complement of section F, that is to say C#, D, D# and E; Fig. 58 shows this, using a symbol derived from mathematics ($\bar{\text{F}}$) to indicate the complement of F. So here we have the literal inclusion of a complement. Naturally, then, we can also have the inclusion of a complement under transposition. Actually there are three such relationships between the sections of Op. 19/6: E includes both the transposed complement of B and the transposed complement of C, while B in-

Fig. 58

Fig. 59

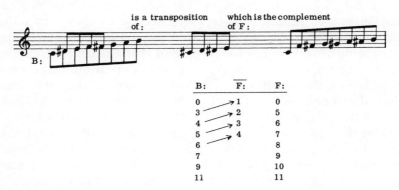

B:	F:	F:
0	1	0
3	2	5
4	3	6
5	4	7
6		8
7		9
9		10
11		11

cludes the transposed complement of F. Fig. 59 spells out the last of these: you can work out the other two for yourself if you want to. And, again as you would expect, there is a final way in which two sets of notes can relate to each other, which is when one includes the complement of the other under inversion. There is one instance of this in Op. 19/6: the complement of A includes the inversion of D, and Fig. 60 shows this.

Fig. 60

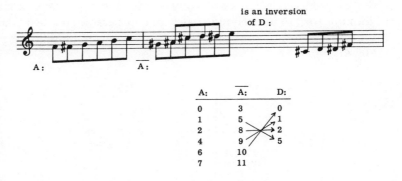

A:	A:	D:
0	3	0
1	5	1
2	8	2
4	9	5
6	10	
7	11	

Unless you have a bent for this kind of thing, all this talk of inversion and complementation may be making your head ache: but if you look back through Figs. 55–60 you'll see that the musical relationships we are talking about are really very simple and straightforward; it is merely that some of them are unfamiliar. And when you take all these relationships together, they can tell you a surprising amount about the structure of the piece as a whole. First let us express the relation of each section to every other section by means of a kind of mileage chart (Fig. 61). You read this like you read the charts that tell you the distance between towns, except that what it is telling you is whether or not we have been able to establish a relationship between the sections in question. If such a relationship exists, then the square is blacked in. For example, if you look at the entries for section C you will see that the only section which relates to it is E. On the other hand if you look at the entries for E, you will see that it is related to every other section of the piece. In other words we have established a pattern of relationships between each of the various sections of the piece that shows what relates to what, and we can make the formal consequences of this more easily visible if we draw a chart like Fig. 62. This embodies precisely the same information as Fig. 61 (the lines between sections represent relationships), and it makes it obvious how everything relates to E, whereas C is as it were out on a limb; there is no direct relationship between C and either the section before it or the section after it. And, if you think about it, this means something very like what Schenker's chart showing an 'interrupted' progression was saying (Fig. 16 above). In each case the analysis is saying that there is not a direct relationship between the two adjacent formations: they only relate to each other indirectly, in that both of them have a direct relationship to some third formation.

We have succeeded in our original aim. We now have what we were looking for, an underlying structure comparable to a Schenkerian

Fig. 61

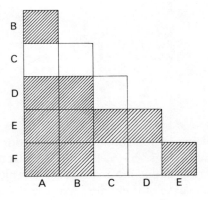

Fig. 62

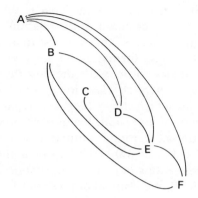

middleground; and it would be quite easy to complete the analysis in the way Kresky completed his, by looking for ways in which surface details in the music 'express' this underlying structure. And though what I have done is not really a proper set-theoretical analysis (as you will see, Allen Forte presents things rather differently), it should have given you some idea of what set-theoretical analysis is about. But the way I did it was not very convenient. I simply talked about 'the harmonic content of A'. But suppose there had been another section with the same harmonic content? Or suppose I had wanted to compare this piece with another one in which the same pitch class formation was found? What is wanted is a standardized way of referring to these pitch class formations wherever they are found. And the basis of set-theoretical analysis proper, as set out by Forte in his book *The Structure of Atonal Music*, is a complete listing of every possible pitch class formation that can appear in any piece of atonal music.

That sounds impossible! But the number of possible formations is reduced to manageable proportions by two restrictions. The first is that only formations of between three and nine different pitch classes are considered. Why is this? Suppose that section E in Op. 19/6 had consisted not of nine notes but of twelve – in other words, that the content of E had been the entire chromatic scale. In this case showing that its harmonic content included that of the other sections would have been totally meaningless: everything is contained within the content of the chromatic scale, from Beethoven's Ninth Symphony to Stockhausen's *Zeitmasse*. At the other extreme, recall what I said in the last chapter about how meaningless it would be to derive music from a single motivic cell consisting of a second (p. 109 above). At either extreme everything can be derived from anything. That is why Forte restricts himself to a central range of sizes in which the relationships you find are likely to be of some significance. So that was the first way in which the number of possible pitch class formations is kept within manageable proportions. The second has to do with the fact that in this kind of analysis we are interested in pitch class formations regardless of the particular transposition in which they occur, and regardless of whether they appear one way up or in inversion. Let us use the content of section D in Op. 19/6 as an example, writing it numerically (but you can read it as music if you like). We do not want to have one name for [0, 1, 2, 5], another name for transpositions like [1, 2, 3, 6] and another name for inversions like [0, 11, 10, 7]; we want all of these to have the same name, so that whenever we come across one of them we will immediately be able to see that it is the same as the others. And this is what Forte does. Each of these is a different version of a single pitch class set – or *pc set*, as Forte abbreviates it – which, as it happens, he calls 4–4. The first 4 means that there are four elements in the set (that is to say, there are four pitch classes in any particular version of it); the second 4 means that it comes fourth in his listing of the sets with four elements. And because there is only one pc set for this formation in all its various transpositions and inversions, the total number of possible pc sets of between three and nine elements becomes surprisingly small: there are in fact 208 of them. Forte lists them in an appendix to his book.

Fig. 63

$$(4) \qquad \begin{bmatrix} 0, & 1, & 2, & 5 \end{bmatrix} \begin{bmatrix} 0, & 1, & 2, & 5 \end{bmatrix} \begin{bmatrix} 0, & 1, & 2, & 5 \end{bmatrix} \begin{bmatrix} 0, & 1, & 2, & 5 \end{bmatrix}$$

Of course you need a set of rules to tell you how to work out the correct name of any particular pitch class formation you may come across, and this is rather like identifying a butterfly from one of those books that ask you a series of questions until there is only one possibility left: it is simple in principle but a bit involved in practice. Let us take four separate versions of the pc set 4–4: the version we found in Op. 19/6; a transposition of it; an inversion; and another inversion, in which the registration is different. As shown in the top line of Fig. 63 these all look different, but we want them all to come out the same. Forte gives a formal procedure for establishing what pc sets these all belong to, and this is useful where you are dealing with very big or rather similar sets, or if you want a computer to do the work for you; but usually it is easier to do it by eye, so I am consigning Forte's procedure to a footnote.[1] First of all you have to establish whether the version you are looking at is in its most compact

[1] Rewrite whatever version you have numerically, with 0 as the lowest note (Fig. 64, line 2). Jot down the last number (for [0, 1, 8, 11] this gives 11); permutate the numbers so the first becomes the last and add 12 to it, giving [1, 8, 11, 12]; subtract the first note from the last and jot this down (12 − 1 = 11 again). Repeat the process of permutation, addition and subtraction until you are back at the first note: this gives you [8, 11, 12, 13] and [11, 12, 13, 20] and hence the new values (13 − 8 = 5) and (20 − 11 = 9). Now select the lowest of the values you've jotted down, which is 5. The normal order of the pc set is the one that gave you this value (that is, [8, 11, 12, 13]), except that you must now write the first number as 0 and subtract its value from the others, giving [0, 3, 4, 5]. Line 3 of Fig. 64 shows this; only inversely-related versions of the pc set look different now. Choose whichever version gives the lower second number, or if both yield the same second number then the lower third number, and so on. All this is essentially the same method as the one I describe informally in the main text.

Fig. 64

form, in the sense of having the smallest possible interval between its highest and lowest notes; you can see that in this case the smallest interval into which the whole pattern can fit is a perfect fourth, which means that all except the final version are already in their most compact form (their *normal order*, as Forte calls it). So you would rewrite the final version, as in the second line of Fig. 63. Next you look at the version you are dealing with in order to see whether the interval between its first two notes is bigger or smaller than the interval between its last two notes. What you are doing here is checking it against its inversion, and you choose whichever gives the smallest interval; so the first two versions in Fig. 63 remain the same, while the last two have to be inverted. And now you turn the notes into numerals in the same way as before, calling the lowest note '0'; this gets rid of the differences in transposition between the versions, so they all come out as [0, 1, 2, 5]. This means that 0, 1, 2, 5 is the *prime form* of this pc set. And now you simply look up [0, 1, 2, 5] in the appendix to Allen Forte's book, where you find the following entry:

4-4   0, 1, 2, 5   2 1 1 1 1 0

4-4, as I said, is the name of the pc set; 0, 1, 2, 5 is its prime form; and 2 1 1 1 1 0 is its interval vector, which I shall explain shortly. And what happens if you cannot find the prime form you are looking up in Forte's table? You check your calculations, because you have made a mistake.

If you are thinking that this isn't musical analysis, then you are right, because all that it achieves is a standardized way of naming the pc set. No musical decisions have been involved; and it would not in the least matter what you called the pc set, or which version of it you took as the prime form, provided that you were always consistent. But from now on you can begin to draw genuine analytical conclusions, since the various pc sets you discover in a piece can relate to each other in a number of ways. For example, you might find that two sets were similar, in that they both contained a third, smaller set which also functioned as an independent musical element. Or you might find that the various sets used in a piece all shared the same or similar *interval vectors*. This, you remember, was the six-digit number Forte gives for each pc set in the appendix to his book; for 4-4 it was 2 1 1 1 1 0. This simply means that if you look at the intervals between all the different notes of the pc set in any given version of it, and assume octave equivalence, you will find two minor seconds; one major second; one minor third; one major third; one perfect fourth; and no augmented fourths. Of the 208 pc sets, there are only 19 pairs that share the same interval vector; Forte calls these *Z-related* sets and puts a 'Z' in their name (for example 6–Z6), so that when you find one of these pc sets in a piece you are alerted to the possibility that interval vectors will play an important unifying role in it.

But much the most important way that different pc sets can be related, in Forte's eyes, is through their being members of the same *set complex*. Now, a set complex is a grouping of pc sets, rather in the same way that a pc set is a grouping of individual pitch class patterns; except that there is an important difference, in that a pc set is a grouping of equivalent patterns of the same size, whereas a set complex consists of a pc set plus all the pc sets of *different* sizes that can be included within it through various types of relationship. You might find it useful to think of this by analogy with a tree: the leaves belong to the set 'leaf' and the branches to the set 'branch', whereas the complex 'tree' includes the leaves and the branches, along with the trunk, the twigs and so on. Actually we have met a set complex before, though not under that name. When we looked at Op.19/6, we found that the sets of all its sections were included within the set of section E: that is, E either included the notes of the other sections, or it included them when transposed, or it included them when inverted, or else it included the complement of one of these. And this means that the sets of all of the sections of Op. 19/6 are members of the complex about the set of section E – as are also a large number of other pc sets which do not appear in this piece. When everything in a piece can be derived from a single set complex in this way, Forte calls the structure *connected*, and the main thing a set-theoretical analyst is trying to do when he analyzes a piece of music is to show how apparently unrelated pitch formations in it do in fact belong together by virtue of their common membership of a set-complex.

Forte's name for the pc set in section E of Op. 19/6 happens to be 9–4 (meaning, you remember, that it comes fourth in his list of sets with nine elements), and he would refer to the complex about this set as K(9–4). Actually it would be more correct to call it K(3–4, 9–4). This is because any set-complex involves the principle of complementation, and 3–4 is the complementary pc set to 9–4 (Forte aligns sets in his list so that complementary sets have the same order number). What this means is that K(9–4) automatically includes K(3–4), and K(3–4) automatically includes K(9–4) – in other words, there is only one set complex for 3–4 and 9–4, and therefore there really ought to be only one name for the complex: K(3–4, 9–4). However, people find it more convenient to refer to the complex either as K(3–4) or K(9–4) – depending whether it is pc set 3–4 or 9–4 that is appearing in the music – so you have to bear in mind that both names actually refer to the same thing.

Because of this principle of complementation, there are considerably fewer set complexes than there are pc sets – 114 as against 208 (the number is a bit more than half because there are a few sets that do not have complements – for example, the complement of the whole-tone scale is the whole-tone scale). However, though there is a manageable number of set complexes, there is a difficulty with them, and it is a difficulty which is rather typical of set-theoretical analysis. This is that the set complex associates so many pc sets with one another that the relationship can verge on the meaningless. As Forte says, 'examination of a particular composition . . . might yield the information that every 4-element set represented in the work belongs to K(3–2). Yet K(3–2) is but one of seven set complexes about sets of cardinal 3 which contain *all* 4-element sets . . . Reduction to a useful and significant subcomplex is evidently needed' (p. 96). So he defines a special type of relationship which holds only for certain members within a given set complex, which he calls the *subcomplex Kh* and to which he ascribes a particularly high degree of significance.

What exactly is the difference between the complex K and the subcomplex Kh? To understand this we have to look in a bit more detail at what it means for two pc sets to be members of the same set complex. Let us go back to the sets we found in Op. 19/6. You remember that we regarded one set as related to another *either* if one included the other (whether literally or under transposition or inversion) *or* if it included (or was included within) the complement of the other. For example, Fig. 56 showed how the set of B included that of D, whereas Fig. 59 showed how it included the complement of F. Now these relationships do not work the other way round: that is, the set of B neither includes nor is included in the set of F, and equally it does not include nor is it included in the complement of D. Either the one condition of set-complex membership is fulfilled or the other; but in neither of these cases are both conditions fulfilled. Sometimes, however, both conditions can be. Look at the relationship between the sets of E and A. In Fig. 57 I showed how E included A under inversion. But I could equally well have shown how E included the complement of A under inversion: Fig. 65 shows how. So here both conditions for membership of a set complex are fulfilled. And that is what defines the subcomplex Kh.

Fig. 65

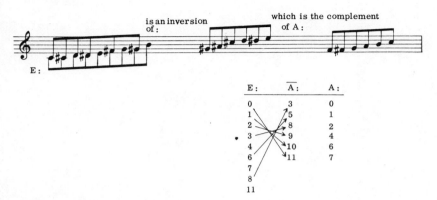

Now, in the analysis I gave of Op. 19/6 I regarded sets as related if they were in the relation K – if either condition of set membership was fulfilled, that is to say.[1] But it would have been possible to distinguish two grades of relationship, one corresponding to K and the other to Kh. Let us see how this would have affected our interpretation of the piece. Fig. 66 shows an improved version of the 'mileage chart' I gave before, while Fig. 67 refines the earlier form-chart (Fig. 64) by showing K relations between sections in a dotted line and Kh relations in a solid one. If we had considered *only* the Kh relations, then our analysis would

Fig. 66

	A	B	C	D	E
B	Kh				
C					
D	K	K			
E	Kh	K	K	Kh	
F	K	K			K

---

[1] Strictly this is not correct. Part of Forte's definition of a set complex is that two sets cannot be in relation K if they are of the same size (that is obvious, since otherwise they would be the same set) or if they are of complementary sizes – so that 4–n cannot be a member of K(8–m). It is true that relationships between sets of complementary sizes are not as general in their scope as true K-relations, and such sets can never be in relation Kh. But it is sometimes useful to regard them as related all the same, and I have done so in my analysis of Op. 19/6. You could always call such sets 'L-related' to avoid confusion.

Fig. 67

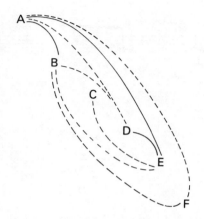

not have made a lot of sense: it would not have shown what sections C and F were doing in the piece at all. But the Kh relations do make sense when seen as reinforcing certain of the K relations: they underline the special role of sections C and F (C being a kind of counter-subject, and F a coda) in contrast to the continuity of the rest of the piece.

In his book Forte goes into a great deal more detail than I have been able to give. But if you understand what a pc set is and how to identify one, and if you know what a set complex is and what the subcomplex Kh is, then you have a basic working knowledge of set-theoretical analysis; so what is more to the point than elaborating the theory is to see it in action by working through one of Forte's analyses. Forte devotes ten pages of his book to *Excentrique*, the second of Stravinsky's Four Studies for Orchestra, which is a reworked version of one of his Three Pieces for String Quartet. As before, the first step in the analysis is to chop up the music into formal sections, and Fig. 68 shows how Forte does this.[1] In this piece some of the sections are very similar to others, so Forte labels them in the traditional way, with A^2 being a variant of A^1 and so on. The rest of the analysis is in effect based on this 'condensed score', as Forte calls it, which omits instrumentation, rhythms, dynamic markings and immediate repetitions – or more correctly, it includes these things but only by implication, in that they are the basis for the division into sections. So that you can see just how

---

[1] I have added bar numbers to Forte's chart, which is on pp. 132–3 of *The Structure of Atonal Music*. In discussing Forte's analysis I make a few minor additions to it where these are necessary for clarity.

Fig. 68 Forte, condensed score of Stravinsky's *Excentrique*

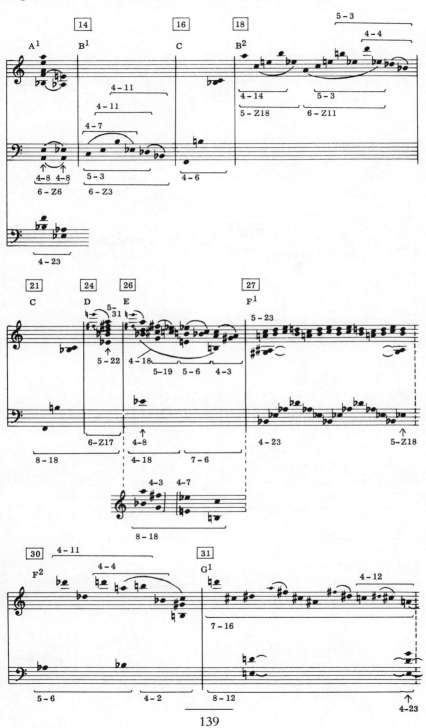

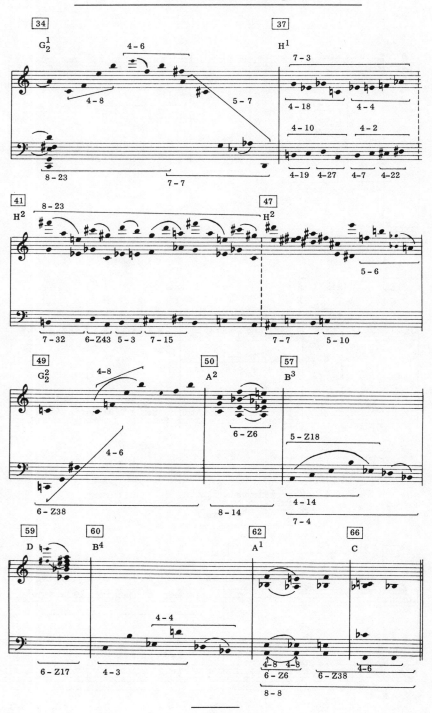

Fig. 69 Short score of *Excentrique*, bars 1–25, with Forte's segmentation

141

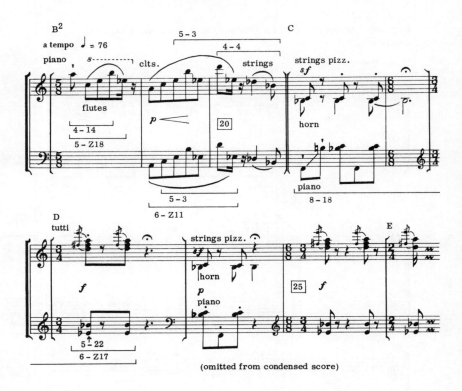

(omitted from condensed score)

the condensed score compares with the original, Fig. 69 shows the first twenty-five bars of *Excentrique* in short score, with everything Forte marks in his condensed score superimposed on it.

As well as the formal sections, Figs. 68 and 69 show the pc sets that Forte indentifies in the music. Sometimes, as in B[1] and B[3], there is a single pc set corresponding to the section as a whole; this implies that the section is functioning as a single harmonic unit, which is what we assumed throughout when analyzing Op. 19/6. Why then does Forte also pick out smaller pc sets within these sections? Because he sees them as having some kind of motivic function. Take set 5–3, which Forte picks out within section B[1]. This turns up again in section B[2], and if you look at Fig. 69 you'll see how it allows you to rationalize the clarinets' phrase there in a rather neat way (bars 19–20); that is why it was worth picking it out in section B[1]. On other occasions, however, there is not a single pc set corresponding to an entire section: B[2] and B[4] are examples of this. In both these cases Forte is saying that the section does not function as a single harmonic block: it is made up of several independent sections – independent in the sense that each may appear in whatever transposition or inversion. But such a section may still be unified in the same way that Op. 19/6 as a whole was unified, through its structure being connected: meaning, you remember, that its various component sets were all members of a single set complex. Fig. 70 spells out how this works for both B² and B⁴. You can see how in each section every note belongs to some pc set that in turn belongs to the complex about 6–Z3; so that 6–Z3 is the *nexus set* of both sections, and in fact of all four sections of B-material (B¹, B², B³ and B⁴). It is not very convenient to have to work out set-complex relations like this every time, however, so Forte helpfully tabulates the relations between all the pc sets he regards as important in this piece. Fig. 71 shows this table: it is simply a more complicated version of the kind of 'mileage chart' we have already met, allowing you to see the relations between any two sets at a glance.

Fig. 70

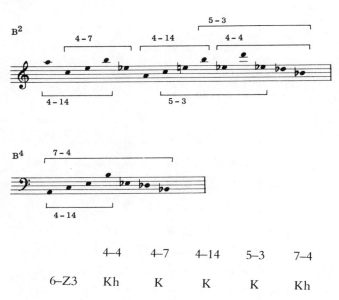

	4–4	4–7	4–14	5–3	7–4
6–Z3	Kh	K	K	K	Kh

What has been achieved so far? The music has been divided into sections, and some – though not all – of these sections have been shown to be unified through membership either of a single pc set or of a single set complex. (You cannot see from Fig. 68 whether sections like B² and B⁴, or for that matter B as a whole, are connected, so Forte comments

Fig. 71

	4-2	4-3	4-4	4-6	4-7	4-8	4-10	4-11	4-12	4-14	4-18	4-19	4-22	4-23	4-27	5-3	7-4	7-6	7-7	5-10	7-15	7-16	5-Z18	5-19	5-22	5-23
5-3	Kh	Kh	K	K	K	Kh	K	Kh	K	K	K	K	K		K	Kh	K		K	K	K	K		K		K
7-4	K	K	Kh	K	K	Kh	K	K	K	K	K	K	K			K	Kh			K						K
7-6	K	K	K	Kh	K		K	K	K	K	K	K	K		K	K	K	Kh		K						K
7-7	K		K	K			Kh	Kh	Kh	K	K	K	K		K	K			Kh	K						K
5-10	K	Kh	K	K	Kh	Kh	K	K	K	K	K	K	K	K		K	K		K	Kh					Kh	Kh
7-15	K		K	K			K	K	K	Kh	K	K	K	K	K											
7-16		Kh		K	Kh		K	K	Kh	Kh	K		K	K	K	K				K						K
5-Z18	K	K	K	K	K	K	K	Kh	Kh	Kh			K	K	K	K				K					K	K
5-19	K	K	K	K	K	K	Kh	K	K	Kh	Kh	K	K	K	K											
5-22				K	K				Kh	Kh	Kh	Kh	Kh	K	Kh	K	Kh									
5-23	K	K	K	K	K	K	K	K	K	K	K	Kh	Kh	K	K	K										
5-31										Kh	K					K										
7-32	K	Kh	Kh	K	Kh		K	K	K	K	K	K	K	Kh	Kh	Kh	Kh	K	K	K	K	K	Kh	K	Kh	K
6-Z3																	Kh									
6-Z6/38	Kh	K	Kh	K	Kh	Kh	Kh	Kh	Kh	Kh	Kh	Kh	Kh	Kh	Kh	K	K	K	K	K	K	K	Kh	K	Kh	K
6-Z11	K	K	K	K	K	K	K	K	K	K	K	K	K	K	K	K	K	K	K	K	K	K	K	K	K	K
6-Z17/43																										

144

on this verbally in his text.) But this is not true of the piece as a whole: there is not any one nexus set from which every section of the music can be derived, as was the case in Op. 19/6. So the main part of Forte's analysis is taken up with examining the relations between pairs of sections, in order to see how the piece's form emerges out of the inter-relationships of its various sections. Fig. 72 shows Forte's conclusions, and essentially it has the same kind of meaning as our form-charts of Op. 19/6 (Figs. 62 and 67), except that it is at a more abstract level in that 'B' stands for a group of sections rather than a single section.

There is an important difference that is not so obvious, though. The form-charts for Op. 19/6 showed whether sections were connected – connected, in this sense, meaning a strict, mathematical relationship that you could get a computer to work out for you, if you wanted to. But Forte's chart of the form of *Excentrique* does not show whether its sections are connected, but whether they are 'associated', as he puts it. He defines what he means by association this way: two sections are associated either if their structure is connected, or if they have at least one explicit set in common, or both (pp. 131–3). Now this again sounds like something you could program a computer to decide for you. But in fact it is not, or at least the computer would not make the same decisions as Forte does. Let us take as an example the relationship between sections B and C. Forte says that 'the set-complex structure of this pair is connected but trivial in the sense that the nexus sets are the same as those for B alone. Although 4–6 is in Kh(6–Z11), there is no explicit derivation, and therefore the pair is not regarded as associated' (p. 137). And so if you look at Fig. 72 you will see no line between B and C. But this flatly contradicts the definition for association which Forte himself gave, since B and C do form a connected structure, and what makes it all the more illogical is that just the same relationship exists between sections B and F, which Forte *does* regard as associated.

Forte's interpretation here may be illogical, but that does not necessarily mean it is analytically bad. What it means is that he is making the same kind of informal judgment about the music as a Schenkerian analyst is constantly making: in other words, Forte is using the apparatus of set-theoretical analysis as a heuristic device, a mechanism that proffers possible relationships which he then assesses for their musical significance – much as the technique of Schenkerian analysis suggests possible relationships which the analyst can choose to accept or reject as he sees fit. Admittedly there is a difference in that the relationships suggested by set-theoretical analysis are that much more abstract, that much more removed from the music, so that it is difficult

145

Fig. 72 Form-chart of *Excentrique*

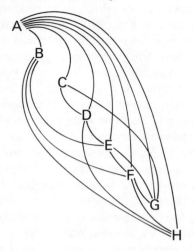

to make a judgment about them in musical terms: it is possible to complete a set-theoretical analysis and still feel that you have not really got to know the music, which is something that could not possibly happen with Schenkerian analysis, and I cannot help feeling that this casts doubt on the practical value of set-theoretical analysis. What is beyond doubt, however, is that whatever merit a set-theoretical analysis may have does not derive from its being objective and scientific, in the sense that a mathematical proof is objective and scientific. It is easy to be duped by the appearance and terminology of a set-theoretical analysis into thinking that it is like a mathematical proof. But it is not, and the fact that informal judgments come into the interpretation of the results is only part of this. Much the most important respect in which a set-theoretical analysis is not objective and scientific concerns the very beginning of the process, the initial segmentation of the music: that is to say, the way the analyst divides the music up into formal sections, and his decision as to which pc sets to pick out within these sections. Apart from final details of interpretation, everything in the analysis depends on this segmentation because it is here that all the *musical* decisions are made. Identifying the pc sets, working out the relations between them and deciding what sections are connected: all these are decisions about the music, not musical decisions – they involve no musical judgment and could just as well be made by a computer. So no set-theoretical analysis can be more objective, or more well-founded musically, than its initial segmentation.

Fig. 73 Imbrication

Actually it would be possible to carry out this segmentation in a rigorously objective manner. There is only one way this can be achieved: by considering every possible group of adjacent notes in the entire piece, regardless of whether the grouping makes musical sense or not. Forte calls such a process *imbrication*, and he does occasionally use it for short sections where the music does not project any particular grouping (Fig. 73 shows how it works). But you can imagine that in anything but the tiniest piece, such a procedure would give rise to a quite unmanageable number of groups, most of them totally without musical significance – 'of no consequence with respect to structure', as Forte puts it. So, he continues, 'editing may be required' (p. 90). And how is this editing to be done? The criteria will vary with each context, Forte replies, and 'it seems virtually impossible to systematize these in any useful way' (p. 91). But chief among them, he adds, are looking for sets that recur within or between sections, and looking for sets that are linked with others through membership of complexes.

Something highly unscientific is happening here! To see what, let us take a specific example: the association Forte makes between A and B in *Excentrique*. These groups of sections are connected, but only weakly, so Forte is looking for some way in which the musical foreground projects the relationship between them. He finds this in the link between A^2 and B^3, that is, in bars 51 – 8. The first four notes of B^3 (bar 57) project pc set 4–14; this is just the same as it was before, in B^2. And the two chords in A² (bars 53 – 6) are also just the same as they were before, in A¹. What is different is the G – C – G – C formation at the beginning of A² (bar 51). Actually there was a similar figure in A¹ (bars 5 – 6), but there the notes were E and A, so that they made no difference to the pitch class structure (E and A are both included within the two chords). In A², however, this figure makes a great deal of difference to the pitch class structure, since G and C are not included in the chords. As Forte puts it, 'this simple transformation has a remarkable consequence, for A² then has as its total content pc set 8–14, and the first four notes in B³ form the complement, 4–14' (p. 136). And, from the point of view of set-theoretical analysis, no surface formation could more strongly project a structural relationship than the appearance of a pc set and its complement, one after the other.

Now if you are following the analysis by looking at Forte's 'condensed score', all this looks convincing. But if you take the trouble to refer back to the original score (which Forte's condensed score does not encourage, since it omits bar numbers) then you will find something that the condensed score does not show. Fig. 74 shows what this is by superimposing Forte's analysis on the original score. The G – C – G – C pattern in bar 51, which is played in harmonics by a solo cello, follows the previous section without a break (Forte's G_2^2).[1] And then, before the two chords in the woodwinds, there comes a silence of nearly two bars – the longest notated silence of the piece, in fact. Yet Forte is asking us to think of what comes before and after this silence as making up a single pitch formation, that is to say the complement of the first four notes of bar 57. Would it not be much more natural to think of the two–bar rest and the change of orchestration that coincides with it as forming a structural division, rather than reading a single pitch formation right across it? It would, but it would spoil Forte's explicit association between A and C! What is happening, then, is that Forte is using analytical results to decide what the basic facts are – that is to say, as a means of determining the segmentation on which the results depend. Such a self-validating procedure flies in the face of scientific method.

No analyst approaches music dispassionately and objectively. The Schenkerian analyst sees fundamental structures wherever he looks. The motivic analyst cannot see a bar of music without motivic connections springing to his mind. If the set-theoretical analyst sees what he wants

[1] G_2^2 means that this is the second half of a larger section G^2, itself a variant of G^1. Note the piano glissando: Forte ignores this in his condensed score, and therefore in his analysis. Obviously it would be rather ridiculous to derive every note of the glissando from a pc set! This is an example of objectivity being tempered by common sense.

Fig. 74 *Excentrique*, bars 49 – 58, with Forte's segmentation

to see, that is because he is human; it does not mean his analysis is invalid or meaningless. What it does mean, however, is that whatever validity or meaning it may have must be a musical one, not a scientific one. In other words a set-theoretical analysis is like any other kind of analysis: it is good if it is in some way useful or enjoyable, and good for nothing if it isn't.

III *Semiotic Analysis*

The second main example of the formal approach to music is semiotic analysis. This originated in France and it is still stronger in French-speaking countries (including Canada) than elsewhere. Semiotic analysis of music is intended as a branch of a general science called 'semiology' – that is, the study of signs. (This means that semiotic analysts have closer links with fields of study outside music than do, say, Schenkerian analysts.) But what does it mean to study music in terms of signs? One way, of course, would be to concentrate on what music means and the way in which musical structures embody or communicate meanings; but the whole business of musical meaning is so difficult to handle that in practice a different approach is required. This approach is rather like how linguists analyze speech: first, by deciding what the building-blocks of linguistic meaning are; and, second, by investigating how these building-blocks are related to each other in any particular example of speech. In the same way, analyzing a piece of music semiotically means, first, chopping it up into units possessing some degree of significance within the piece; and, second, analyzing the way in which these are distributed throughout the piece, with a view to discovering the principles that govern this distribution (for this reason, such analysis is sometimes called *distributional analysis*). Now this procedure is essentially the same as what is done in set-theoretical analysis, and the means by which it is done rather resembles Reti's motivic analysis; so that it is possible to understand a good deal about semiotic analysis without getting too involved in the rather complicated theorizing on which it is based.[1] This section is based on two examples of semiotic

[1] For the theoretical background see Jean-Jacques Nattiez, *Fondements d'une semiologie de la musique* (Paris, 1975); an English translation is due to be published soon, by Faber. There is also an introductory article called 'Music and Semiotics: the Nattiez Phase' by Jonathan Dunsby, in *The Musical Quarterly*, LXIX (1983), pp. 27–43. One extremely detailed analysis by Nattiez, of Varèse's *Density 21.5*, is available in English: *Music Analysis*, I (1982), pp. 243–340.

analysis – examples which do not by any means exhaust the repertoire
of semiotic techniques, but which do give some idea of what semiotic
analysts are trying to do and why. The first is an analysis of Debussy's
Syrinx for flute, and it is by Jean-Jacques Nattiez, the leading figure in
musical semiology. The second is by Elisabeth Morin, and this is a
comparative analysis of two sixteenth-century variation sets on the
song 'John come kiss me now' – one by William Byrd and the other
by John Tomkins, half-brother of the more famous Thomas
Tomkins.[1]

As I said, semiotic analysis proceeds through a number of stages
and, as in set-theoretical analysis, the initial stage is segmentation. Fig.
75 shows Morin's initial segmentations of Variations 1 and 11 from the
Byrd set, together with the original music. What she is doing is aligning
recurrent rhythmic and melodic motives underneath each other – recurrences which may be literal (as in the first three melodic lines of
Variation 1 – see p. 154) or modified (as in the fourth line, where the
figure appears in sequence). Really it is patterns of recurrence that
determine where one motivic unit ends and the next begins; recurrence
is in other words the principal criterion on which the process of
segmentation is based. Reading down the columns, then, gives the
various appearances of a motivic type; whereas reading across the columns, from left to right, gives the number of different motivic types (or
paradigmatic headings as semiotic analysts call them) that appear in a
given piece of music.[2] And reading from left to right and from top to
bottom – as in an ordinary score – reconstitutes the original ordering of
the music (except that Morin presents each hand separately). Although
all that has happened is that the original score has been physically
reconfigured, it is already possible to see at a glance such things as the
more fragmentary and assymetrical motivic construction of Variation
11 as compared to Variation 1 – something that is not quite so apparent
in the performance score. In their clumsy jargon, semiotic analysts use
the term 'explicitation' for this process of bringing hidden or implied
aspects of musical structure out into the open.

[1] The Nattiez analysis is on pp. 330–54 of *Fondements d'une semiologie de la musique*;
Morin's is published in book form as *Essai de Stylistique Comparée* (Montreal, 1979)
and includes an English translation.

[2] Strictly speaking, paradigmatic headings (also known as paradigmatic planes)
aren't restricted to motifs, in the traditional sense. At the same time, semiotic
analysis in practice concentrates on motifs and melodies, just as set-theoretical
analysis in practice concentrates on harmonies; so the two approaches are in a way
complementary. Note that recurrence is one of Forte's criteria for segmentation
(*The Structure of Atonal Music*, pp. 83, 85).

Fig. 75 Morin, paradigmatic analysis of Byrd's variations 1 and 11

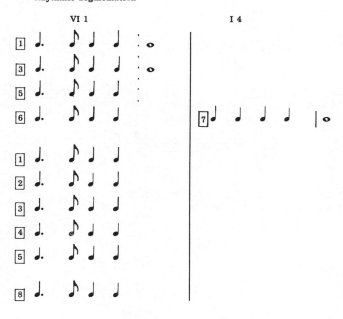

Right hand

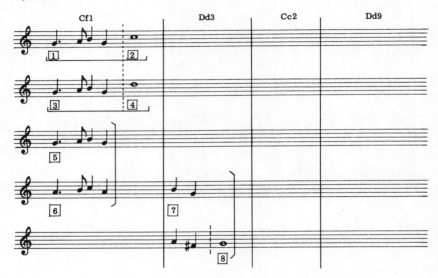

Left hand

Variation 11

Rhythmic segmentation

Fig. 76 Debussy, *Syrinx*

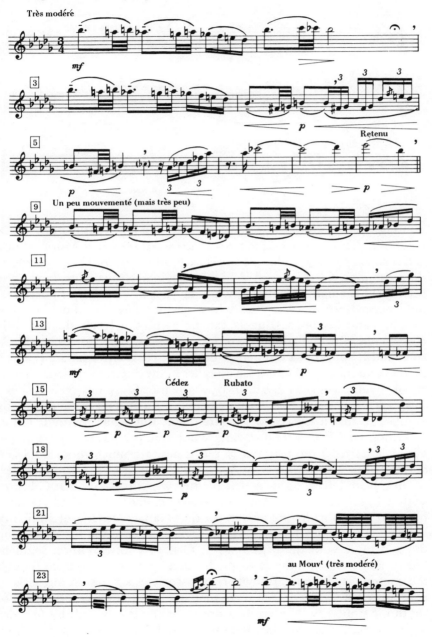

Fig. 76 reproduces the score of *Syrinx*, and Fig. 77 is Nattiez' initial chart of it. This uses the same two-dimensional format as Morin's but it is not so easy to read. Nattiez labels each motif: A, B, C . . . indicate different motivic types and A1, A2 . . . indicate variants (just as in traditional thematic labelling), while z, y, x . . . identify figures that only occur once or twice and which he therefore does not regard as paradigmatic headings. But as can be seen, the labels do not fully correspond with the arrangement into columns; why, for example, do A, B and C appear in a different order in the chart and why are D and E in the same column? The explanation lies in the different musical character of *Syrinx* as against Byrd. In Byrd the motifs are relatively disjunct from each other and the divisions between them tend to be metrically regular, so that it is easy to separate them. But while *Syrinx* is full of repetition (and if it were not, how would the process of segmentation ever get started?) the patterns of recurrence are much more fluid and assymetrical. The reason why A, B and C appear in the wrong order, reading from left to right, is that Nattiez wants to show that C begins with a figure similar to that with which A ends. The fluid relations between motifs in *Syrinx* also mean that Nattiez' criteria of similarity have to be more flexible than Morin's. Nattiez' criterion for associating the end of A with the beginning of C is that the common segment begins and ends with the same pitch classes (G♭ and D♭), even though the contour is different. Elsewhere he associates figures on the basis of contour, even if they do not share first and last notes; or on the basis of rhythmic similarity (Nattiez does not separate melody and rhythm into different charts, like Morin). Because vertical alignment is used to show

Fig. 77 Nattiez, first paradigmatic analysis of *Syrinx*

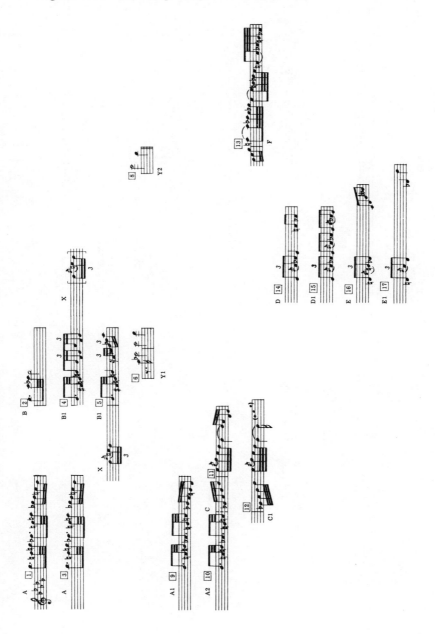

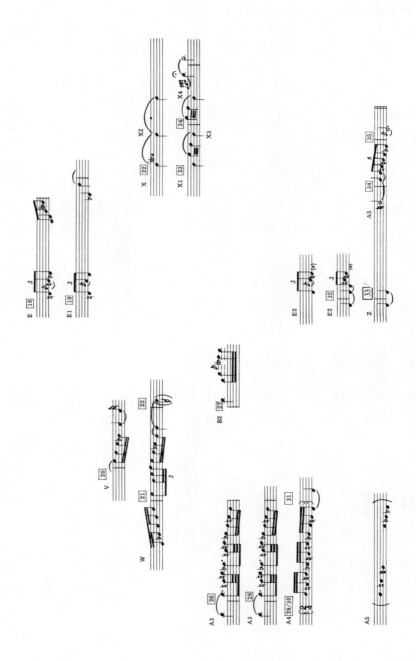

Fig. 78 Nattiez, second paradigmatic analysis of *Syrinx*

such less obvious overlaps between different motifs, the strict separation into distinct columns characteristic of Morin's chart is not possible here; Nattiez' chart is essentially no more than an unusually sophisticated version of the traditional motivic table used by such analysts as Reti. For this reason, and using this first chart as a basis, Nattiez also presents a second chart (Fig. 78) in which the long and irregular motifs of the first chart are split into their component figures and arranged more strictly in a series of columns; each separate figure is numbered and, as you can see, Nattiez breaks the piece down into sixty-six different ones. It is this second chart that is the basis for later stages of his analysis.

This first stage of a semiotic analysis is known as a *paradigmatic analysis* because it consists of extrapolating the units of significant structure in music; it results in a list of paradigmatic types, so that the temporal aspect of the music is discounted. The second stage of the analysis is known as *syntagmatic analysis* and here attention returns to the temporal aspect of the music. What happens is that the distribution of these paradigmatic units in time is analyzed so as to discover the rules underlying this distribution. (Again there is a comparison with Reti's concept of thematic patterns.) Before seeing how Morin and Nattiez do this, it would be useful to clarify what is involved by turning to a simpler case, and an unusually simple example of this second stage of semiotic analysis is Marcelle Guertin's study of the initial themes from Book One of Debussy's Preludes.[1] Fig. 79 shows what looks like simply a series of paradigmatic tables for each theme; but it is more subtle than it looks, because the horizontal alignments between themes are intended to indicate an equivalence of function between the component parts of the various themes. The labels explain this. By X, X^1, Y and U Guertin respectively indicates an initial unit; a variant of the initial unit which remains within the same pitch range; a variant of the initial unit which extends its pitch range; and a reduced repetition, based only on the first fragment of the immediately preceding unit. (Ʉ means a transposed version of U.) These labels – and there are others of lesser importance – show the pattern of relationships between the component parts of a theme, and because they refer to relationships, and not to the particular materials being related, they can be abstracted from their context and presented in the form of a symbolical table (Fig. 80). This in turn can be reduced to a simple generative rule which can be applied to all instances (Fig. 81). In this formula, as in semiotic analysis generally, the

---

[1] This has been published, along with an English translation of Nattiez' analysis of *Syrinx*, in *Three Musical Analyses* (Toronto Semiotic Circle, Victoria University, Toronto, 1982).

Fig. 79 Guertin, analysis of themes from Debussy's Preludes, Book 1

Fig. 80

I	II	III	IV	V	VI	VII	VIII	IX	X	XI	XII
X	X	X	X	X	X	X	X	X	X	X	X
	℧				℧			UM UM			
X¹	Y	Y	Y	X¹M	Y	Y	X¹	Y	Y	Y	X¹
U	*	U	U	℧	*	U*	U		U*	U	
U U			U U								
U+ *		U¹ U U¹ *	℧+ ℧¹+ *	℧¹ ℧¹¹				℧S ℧S¹ ℧S ℧S¹ ℧S¹— *			
								Z			Z
						θ		θ *			θ *
				X₂							
				Y₂							
				V							
				V¹ *							

Fig. 81

a) $X \;+\; \left\{ \begin{array}{c} X^1 \\ Y \end{array} \right\} \;+\; \left\{ \begin{array}{c} U \\ ℧ \end{array} \right\}$

b) $X \;+\; \left\{ \begin{array}{c} ℧ \\ ℧M \end{array} \right\} \;+\; Y$

(with crossing arrows between the last two terms of a) and b))

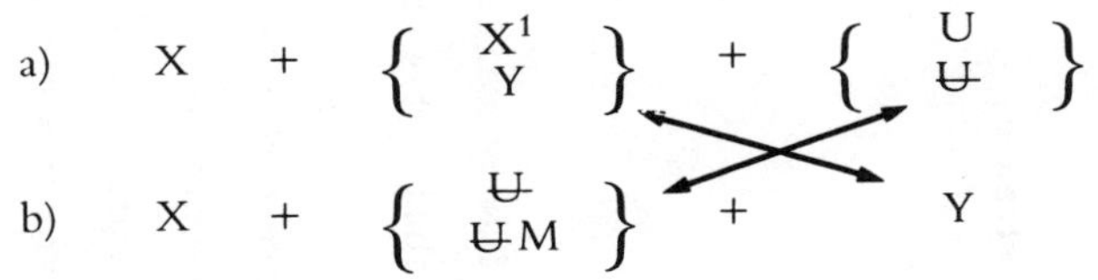

braces represent equivalent classes – for instance in (a) X¹ and Y are interchangeable, they have the same function. Rule (a), then, is read as saying that an initial theme from Book One of the Preludes will be formed of an initial unit; plus a repetition of it which may or may not extend its pitch range; plus a reduced repetition which may or may not be transposed. And rule (b) says that the order of the last two units may be reversed (with a few modifications).

This achieves the aim of semiotic analysis – to find a general rule

Fig. 82   Nattiez, feature list for *Syrinx*

E	contains a chromatic element
F^1	ascending motion
F^2	descending motion
G^1	conjunct motion
G^2	disjunct motion
H^1	"black keys"
H^2	whole-tone scale
I^1/x	identity of initial and final of same unit /x
I^2/x	identity of initial and final of this unit with initial and final of unit x
J^1	resting point
J^2	type of variation with respect to the resting point
K^1/x	belongs to a whole-tone progression, the initial of which is x
K^2/x	belongs to a semi-tone progression
K^3/x	belongs to an arpeggiated progression

A^1
A^2
B^1
B^2

B^3 B^4 B^5 B^6

D^1 D^2 D^3 D^4 D^5 D^6

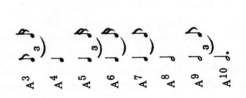

A^3 A^4 A^5 A^6 A^7 A^8 A^9 A^{10}

C^1 C^2 C^3 C^4

L — to-and-fro motion

M^1
M^2
M^3
M^4
M^5
M^6
M^7
M^8

N^1 — transposition, a third down
N^2 — transposition, a second down
N^3 — transposition, an octave down
0 — substitution of E flat for E natural

governing the distribution of significant units within a given piece or repertoire – but it is obvious that this is an unusually simple case, one that involves only the most rudimentary relationships between one musical unit and another. Usually semiotic analysis requires that the units identified in the first stage of the analysis be subjected to a more precise and systematic description, before the relationships of transformation existing between them can be determined and their distribution analyzed accordingly. In both Nattiez' and Morin's analyses this is done by classifying the musical units in accordance with a list of characteristic features, but the list of features each uses is different (Figs. 82 and 83). In a way this is a pity: wouldn't semiotic analyses be more useful if they all used the same list of features so that one analysis could be directly compared with another in detail? The justification (which I don't consider wholly convincing) is that the purpose of such a list is to identify the features that are important for the relationships between units within the particular context of a given piece or repertoire of pieces; hence the list of features has to be compiled specially for each application. It is this that explains the curiously quirky nature of Nattiez' list, which is an amalgam of quite different kinds of categories: some formal and generally applicable (M^1 = one semitone down and two up), some precise but not so generally applicable (0 = substitution of $E^\flat$ for $E^\natural$), and some quite informal (L = to-and-fro motion). And the same kind of informality is evident in the way Nattiez applies this feature list (Fig. 84 shows the beginning of this, the numbers corresponding to Fig. 78): why is unit 10 marked as containing a chromatic element (E) when unit 3 is not? would unit 3 count as conjunct (G^1) if the $E^\natural$ had been notated as $F^\flat$? These are free analytical decisions, not deductions, and Nattiez does not explain or justify them.

It is possible to see, at least in principle, how this kind of classification by feature could give rise to some kind of distributional analysis, but Nattiez does not take the analysis any further (the reason will become clear later). Morin, on the other hand, does, but the way she employs classification by features is rather different. Her feature list[1] catalogues intervallic and rhythmic structures in a more comprehensive and systematic manner than Nattiez'; a consequence of this is that each paradigmatic unit is characterized by two features (one relating to pitch and one to rhythm), whereas the number of features was quite variable with Nattiez. Morin's feature list is in other words more general, more

---

[1] The symbols at the top of Morin's initial segmentation charts, both for pitch and rhythm, refer to the feature list.

Fig. 83   Morin, feature list for *John come kiss me now*

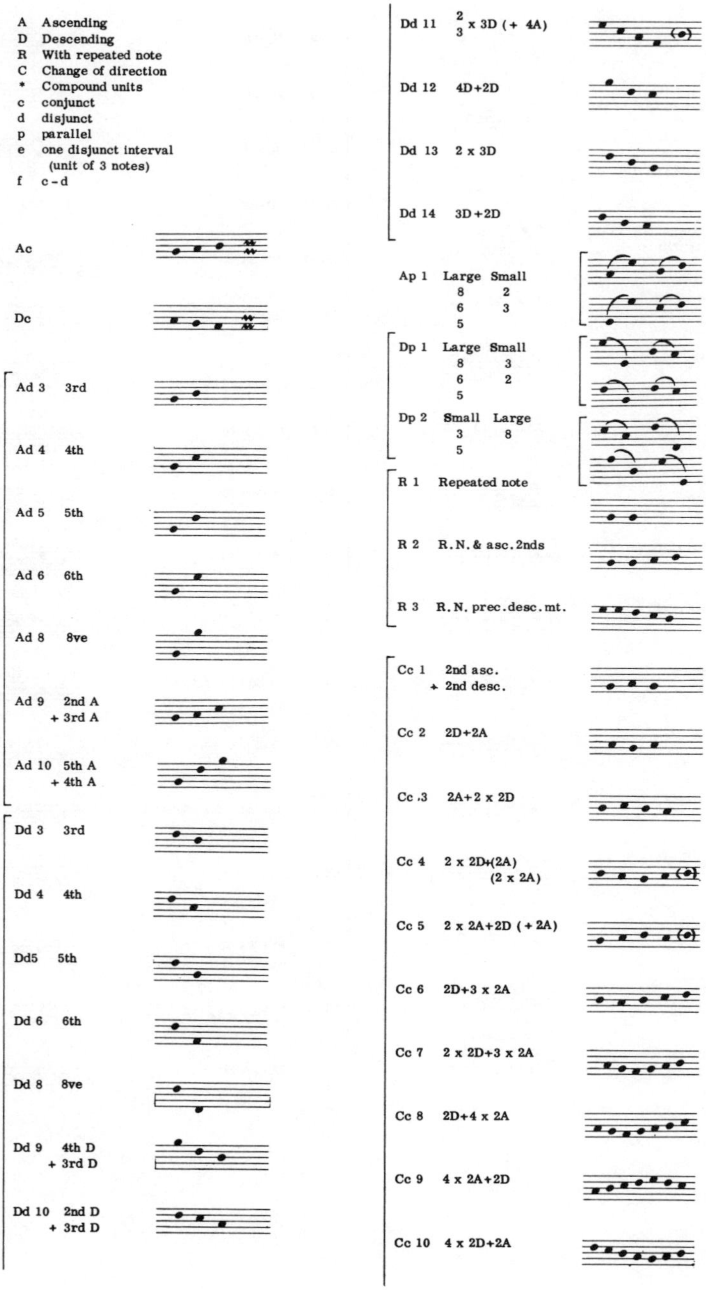

A   Ascending
D   Descending
R   With repeated note
C   Change of direction
*   Compound units
c   conjunct
d   disjunct
p   parallel
e   one disjunct interval
     (unit of 3 notes)
f   c – d

Ac

Dc

Ad 3   3rd

Ad 4   4th

Ad 5   5th

Ad 6   6th

Ad 8   8ve

Ad 9   2nd A
        + 3rd A

Ad 10   5th A
        + 4th A

Dd 3   3rd

Dd 4   4th

Dd5   5th

Dd 6   6th

Dd 8   8ve

Dd 9   4th D
        + 3rd D

Dd 10   2nd D
        + 3rd D

Dd 11 $\frac{2}{3}$ x 3D (+ 4A)

Dd 12   4D+2D

Dd 13   2 x 3D

Dd 14   3D+2D

Ap 1   Large   Small
         8   2
         6   3
         5

Dp 1   Large   Small
         8   3
         6   2
         5

Dp 2   Small   Large
         3   8
         5

R 1   Repeated note

R 2   R.N. & asc. 2nds

R 3   R.N. prec. desc. mt.

Cc 1   2nd asc.
       + 2nd desc.

Cc 2   2D+2A

Cc .3   2A+2 x 2D

Cc 4   2 x 2D+(2A)
                (2 x 2A)

Cc 5   2 x 2A+2D (+ 2A)

Cc 6   2D+3 x 2A

Cc 7   2 x 2D+3 x 2A

Cc 8   2D+4 x 2A

Cc 9   4 x 2A+2D

Cc 10   4 x 2D+2A

Cc 11	2 x 2A+2 x 2D	
Cc 12	2 x 2D+2 x 2A+2D	
Cc 13	2 x 2A+3 x 2D	
Cc 14	2D+2A+2 x 2D+2A or trill	
Cc 15	3 x 2D+2A	
Cd 1	3D...6A	
Cd 2	5D...6A	
Cd 3	(5 (6D...2A (8	
Cd 4	3A...3D	
Cd 5	3D...2A	
Ce 1	2A+3D	
Ce 2	3A+2D	
Ce 3	3A+4D	
Ce 4	4A+3D	
Ce 5	4A+2D	
Ce 6	5A+2D	
Ce 7	8A+2D	

Ce 8	3D+5A	
Ce 9	2A+5D	
Ce 10	3D+4A	
Ce 11	4D+3A	
Ce 12	4D+2A	
Ce 13	5D+4A	
Cf 1	2 x 2A+3D (Theme)	
Cf 2	3D+2 x 2A	
Cf 3	3A+2 x 2D	
Cf 4	3A+3 x 3D	
Cf 5	2A+2D+3D	
Cf 6	2 x 2A+3D+2 x 2A	
Cf 7	2D+3 x 2A+3D	
Cf 8	2D + 3A + 2D + 2A + 2 x 2D (trill)	
Cf 9	2 x 2A+ (4D (5D (6D (8D	
Cf 10	4A + 2 x 2D	
Cf 11	(8 (6 D+2 x 2A	
Cf 12	2A+3 x 2D	

I	In crotchets	I 1 |	**V**	In triplets, sextuplets or duplets (cont.)	V 10 in [notation]
		I 2 ||			V 11 [notation]
		I 3 |||			V 12 [notation] or [notation]
		I 4 ||||			V 13 series of [notation]
II	In quavers	II 2 [notation]			V 14 trill
		II 4 [notation]			V 15 [notation]
		II 5 [notation]			V 16 [notation]
		II 6 [notation]	**VI**	Dotted rhythm	VI 1 [notation] (Theme)
		II 7 series of quavers			VI 2 [notation]
III	In semiquavers	III 2 [notation]			VI 3 [notation]
		III 4 [notation]			VI 4 [notation]
		III 5 [notation]			VI 5 [notation]
		III 6 series of semiquavers			VI 6 [notation]
IV	Composite rhythms	IV 1 [notation]			VI 7 [notation]
		IV 2 [notation]			VI 8 [notation]
		IV 3 [notation]	**VII**	Syncopation or off-beats	VII 1 [notation]
		IV 4 trills			VII 2 Syncopated crotchets
V	In triplets or sextuplets	V 1 [notation]			VII 3 in crotchets finishing in quavers
		V 2 [notation]			VII 4 [notation]
		V 3 [notation]			VII 5 [notation]
		V 4 [notation]			VII 6 [notation]
		V 5 [notation]			VII 7 [notation]
		V 6 [notation]			VII 8 [notation] or [notation]
		V 7 [notation]	**VIII**	Other rhythmic figures	
		V 8 [notation]			
		V 9 [notation]			

neutral, than Nattiez'; it embodies less interpretation, less consideration of the individual musical context. However, Morin uses her feature list as a means of progressing to a further stage of analytical abstraction, in which freedom of analytical choice returns. Fig. 85 shows, at the top, the classification of syntagmatic units according to the list of features (this merely clarifies Fig. 75, adding no new information); and, below, the subsequent stage of abstraction. This lower chart is comparable in what it is saying to Guertin's symbolic chart of the Debussy Preludes (Fig. 80): instead of representing the properties of each syntagmatic unit, in isolation, it shows the relations between syntagmatic units within each variation. Just as in Guertin's chart each first unit was labelled X, so here each first unit is labelled Aa – the 'A' referring to melodic types (as in Nattiez, variants are A_1, A_2 . . . and different types

Fig. 84

1	[music]	c^1	E			$K^1/$ si (F^2)	M^1
2	[music]					$K^1/$ si (F^2)	N^2
3	[music]	B^3		F^2 G^1		$K^1/$ si (F^2)	
4	[music]	c^1	E				M^4
5	[music]	A^8					
6	[music]	$c^1 + A^8$	E		$I^1/$ si		M^5
7	[music]				J^1(fa♯sol♮) J^2 $(K^2/$si$(F^1))$		
8	[music]	c^3					
9	[music]	B^2					
10	[music]	B^2 ap	E		$I^1/$ré		M^3
11	[music]	A^3					

B, C . . .), and the 'a' referring to rhythmic types. A careful comparision of the two charts shows certain discrepancies between them: for instance, in Variation 11, Cc1 (bar 3) and Ce1 (bar 4), which were originally classified as separate paradigmatic headings, are now amalgamated with Cc2 (bar 1) as variants of B.[1] This is not a mistake but a refinement of the initial description, in the light of the particular context of this piece and the variation set as a whole; the motivic homogeneity of the piece, Morin is implying, is such that the two inversely related forms of the figure, and the expansion of the second to a third, can all be regarded as variants of a single idea (but, like Nattiez,

[1] Refer back to Fig. 75 if you can't remember what Cc1, Ce1 and Cc2 refer to.

Fig. 85 Morin, Syntagmatic analyses of Byrd's variations 1 and 11

The figures indicate the bars; the dots indicate the beats.

1 . . . . 2 . . . . 3 . . . . 4 . . . . 5 . . . . 6 . . . . 7 . . . . 8 . . . .

VARIATION 1

Cf1–V'1	Cf1–I'1 1	Cf1–I'1 1	Cf1–I'1 1	
Cc2–I'1 1	Dd9–I'1 1	Cc2–I'1 1	Dd3–I 2 Dd3–I 2	Dd9–I'1 1

VARIATION II

Ac Cc2	Ac Cc2	Ac Cc1	Ac Cc1 Cc1	Ac + Ad3 + Dd5	Ac + Cc2 Cc2 Cc2 Cc2	Cf1 Cc2	Cf1 Cc2	Cf1
+	+	+	+		+	+	+	
II'2 II2	II'2 II2	II4 II'2 II'2	II4 II'2 II'2	II8 + II2	II'4 II'2 II'2 II'2 II4	II'2 II4 II'2	II'2 II4 II'2	II4
Ac–II'3	Ac Cc2	Dc–I'2	Dc–I'2	Ac–II4	Ad + Dd5			
	+	+						
	II'2 II2	II'2 II3						
	Dc–I'III		II4					

Capital letters: melodic units
Small letters: rhythmic units

Figure: mel. or rhyth.
transformation

Mes	1	2	3	4	5	6	7	8
Var.								
1	Aa / B	Ca	Aa / B	Ca	Aa / B	A'a	D–D b	Ca
11	Aa + Bb / Cd	A'a + B'b Aa + B;b A'₁ + B'b / Dc	A;c + B;a / Dd₁	A;c + B;a / Ab₂	A;c + B3a + B;a/A;c + B;c + F;₁ A;c + B;a + B;a + B;a / Dd₁ F₁b-F-b1	Ec + B;a	E'c + B;a	E'c

177

she does not actually explain or justify this). With the completion of the syntagmatic analysis, then, the paradigmatic classifications with which the analytical process began are verified, or else they are modified so that the music is reduced to a minimum number of paradigmatic headings, each of which may appear in a variety of different guises.[1]

Unlike Guertin, Morin does not attempt a generative rule for the distribution she finds. What, then, is the point of her protracted and complicated analytical procedure? It is important here to remember that what she is analyzing is not the two variations that I have been discussing but a total of thirty-two variations by two different composers; and the successive categorizations she makes highlight characteristics which some of the variations have while others do not, or structural patterns found within certain groups of variations. Fig. 86 is typical of the use Morin makes of her findings. It makes visible (or explicitates) the thematic diversity of Byrd's variations as against Tomkins's, and Byrd's organization of his variations in terms of blocks with an overall shaping of the whole as against Tomkins's regular alternation of two textural types. Perhaps, she suggests, this is why Byrd's set is better than Tomkins's. Now, it is tempting to say: do we need semiotic analysis to tell us that? Do we even need semiotic analysis to establish the categories in Fig. 86? Does the whole process tell us anything we could not have discovered informally? Not according to Morin: at any rate she admits that 'a certain number of these conclusions could no doubt have been obtained from attentive listening', and that her conclusions are more or less the same as William Apel's (Vol. 1, pp. 105–6). But, she adds, semiotic analysis allows the observations on which such intuitive judgments are based to be described in precise detail, and in a form that can be communicated from one analyst to another; and this is a sound argument, one which applies as much to Schenkerian analysis as to semiotic analysis. And if there does sometimes seem to be a discrepancy between effort expended and conclusions drawn, this is true of many forms of advanced analysis. The more serious objections to semiotic analysis lie elsewhere, and they fall under two headings.

The first of these is an objection I raised to set-theoretical analysis, and it has to do with the initial segmentation with which the whole

Opposite page: **Fig. 86**   Morin, Comparison of Byrd's and Tomkins's variation sets

[1] This is parallel to the way set-theoretical analysis reduces the harmonic formations of music to a minimum number of pc sets each of which may appear in different transformations.

FORM	BYRD 1	2	3	4	5	6	7	8	9	10	11	12	13	14	15	16	TOMKINS 1	2	3	4	5	6	7	8	9	10	11	12	13	14	15	16
Variation:																																
Theme: appears in upper voice	XX	XX	XX	XX	XX	XX	XX	XX	XX	X		X		X	XX		XX	XX	XX	XX	XX	XX			XX	XX		XX		XX	X	XX	XX
interm. "						X				X	X	X	X			XX	X					XX		XX			XX			X		
lower "										X	X			XX										XX		XX		XX				
Number of figuration voices: –one voice (linear)								XX	X	XX	X	X	XX	XX				XX		XX		XX		XX			XX		XX		XX	
–2 parallel voices forming one (linear)					X		X				X								XX						XX		XX					
–number of voices changes in course of variation		X		X		X				X	X	X					X												X			
–several voices	XX	XX	XX	XX	XX	XX	XX		Xx	x	X		X	xx		XX	XX	XX		XX		XX		XX			XX		XX		XX	XX
Imitation from one voice to another	Xx	XX	XX		X	X	XX		X		X	X		XX	XX	XX	XX		XX		XX		XX		XX		XX					XX
Overlapping (strettos)		X		X			XX							XX	X			XX				X		XX						XX		XX
Units of one half-beat or less								X						XX						xx				XX			X		XX			
" " one beat								X	XX	XX	X	XX	XX	XX	X		XX		XX		XX		X	X		X	XX			XX	XX	XX
" " two beats	XX	XX	XX	X	XX	XX		XX	X		X				X	XX	XX		XX		XX		XX			X		X				XX
" " more than two beats				Xx	X		XX										XX		XX		XX		XX									XX
Fractioned units				X							X							XX	X			XX	X		XX	X	XX	XX	XX	X	XX	XX
Regrouped units			X			XX		XX	XX	XX	X	XX	XX	XX	X			XX		XX		XX		XX	X		XX	XX	XX	X		
Symmetrical units	XX	XX	XX	XX	XX	XX	XX	XX	X	X	X		X		XX	XX	XX	XX		XX		XX	XX	XX	XX	XX	XX		XX	XX	XX
Asymmetrical units				X					X	X	X	XX	X	XX	X					XX		XX			xx	xx		XX			XX
Variation may be divided in two at bar 5	X	X	X	X	X	X	X	X	(X)	X	X	X	x	X	X	X	X	X	X	X	(X)		X	X	X	X	X	X	X	X	X
unit spans bars 4-5													x					x		x											
Change in melodic or rhythmic material at bar 5, material added or new manner or transforming it		X	X	X	X	X	x	X	X	x		X	X		X	X	x		x			x	X		x	X					
Same melodic or rhythmic material throughout variation	XX						XX			XX	XX			XX	XX	XX	XX	XX	XX	XX	XX	XX		XX	XX	XX	XX	XX	XX	XX	XX
Material carried over from preceeding variation, as is or transformed		XX		X	X				XX		X		X										X	X							
Connection between end of var. and following one (same material)				X				X	X																					

analytical process begins. The classification of segments into paradigmatic headings which happens at this stage is reversible later; as we
saw, Morin modified her initial classifications in the light of what she
discovered, and in a sense the initial paradigmatic classification is redundant since feature analysis of the individual segments supplants it –
so that its main role in the initial stage is to provide criteria for the
segmentation itself (one unit being defined as such through its
reiteration by a second unit).[1] But the segmentation itself is not reversible in the same way – and all subsequent stages of the analysis
depend on it. A simple illustration of what is involved is Morin's
segmentation of the left-hand melody of the first Byrd variation into a
pattern beginning D – C – D – B (see column Cc2 on p. 154: here the
segmentation involved is horizontal rather than vertical, but the same
principles apply in either case). Would it not be more musical to read the
musical line as beginning with a B instead of a D?[2] This is important
because, if this were done, then the Cc2 class would disappear (the line
would be identified as Cf1) and the final syntagmatic analysis would be
quite different because classes A and B would be the same. The
difficulty is that here, as often, semiotic analysis provides no criteria for
deciding which is the correct segmentation. In fact it is not really clear
what sort of thing the segments are meant to be. Should they simply
correspond to downbeats, pauses, rhythmic or textural homogeneity
and the like – so that they're primarily descriptive – or are they meant to
embody analytical interpretation of some sort? Nattiez says that 'people
decide to associate several units in a single paradigm because of semantic
or psychological criteria that they do not express consciously. We do
not seek to downgrade the role of intuition at the outset of the analysis',[3]
and for this reason he recommends that a semiotic analysis be based on
the superimposition of a number of separate interpretations rather than

[1] What, then, happens if the relation between segments is not one of simple
recurrence at all but of some more complex transformational relation? The
answer, of course, is that there are no criteria on which to base the initial segmentation. The result of this in practice is the limitation of semiotic analysis to
such styles (Debussy, imitative counterpoint, certain exotic musics) as are characterized by literal repetition. This limitation is not very compatible with the aim of
creating a general theory of sign structures in music.

[2] If it is authentic, then the different notation of bar 5, where the B lasts three beats,
contradicts my interpretation there, but by the same token it would confirm it
elsewhere! Rather than relying on notational details it is better to ask: what would
be the right way to orchestrate the piece? Would you orchestrate bar 5 differently
from bars 1 and 3?

[3] From the revised translation of Nattiez' text in *Three Musical Analyses*, p. 11.

merely on one. Doesn't this imply that what the semiotic technique is really telling us about is not the music as such but analysts' interpretations of it? In which case, instead of basing the process on an analysis of patterns of recurrence in the score, would it not be more useful to begin with some more subtle analysis of the music – say a Schenkerian one – and apply the semiotic techniques to that?[1] Shouldn't we see semiotic analysis as a sophisticated means of presenting and refining analytical findings rather than as a way of making basic discoveries about the music? But in this case what are we to make of the claim that semiotic analysis is objective and scientific? I don't know the answer to these questions, so that the first difficulty with semiotic analysis – as with formal analysis in general – is that while it allows us to make precise statements about music, it doesn't always seem too clear precisely what we mean by these statements.

The second major objection to semiotic analysis has to do with the conception implicit in semiotic analysis – and in formal analysis in general – of music having meaning purely by virtue of abstract relations existing between its component parts. That, after all, is the rationale for basing the analysis on the score (rather than on the experience of the music), and for analyzing it in terms of the patterns made by symbols at increasing levels of abstraction. The problem is this: how much of what matters about music is retained in the translation from sound-experiences to abstract categories such as 'ascending conjunct line'? Can we say anything important about the experience of a given line simply by classifying it as the opposite of lines which are descending or disjunct? Aren't we in danger of making precise statements about musical scores which have only the vaguest connection with the music we experience? I think the answer is that it depends upon the music. Considered individually, the variations on 'John come kiss me now' studied by Elisabeth Morin are not of very great musical interest; after all, each is only eight bars long. The interest comes largely from the fact that they are variations – that is, from the relations between the different variations, the overall patterns of evolution through groups of them and so forth. Morin's analysis is of considerable interest because it is exactly such relationships that she deals with, and her conclusions are reasonably

---

[1] Allen Forte has recently been doing something rather like this. He has been analyzing nineteenth-century music in terms of more or less Reti-like motifs (short intervallic patterns which can be transformed by inversion, retrogression and so forth), but instead of simply looking at the musical surface, like Reti, he uses Schenkerian techniques to discover them at middleground level as well. See his 'Motivic Design and Structural Levels in the First Movement of Brahms' String Quartet in C minor', *Musical Quarterly*, LXIX (1983), pp. 471–502.

secure because thirty-two variations is a reasonably large set of data for generalization. By contrast, Marcelle Guertin's analysis of the twelve themes from Debussy's Preludes is of less interest because it is individually that the Preludes are of musical value – through their individual sonorities, harmonic qualities, expressive or illustrative characteristics – and not just by virtue of the structural relationships between them as a set. And the generative rule Guertin extrapolates from them would be more convincing and indeed useful if it were based on a larger set of data.

Perhaps you can now guess why Nattiez left his analysis of *Syrinx* incomplete. He offers it more as a demonstration of a method than as an illumination of Debussy's music. He considers the segmentations and categorizations resulting from the analysis of a single short piece as purely provisional. They would only become reasonably certain, and hence of real scientific value, if they were verified by comparison with a whole range of other pieces belonging to the same repertoire. In fact he sees the importance of semiotic analysis as lying not so much in what it can say about sign structures within individual pieces of music, but in what it can say about the relations between different pieces. In other words he thinks the real topic of semiotic analysis should be musical style.[1] This shift from the analysis of the individual work to the analysis of a repertoire is probably appropriate given the emphasis formal techniques of analysis lay on abstract relationships, but it means that the aims of the analysis become very different from those of the approaches we have considered up to now. The next chapter clarifies these aims.

---

[1] These last sentences refer to the revised version of Nattiez' analysis published in *Three Musical Analyses*, and they represent a change of heart. At the time of the first version, published in 1975, he did not believe the application of semiotic analysis to individual compositions to be so severely limited.

Chapter Five

TECHNIQUES OF
COMPARATIVE ANALYSIS

If you think that the point of analyzing music is to make objective discoveries about the music's structure, rather than to make intuitive judgments about it, then you have to start by doing one of two things. The first possibility is to devise a theory that allows you to explain the music in terms of some kind of explicit principles of organization. The second is to adopt a comparative method, measuring different pieces against each other; you do not need an explanatory theory in order to do this, you just need some kind of yardstick to make the measurements.

Now, it was the first of these two approaches that we encountered in the last chapter, and we discovered that though analyzing music by means of formal techniques looks very scientific and objective, it is not so in reality: even set-theoretical analysis depends on more or less intuitive segmentation of the music. Let us just think what it would mean for an analysis to be genuinely scientific and objective. It would mean that you could get the right results simply by following given procedures correctly: intuitive judgments about the music (I feel that . . .) would not be involved. This means that if an analytical method were really scientific and objective, then you ought to be able to get a computer to do the analysis for you -- you feed in the music, and out comes the analysis. And people have tried to get some of the analytical techniques we have discussed to run on computers, so as to check just how objective these techniques really are.

For example Michael Kassler, who was formerly one of Babbitt's students at Princeton, has been trying to write a computer program that will carry out a Schenkerian analysis on any music you feed into it. As far as I know he has not fully achieved this yet, but he has implemented a program which takes a Schenkerian middleground as its input, and

Fig. 87

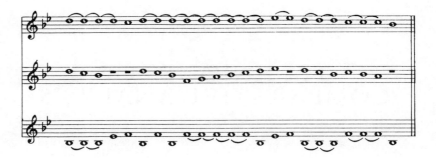

derives this from one of the three forms of fundamental structure (Fig. 13 above). For example, you might type in the music shown in Fig. 87 (you do this by means of an alphanumeric code, but we need not bother with these details). What is this strange music? It is a middleground graph of Haydn's *St Anthony Chorale*, only it has been translated into a version the computer can understand. You can see this middleground graph in conventional Schenkerian notation at the top of Fig. 88. The version you type into the computer is the same, except that it has been divided up into three consistent lines; and, though it looks odd and contains some uncouth counterpoint, this is a perfectly intelligible way of notating the Schenkerian middleground. What does the computer do once you have fed this music into it? It produces a string of letters and numbers which, when transcribed back into musical notation, looks like Fig. 88.[1] Line (1) is the same as Fig. 87; the only difference is that I have put everything on one stave. Compare it to line (2). The two lines are the same, except that line (1) has three extra notes – the D, C and B♭ at the beginning of the middle line, which are marked with a square bracket. In other words, line (1) includes a prolongation that line (2) does not; or to put it the other way round, line (2) is a reduction of line (1) in that it omits the prolongation. And if you scan through the entire chart you will see that every line relates to the next one in this way; as you work downwards each line removes something from the previous one, until only the fundamental structure is left. So the computer has

---

[1] This chart is adapted from Kassler's alphanumeric notation in his article 'Explication of the Middleground of Schenker's Theory of Tonality' (*Miscellanea Musicologica: Adelaide Studies in Musicology*, 1977). I have simplified the presentation by carrying out the rules of transposition and octave adjustment at the beginning instead of half way through; I have also corrected a misprint in line 6 (G5) and an apparent anomaly of ordering in line 7.

Fig. 88 Kassler's explication of a Schenkerian middleground

[1] By 'lyne' Kassler means what I called a 'structural voice' on pp. 39ff above.

reduced the middleground to a background, and it has done this simply by following a set of explicit rules. The program in fact basically consists of a set of rules specifying different prolongations: on the right of the chart you will see the name of the rule that links each line to the next one, and though Kassler does not spell out these rules in his article, you can see quite clearly how they work. These rules correspond more or less closely to the various types of prolongation that Schenker described in his *Free Composition*, and Kassler sees himself as explaining Schenker's theory in the sense of providing precise definitions of things that Schenker himself only outlined impressionistically.

Will this put Schenkerian analysts out of a job? I don't think so. Bear in mind that the computer did not start off with the *St Anthony Chorale*, but with an analysis of it. What Kassler's program shows is that the background of a Schenkerian analysis is implicit in its middleground. But this is really quite obvious if you think about it. A middleground is the music seen in the light of a background structure. As I said earlier (p. 41), all the analytical work is contained in the middleground: the background is just a means of arriving at the middleground, and of communicating it intelligibly to other people. So it is not particularly surprising that a computer can work out what background is implied in a middleground analysis. What would be much more surprising would be if a computer managed to come up with a passable Schenkerian middleground on the basis of the actual music – in this case, of Haydn's *St Anthony Chorale*. Kassler does not seem to regard this as too much of a problem for, he says, 'collectively the foreground prolongation techniques must account for many more notes than the middleground techniques, but since nearly every foreground technique closely resembles a corresponding middleground technique which Schenker called by the same name, the research reported here should extend readily to an explication of Schenker's entire theory' (p. 72). I do not want to put myself in the position of those who scoffed at the Wright brothers, but I can see reasons to doubt this. One is that I do not see how a computer can take proper account of all the surface features which play such an important role in music and which are therefore so vital to sensible Schenkerian analysis – things like rhythm, dynamics, articulation, timbre, effects of contrast, or playing on the listener's expectations. As I said in Chapter 2, you omit these things from a Schenkerian graph but you certainly do not omit them from your analysis – if your analysis is any good, it will be the result of careful consideration of all these things. I do not doubt that a suitably programmed computer could deduce a fundamental structure from just about any tonal score: music is so rich in its patterning that such things can almost always be done. But I do doubt that an analysis done this way, without a sensitive consideration of surface features, could be a useful and sensible analysis – in short, that it could be a *musical* analysis.[1]

In another project, a computer was programmed to identify suspensions and other types of dissonance in Josquin's Masses.[2] Here the computer really was analyzing. It scanned a transcription of the actual score, classifying dissonances according to rules based on such things as intervals between simultaneous or successive notes, the direction of resolutions (up or down) and their metrical position. The computer would analyze the music according to these rules and would classify the dissonances it found according to them; it also made a reduction of the music, showing the consonant formations from which the dissonances were derived. The researchers then sifted through the results in order to discover mistakes – 'mistakes' here meaning discrepancies as against how a human analyst would have classified the dissonances. They would then use these mistakes as the basis for modifying the rules, and then the modified rules would be tested by means of another computer analysis of the music . . . and so on. The purpose of all this was to refine the theory of dissonance on which the rules were based – refine both in the sense of making the theory precise and explicit, and of achieving the best fit between theory and application. So although the process was analytical, the motivation was primarily theoretical; as in Kassler's work the point of using the computer was not so much its ability to yield large quantities of analytical data, as the rigour of method and definition which the use of a computer program guarantees.

However, most of the applications of computers to musical analysis have been designed to take advantage of the large quantity of information a computer can handle, and with the aim of making some kind of practical discovery about the music. The Josquin project gives

---

[1] Lerdahl and Jackendoff have developed a systematic approach to surface features that leads to more or less Schenker-like analyses; see *A Generative Theory of Tonal Music*, p. 203–10, for their analysis of the *St Anthony Chorale*. But though their technique is systematic, it is not computational: as they say, 'achieving computability in any meaningful way requires a much better understanding of many difficult musical and psychological issues than exists at present' (p. 55).

[2] P. Howard Patrick, 'A Computer Study of a Suspension-Formation in the Masses of Josquin Desprez', *Computers and the Humanities*, 8, 1974, pp. 321–31; Patrick and Strickler, 'A Computer-Assisted Study of Dissonance in the Masses of Josquin Desprez', *Computers and the Humanities*, 12, 1978, pp. 341–64.

us an example of this too.[1] Here the motivation was historical rather than theoretical. There had long been a suspicion that the *Et in Spiritum* section of Josquin's *Missa L'homme armé* was a later addition. This is because it does not appear in any of the earliest manuscripts. However, documentary sources cannot prove this suspicion. So the idea was to see whether it could be confirmed on stylistic grounds. If this section's style stands out from the rest of the mass then the evidence, while still circumstantial, becomes very strong. The problem is to find a way of measuring style that allows for the possibility that Josquin decided to write this particular section in a rather different style from the rest – perhaps a more experimental style, or a more old-fashioned one. Equally, if the section was composed later, its composer might well have tried to imitate Josquin's style. So the best criterion would be something that a composer would not be likely to control consciously, but which would typify his style whatever he was consciously trying to achieve. The criterion that the researchers hit upon was the proportion of incomplete triads in the music (that is, chords in which there are only two pitch classes though there are three or more voices). Complete triads were much commoner in the mid sixteenth century, when *Et in Spiritum* first appears in the manuscripts, than they were when the rest of the Mass was composed, fifty years earlier. And because an overall triadic sonority is a kind of compositional habit of mind, it would be difficult for a later composer to imitate Josquin's style accurately in this respect, even if he were trying to. We are not so much concerned with the outcome of this trial (the verdict was guilty) as with the method involved. An objective comparison is being made between a number of pieces of music – the various sections of the mass – and the comparison is based on a single measure of the music's style. This measure is chosen to reflect the composer's underlying habits of mind rather than his conscious intentions. And the purpose of this exercise is not to make a musical discovery – it does not make us hear the music differently, as a Schenkerian analysis does – but a discovery *about* the music. The discovery itself is historical.

Here, then, we have an example of the comparative method – the second way in which you can analyze music objectively. Techniques of this sort can be considerably more sophisticated, and can be used to resolve questions that might not at first seem to lend themselves to such precise treatment. How, asks Fred T. Hofstetter, can you test some-

---

[1] A. Mendel, 'Some Preliminary Attempts at Computer-Assisted Style Analysis in Music', *Computers and the Humanities*, 4, 1969–70, pp. 41–52.

thing like Cobbett's statement that 'the spirit of nationalism is felt in all of the best chamber music'? By looking for some measurable stylistic criterion which will show whether 'composers differ from one another as a function of their nationalities'.[1] What would be a suitable criterion for this? Again, what is wanted is unconscious stylistic habits 'which the composer leaves like fingerprints upon the music he creates' (p. 119). This time the analysis was based on the relative frequency with which different intervals occur in a single musical line – either between a pair of notes, or within groups of three or four successive notes. If there are four notes, then so many different combinations of intervals are possible (29,791 to be exact) that there would be little point in comparing their distribution unless you had the most enormous quantity of music under analysis; for this reason Hofstetter's classification of intervals becomes successively coarser as larger groups are considered – in the case of groups of four notes, the only distinction made is between steps and leaps. So much for the criterion of stylistic comparison. The other important thing to consider in making an analysis of this sort is the selection of the basic data – that is, the choice of chamber music which is truly representative of the various national styles. What governs this selection? First, the sample must be reasonably large; obviously any results derived from the first ten notes of one work from each of the various national schools would be pretty meaningless. Second, factors other than nationality must as far as possible be eliminated. For example, music for oboe probably involves smaller average interval sizes than music for violin, since rapid changes of register are much easier on the violin; in which case if you compare a Czech violin piece with a French oboe piece, you do not know how far differences in intervallic distribution reflect the difference in medium rather than the difference in nationality. Again, it might be that early works in general show different intervallic distributions from mature ones, or that programmatic works show different distributions from non-programmatic ones; so these factors, too, must be kept constant within the sample. In this instance Hofstetter fulfils these conditions by basing his analysis on melodies from two mature, non-programmatic string quartets by each of two different composers from each of the four main national styles of nineteenth-century chamber music (French, German, Czech and Russian). The rest of the analysis is purely a matter of statistics, the result of which is that style does vary with nationality, that it

[1] F. T. Hofstetter, 'The Nationalistic Fingerprint in Nineteenth-Century Chamber Music', *Computers and the Humanities*, 13, 1979, p. 105.

corresponds to geographical distribution on an east–west axis, and that the most distinctive style is the Russian. In other words objective confirmation of Cobbett's intuitive statement is achieved. Or is it? Obviously the method itself is objective, in that it involves verifiable mathematical deductions. The application of the method can be questioned, however. Is the sample large enough? Is the intervallic categorization fine enough? Are there other and perhaps more important factors which ought to have been considered, for instance the speed of the music (perhaps fast music tends to use smaller intervals, or more arpeggios?) Again, is it sense to use Dvořák as a representative of Czech nationalism when he was so heavily influenced by Brahms? And one might criticize the way in which the results are presented: how do we know what to make of the differences in interval distribution *between* the different nationalities when we have not been told how big the differences *within* each nationality were? And the most basic question is, how appropriate is intervallic distribution as a stylistic criterion? Would other stylistic criteria yield similar or contradictory results? Obviously resolving these questions would require a large number of ancillary studies, and in the absence of these one cannot be sure that this analysis is objective in the sense that it supports the generalization that is made from it. If this is not the case, then it is only objective in the sense that anybody who chooses the same pieces of music and carries out the same operations on them will arrive at the same results; and this is a much narrower and less useful kind of objectivity.

Fig. 89

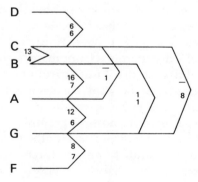

The same kind of techniques are widely used in the study of non-Western music, and the same questions of objectivity arise here too.

Many (though not all) ethnomusicologists are interested in cross-cultural comparisons of music, and the basic technique for making such comparisons is to choose some quantifiable characteristic which you believe to be significant for musical style. In fact the relative frequency of melodic intervals is often used as a stylistic criterion by ethnomusicologists, though not in such a sophisticated way as in the computer study we have just looked at. Ethnomusicologists tend simply to count successive intervals between pairs of notes. But even such a straightforward technique as this can be applied in different ways. You could count how often the various intervals (minor second, major second and so on) appear in the music of one culture as against the music of another. Or you could compare the distribution of rising to falling intervals. This is what is being done in the analysis shown in Fig. 89, which is based on a song from Madagascar called 'Zaodahy' (Fig. 90).[1] The chart shows the number of rising or falling intervals between each pair of pitches in the voice part (I have omitted the zither, though obviously it could have been included too). For example, it shows that C falls to B thirteen times and B rises to C four times. Why do these figures appear at the extreme left of the chart? Because the horizontal axis represents interval size. The smallest interval in this song is the minor second, the only example of this being between B and C. But there are four major seconds, which appear next; there is one minor third (betwen C and A); and so on, until every interval that appears in the song under analysis has been accounted for. And what use is this chart? In itself, very little. For example, if you look at the numbers, the most striking thing is that the perfect fourth from G to C occurs no less than eight times rising but never falling. But this merely reflects the upbeat with which the tune begins. It is easy to imagine that if the text had happened to have one syllable less, then this upbeat would have been omitted. However, the chart is not meant to be used this way. It is intended as a means of making comparisons. It would be possible to make comparisons *within* this particular song. Fig. 91 compares the frequency with which the various intervals occur in each of the three verses of 'Zaodahy'. It shows one or two possibly significant trends. For instance, the third verse has nearly as many falling intervals as the first

[1] This song was collected and transcribed by Norma McLeod, and I have taken from Marcia Herndon's 'Analysis: The Herding of Sacred Cows?', *Ethnomusicology*, 18, 1974, pp. 219–62. Herndon uses it, as I do, to exemplify different analytical techniques. The present analysis is mine but follows the technique described by Mervyn McLean in 'A New Method of Melodic Interval Analysis as Applied to Maori Chant', *Ethnomusicology*, 10, 1966, pp. 174–90.

Fig. 90 *Zaodahy*

two, but rather fewer rising ones; this quantifies the way in which the music settles down onto its final cadence in the third verse. In a large and complex piece – which 'Zaodahy' is not – internal comparisons of this sort might be quite revealing. However the technique is really meant for making comparisons *between* a large number of songs. For this purpose Mervyn McLean, who developed this particular kind of graphing, analyzes the intervals in accordance with their relationship to the tonic. For example he counts how many major thirds occur above the tonic, how many below it, and how many spanning it. And having assembled a large quantity of data he then analyzes it mathematically to see if it correlates with various factors that might reasonably be expected to have an influence on musical style. Thus he finds that there are minor differences between the songs of the various Maori tribes represented in his data, but that there are larger differences corresponding to the song type (laments, lullabies, entertainment songs) regardless of the tribe involved. And from this he concludes that the frequency of melodic intervals is a valid way of distinguishing and characterizing different song styles; one, moreover, that obviates the need for a full rhythmic transcription (generally it is possible to transcribe pitches much quicker than rhythms).

Fig. 91

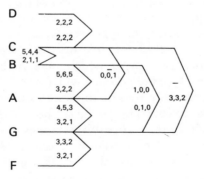

Is this technique objective? One problem may have occurred to you: how do you make an objective decision about which note is the tonic? For example is the tonic in 'Zaodahy' C, as its scale-form would suggest in a Western context? Obviously no: C is treated as a departure-note, not an arrival-note. Then F, the destination note of the song as a whole? Or G, round which the tune most frequently revolves? Clearly no objective decision is possible in terms such as these. On the other hand you can retain objectivity if you simply adopt some formula for defining tonics. For instance, you can define the tonic as the note that appears most frequently. This means of course that what you decide to call the tonic may not correspond to what people would intuitively judge to be the tonic. Does this matter? Ethnomusicologists will tend to say no, provided that the analyst is consistent in applying his criteria. Jan LaRue makes an interesting analogy: 'In measuring two rooms, a yardstick thirty-five inches long will not yield exact yardages, but it will definitely tell us which room is larger'.[1] In other words, he's saying, the information you get by evaluating music in this way may not be significant in itself, but it becomes significant when it is used for comparing different pieces.

This becomes even more obvious when the criteria for evaluation are more restricted than in the case of the interval frequency technique. Charts like Fig. 89 simply omit the time element from the music: the intervals are totalized, regardless of their temporal distribution in the piece. Now, there are complementary techniques for classifying music in accordance with its contour. This means retaining the time element, since contour is a function of pitch and time. But in this case it is necessary to categorize the music's pitch structure in a much more drastically reduced way – otherwise you end up with as many contour types as individual tunes, and consequently with no analysis. Charles Adams wrote an article which summarizes the various ethno-musicological approaches to analyzing contour, and which also sets out a typology of his own.[2] His typology takes account of only four pitch features in any one melody: its first note, its final note, its highest note and its lowest note. The way in which these can be distributed gives rise to fifteen different types of contour which are shown graphically in Fig. 92. (Why are there only two or three notes in some of these? Because several functions are coinciding – the last note is also the lowest note, for instance. 'Zaodahy' exemplifies this: it comes out as $S_1D_1R_1$.) Now it is perfectly possible, and objective, to compare different repertoires of music just on the basis of this categorization into contour types. Adams does this, using songs from two American Indian cultures for the purpose. But he finds that this is not a very useful way of evaluating style; each culture comes out looking much the same. What he did find, however, was that those features that determine the *shape* rather than the *type* of a contour varied significantly as between the one culture and the

[1] *Guidelines for Style Analysis*, Norton, 1970, p. 18.
[2] 'Melodic Contour Typology', *Ethnomusicology*, 20, 1976, pp. 179–215.

Fig. 92 Adams' classification of melodic contours

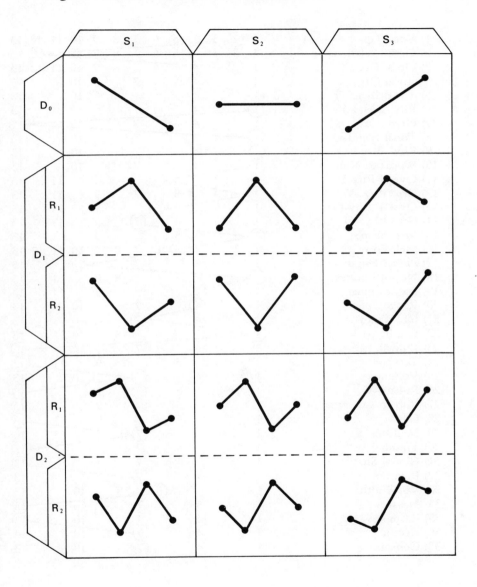

Fig. 93 Cantometric coding of *Zaodahy*

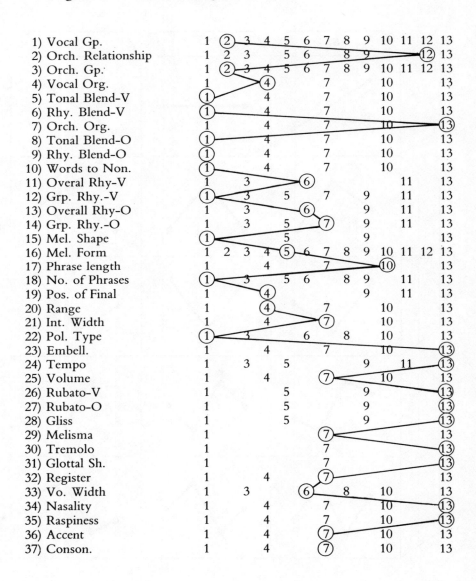

1) Vocal Gp.
2) Orch. Relationship
3) Orch. Gp.
4) Vocal Org.
5) Tonal Blend-V
6) Rhy. Blend-V
7) Orch. Org.
8) Tonal Blend-O
9) Rhy. Blend-O
10) Words to Non.
11) Overal Rhy-V
12) Grp. Rhy.-V
13) Overall Rhy-O
14) Grp. Rhy.-O
15) Mel. Shape
16) Mel. Form
17) Phrase length
18) No. of Phrases
19) Pos. of Final
20) Range
21) Int. Width
22) Pol. Type
23) Embell.
24) Tempo
25) Volume
26) Rubato-V
27) Rubato-O
28) Gliss
29) Melisma
30) Tremolo
31) Glottal Sh.
32) Register
33) Vo. Width
34) Nasality
35) Raspiness
36) Accent
37) Conson.

other. Features of this sort include things like where the highest note is placed in terms of a song's total duration, or the slope between the first and last notes expressed as a proportion of the song's total pitch range. Here, Adams concludes, is a criterion of musical style which is not only objective but useful – that is, it makes reasonably fine distinctions between styles and it is easily applied to any song.

These, then, are two techniques for evaluating and comparing musical styles. In each a single aspect of the music is being used as an index of the style as a whole. And obviously there are any number of alternative traits that you could use for purposes of stylistic comparison. But the most significant results naturally come when you use a large number of different traits together in order to characterize styles. This is what Alan Lomax and his co-workers did in the Cantometrics project, which must be the most ambitious piece of research ever to have been carried out in the field of comparative musicology (this, incidentally, is a useful though unfashionable term for the kind of work this chapter is about). The Cantometrics project – the name means song-measuring – involved the comparison of several thousand songs selected to be as representative as possible of all the world's cultures, and Fig. 93 shows what these comparisons were based on. Again it is 'Zaodahy' that is being analyzed.[1] There are thirty-seven different aspects of the music being considered here – or more precisely we should say that it is being evaluated along thirty-seven dimensions. Some of these relate to the melodic or contoural features we have been talking about. For instance, line 15, Melodic Shape, classes contour into four types (arched, terraced, undulating and descending); the circle round 1 means that 'Zaodahy' is being classed as arched. (There is of course a code book to tell you what the figures mean in each case.[2]) Line 19 measures the position of the final note within the total pitch range of the song; 4 means that the final tonic falls within the lower half of the range. The 4 in line 20 means that the range is somewhere between a minor third and a perfect fifth, which as it happens is an error on the analyst's part. And so on. But there are also many dimensions that evaluate things quite different from anything we have discussed so far, for instance the degree of tonal blend, the ratio of words to music, the use of rubato, and the nasality of the singing. You cannot of course judge the nasality of the singing from a transcription; the Cantometrics project was based on

---

[1] This analysis is also taken from Marcia Herndon's article (pp. 230–1).

[2] Lomax, *Folk Song Style and Culture*, American Association for the Advancement of Science, 1968, Chapter 3.

sound recordings rather than transcriptions, which is an important distinction between it and the techniques we have looked at up to here. On the other hand, how can you evaluate something like nasality in an objective manner? Not, clearly, by means of the kind of explicit formula you can use to define what you mean by a 'tonic'. Lomax's answer, which has not satisfied all his critics, is very simple: with a minimum of training more or less anybody will make the same judgments about such things, and so a consistent measure is achieved even if we cannot actually define what it is that we are measuring.

What Lomax and the various other people who collaborated with him did was to code a very large body of music in this manner, feed the data into a computer, and analyze the results according to all kinds of factors that they were interested in. Some of these factors are obvious, for example geographical provenance. Others are less obvious to musicians and reflect the fact that the cantometrics project was really a piece of anthropological rather than musicological research. One example will have to serve for many. Fig. 94 measures two cantometric variables against the complexity of social organization in the cultures from which the songs come. The solid line represents one of these variables, the wordiness of song texts, while the broken line measures the precision with which consonants are articulated; these two variables correspond to lines 10 and 37 of the initial analysis respectively. In both cases the vertical axis corresponds to the cantometric variable, while the horizontal axis measures societal complexity in terms of food production; X represents the simplest type of food production – hunting and fishing – while IR represents complex agricultural organization involving irrigation. So the chart tells us that there is a more or less linear relationship between wordiness and articulation in songs and complexity in social organization: the more complex a society in this sense, the more wordy its songs are likely to be and the more precisely articulated. And Lomax's overall conclusion, supported by very many correlations of this kind, is that 'song style symbolizes and reinforces certain important aspects of social structure in all cultures' (p. vii). If this seems at first sight a rather far-fetched and extravagant idea, then it is worth thinking a little more about what 'style' actually means in this context. Style is not the way someone chooses to sing but the way in which they sing without making any conscious choice; as Lomax puts it, 'if a culture member sings at all, he has to sing in the style of his people because it is the only style he knows. It is in fact almost impossible for anyone really to change his singing style. It takes years for a non-European to learn opera; it has required half a century for

Europeans to learn to perform American jazz' (p. 28). At the same time style is something to which anybody who belongs to a given culture responds with precision: 'any culture member can immediately sense that something is stylistically wrong about a greeting, a cooking pot, a song, or a dance, without being able to explain why this is so' (p. 12). So what Lomax is doing is using song style as a convenient way of characterizing the stylistic community which underlies all the varied activities of a given culture – its work distribution, sexual mores and social customs as much as its dance or song.

Fig. 94

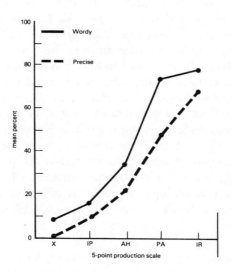

What cantometrics is not concerned with, however, is the individuality of a given song – the particular things that the singer sets out to do in it, rather than the general stylistic background that he takes for granted. In this respect it is very interesting that of all the lines in the cantometric coding sheet, as the initial analytical chart is termed, the ones that produce the least correlation with social structure are those that have the most bearing on the music's technical structure: lines 11, 13, 15, 16, 17, 18, 19 and 22 (p. 36). What this means is that whereas things like wordiness or nasality are rather consistent within a given culture and reflect (or reinforce) its societal patterns, things like melodic shape and form vary pretty much from one performer or occasion to the next. In other words these things have to do with what a particular performer is trying to achieve in a particular song, and not with the taken-for-granted stylistic background. But if this is so, then the problem arises whether there is any sense in attempting to compare such technical features statistically, which is what the techniques for evaluating interval frequencies and classifying contours I described earlier were doing. Don't the figures you derive from such analysis lose all their meaning when you totalize them? If you are going to make meaningful comparisons of interval patterns and contours, don't you need to take account of the context in which they occur? What is involved here is not just a musical issue. It is the contrast between two distinct approaches to anthropology, namely functionalism and structuralism. Without getting bogged down in details, people like Lomax are 'structuralists' in that they sit in armchairs or (as they prefer to call them) laboratories, comparing different songs from all over the world, and drawing grand conclusions about the relationship between musical and societal organization. 'Functionalists' on the other hand spend years in the field studying a single culture, because they think that you cannot even understand a single song unless you understand what it means to a culture member – and that means understanding the whole pattern of social organization that makes up that culture. Functionalists consequently believe that the sort of comparisons made by structuralists are perfectly meaningless. John Blacking, who is a good representative of the functionalist approach in ethnomusicology, argues that objective measures of interval frequencies and so forth are not actually objective in any useful sense, because

> maximum objectivity can be achieved only if the tones of a melody are understood in the contexts of first that particular melody; secondly, the class of melodies to which it is said to belong by its composer and/or performers; and thirdly, the musical tradition to which it belongs. For instance, in some contexts what *sounds* like a rising fourth may really be a falling fifth, transformed because of limitations of vocal or instrumental range. Venda music will probably be misunderstood if it is compared with other styles of music before it is analyzed as a symbolic expression of aspects of Venda culture.[1]

This is all very well in theory, but what does it actually mean in practice? Here is how Blacking analyzes a repertoire of Venda girls' initiaton songs (the Venda are a people living in the Transvaal). The starting point of his analysis is precisely the fact that the Venda

---

[1] 'Tonal Organization in the Music of Two Venda Initiation Schools', *Ethnomusicology*, 14, 1970, p.1.

Fig. 95 Comparative analysis of Venda initiation songs

themselves regard this group of songs as a single repertoire distinct from
the rest of Venda music. So Blacking's basic question is: just what is it
that ties this group of songs into a repertoire, and that distinguishes
them from other Venda music? It is no good asking the Venda; they
cannot say why this should be, they just know that that's how it is. This
is like the situation with language: people know what is right and what
is not, but they can't explain what the linguistic rules that govern this
are. Only a linguist can do that, and he does it by analyzing what people
actually do – that is, the way they talk. Blacking is attempting the same
thing for this repertoire of Venda music. He compares the various songs
of this repertoire with each other in the hope of discovering both what it
is that they all have in common, and the rules of transformation in
accordance with which the same underlying structure can result in a
large number of apparently quite different songs. I find Blacking's
analysis rather hard to follow as he sets it out, so I have compiled a chart
(Fig. 95) which simplifies – perhaps over-simplifies – the central point
he is making. Each of the lines except the bottom one shows a complete
song (they are repeated over and over again in performance). They are
aligned with each other in the manner of a motivic or semiotic chart,
and they have been transposed where necessary so that in each case the
final note is an E. What do we see? All the songs are made up of falling
scale patterns with occasional leaps, but if we compare the songs by
reading the chart vertically, we can see that the same scale pattern is not
always in use at the same time. However, practically everything fits into
one of two scale patterns: either a repeated fall from D to E, or from G
to A. The bottom line of the chart explains this. What Blacking is saying
is that this bottom line constitutes the underlying model which is
common to all the songs and which they elaborate in different ways.
How does the elaboration work? The most important principle is that a
note from either scale may be selected at any point; this rationalizes the
otherwise irregular leaps found, for instance, in songs 61, 25 and 34. Or
both notes can be selected; this rationalizes the chords in all the songs
except 42. Occasionally neither note is selected (songs 12 and 33), and
conversely extraneous notes are now and then introduced; these are
marked by brackets in songs 61, 39 and 34. There are also slight
modifications of the sequence of notes in songs 33, 34 and 42. And
finally rhythm and immediate note-repetitions are free. These, then,
constitute the rules by which a single underlying structure is transformed into the various different songs that make up this repertoire. Now
if you accept all this, then you can see that it might make sense to
compare the underlying structures and rules of transformation found in

songs from different cultures, just as linguists compare syntactical organization in different languages; but that it makes very little sense to compare the surface formations found in songs of different cultures with each other. It would be like trying to understand how languages work by comparing their vocabularies, or analyzing different literatures by comparing how often the letters of the alphabet appear in them. The significant thing about the occurrence of intervals in these Venda songs is the way they fit into the underlying scalar pattern; to totalize them regardless of context is to make them meaningless. Again, distinguishing the various songs on the basis of their scale-type is misleading. While most of the songs are heptatonic (have seven pitch classes), one is hexatonic and two are pentatonic. But this does not mean that there is any significant difference in the way they work; in each case the same underlying structure is there. Really what Blacking is saying is the same as what Schenker said: analyzing surface features of music is pointless unless you do so in terms of the background structure they elaborate.

Let us keep Blacking's arguments in mind and return to 'Zaodahy'. As we do not have other examples of the repertoire to which it belongs, we cannot follow Blacking's procedures precisely. Is there any other way in which we can discover an underlying structure which its surface patterns elaborate? One ethnomusicologist who has analyzed this particular tune in terms of a kind of background structure is Mieczyslaw Kolinski. He adopts various techniques, and some of them – evaluation of slope between first and last notes, classification of scale types – merely involve surface features. However, this is not the case with his technique for analyzing melodic structure. Fig. 96 shows how he analyzes the vocal line of the first verse, that is to say up to bar 10.[1] Essentially this is a simple graphic representation of the score, with the rhythms omitted; this will become quite clear if you compare it note for note with the beginning of the voice part (the little dots represent note-repetitions). The analysis proper lies in the patterns formed by the filled and unfilled circles. These are used to indicate what Kolinski calls 'recurrent movements'. By this he means wave-like contours of pitch that move from one note to another and back again, sometimes several times in a row. The first such movement is indicated by unfilled circles and marked '1'; it rises from G to D, falls to G, and rises and falls once more before terminating towards the end of bar 4. Overlapping with

---

[1] It is taken from 'Herndon's Verdict on Analysis: Tabula Rasa', *Ethnomusicology*, 20, 1976, pp. 1–22. This reply to Herndon's article corrects a number of errors made there.

205

Fig. 96 Kolinski's analysis of *Zaodahy*, bars 3–10

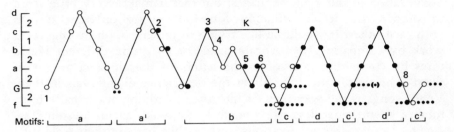

Fig. 97 Kolinski's analysis of 'Zaodahy', renotated

this is a second movement, which is marked '2' and is indicated by the filled circles (filled and unfilled circles are used in alternation so that the different movements stand out from each other on the page). This second movement begins on C, falling to G and ending on the next C. To make it easier to see just how Kolinski is segmenting the music I have drawn up a chart in which the original score of the voice part is chopped up into recurrent movements (Fig. 97); you can see that the tune is entirely made up of such movements with the single exception of the third, which is a unilinear fall from C to B.

Now this kind of analysis is certainly analogous to what Blacking

was doing, or Schenker for that matter, in that it discovers an underlying structure in relation to which the musical surface can be viewed as
a kind of elaboration. What is more, it is objective in a way that
Blacking's way of analyzing probably isn't and Schenker's certainly
isn't, namely that there are clear and explicit rules for doing the analysis
so that any two people should come up with the same result. But is it
objective in the sense of telling us anything meaningful about the song,
or at any rate being the basis for meaningful comparisons between
songs? What exactly is it telling us? It certainly is not telling us about
folk evaluation in the way that Blacking's analysis did; that is to say,
people do not associate their songs into repertoires on the basis of how
recurrent movements are used in them. On the other hand, it does not
seem to be telling us how we experience the music, in the way a
Schenker graph does; at any rate I don't 'hear' the song in terms of
Kolinski's segments. Kolinski seems to think that such movements have
some very privileged psychological status, and for this reason he finds it
meaningful to analyze music from all the world's folksong cultures and
even European art music in this way. The compilations of data look
impressive but I personally have no idea what to conclude from them,
if anything.

Even if one is not quite clear what the theory behind Kolinski's
technique of melodic analysis actually is, it is obvious that the
approach is a theory-laden one. It is because he begins with a theory
that he applies precisely the same method to all melodies. And this
seems to me a pity, because the great advantage of comparative
techniques of analysis is that they allow you to approach music very
inductively. As I said at the beginning of this chapter, you do not need
an *a priori* theory to compare pieces of music; all you need is some
means of comparison which is appropriate to the particular music in
question. And to make the point we shall turn for the last time to
'Zaodahy'.

About the most inductive way of beginning an analysis is to look
for patterns of recurrence. If you are going to be genuinely inductive,
then you need to begin with a relatively full version of the music – a
detailed transcription of voice and zither in this case – since any more
drastic initial reduction of the music will necessarily incorporate *a priori*
judgments as to what in the music is essential and what is not. If you
simply reconfigure the score in terms of patterns of recurrence, in the
manner of semiotic analysis, then you will end up with something like
Fig. 98 (pp. 210–13). (I say 'something like' because you may end up with
something slightly different, depending on how detailed you make the

recurrences and what deviations you admit.) On the basis of what occurs independently of what, we can segment the music and assign a letter to each segment type (these letters are shown at the top of the chart). That gives us the folowing distribution for the song:

Verse 1:	a	a	a	a	c	d	e	d	e	d	
Verse 2:	a	b	a	b	c	d	e	d	e	d	e	d
Verse 3:	a	a	a	a	c	d	e	d*	e	d	f

(d* consists of the second half of d only)

Is there any simple rule governing this distribution? Yes, the song is made up of four essential phrases (a, c, d, e) which are prolonged by means of repetition in the first verse and thereafter by means of transformation (it is transformation that gives rise to b and f in verses 2 and 3 respectively). Can we confirm our identification of a, c, d and e as essential by showing them to have some special function as regards pitch structure? Again yes, because if we pick out the most important melodic notes of each phrase, we find that each consists of an overall melodic motion of a second:

$$a = CB$$
$$c = e = AG^1$$
$$d = FG$$

And adding together each of these essential phrases we get the basic linear motion that underlies each verse, that is to say a scalar fall from C to F that returns (except in the last verse) to G. Now if we view this as the background structure of the song, then we can see two ways in

---

[1] Does this functional equivalence mean c and e should be regarded as belonging to the same essential category? Possibly: Fig. 99 shows how the basic melodic pattern of e elaborates that of c.

Fig. 99

Fig. 98 Paradigmatic analysis of *Zaodahy*

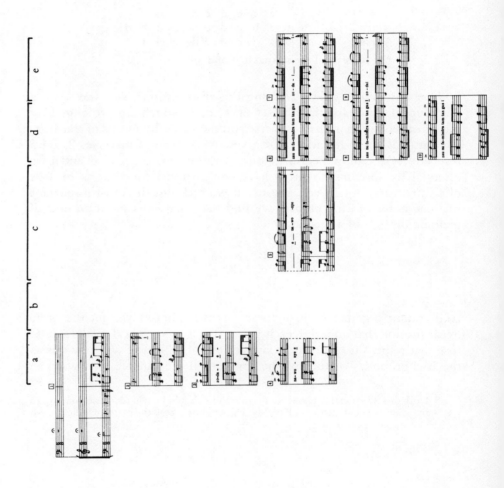

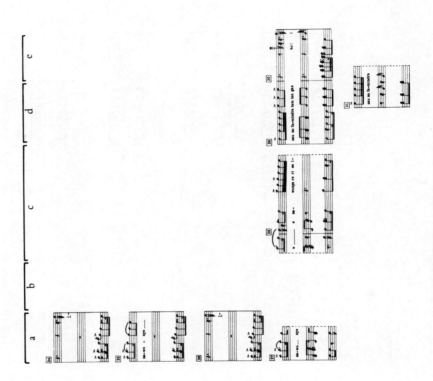

Fig. 100

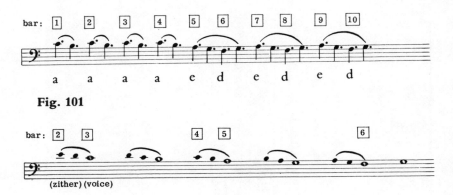

Fig. 101

which it is prolonged at middleground level. One is through a metrically regular pattern of repetitions based on the essential phrases: four repetitions of the first pattern, followed by three of the second (Fig. 100). The other is through a metrically irregular sequential elaboration (Fig. 101).

All this is hardly more than the beginning of an analysis, involving as it does only the simplest induction of regularities in formal distribution and linear motion. But already we have quite powerful indications of the way in which the musical surface acquires its significance through the elaboration of underlying patterns – through *function,* in other words. If one were to use such techniques for analyzing musical function as the basis for comparisons between different pieces of music – whether from one culture or several – then the conclusions might have a degree of musical significance which can hardly be attained merely by evaluations of surface features, however comprehensive and painstaking.

CHAPTER SIX

WHAT DOES MUSICAL ANALYSIS TELL US?

I

As the previous five chapters have showed, there are plenty of clearly defined techniques of musical analysis; but it is not always too clear exactly what these techniques are telling us about the music. In fact, I think there is a good deal of muddled thinking on this topic, which has had two undesirable results: first, the development of analytical approaches that are themselves false or at least wrong-headed; and secondly, false or wrong-headed notions of what it is that we can learn from existing approaches such as Schenkerian analysis. A good way to tackle the question 'what can analysis tell us' is to ask what it is that makes one analysis good and another bad, because this immediately raises the question: good in what sense? good for what?

Now there are some instances where the answer to this is straightforward: one analysis of a piece is good because it is right, and any other is bad because it is wrong. One example of this is a serial note count (see below, p. 294); in most cases there is no doubt which serial parsing is right and which is wrong, and the wrong one is wrong in the same sense as a mathematical error or a misprint is wrong. Actually a serial note count is simply one example of several sorts of analysis whose purpose is to discover what the composer did: uncovering complex proportional schemes in Renaissance polyphony or Bartók, and the secret names encoded in Schumann's or Berg's music, are other examples where an analysis is right or wrong in a purely historical sense – either the composer did what the analyst says or he did not. A more complex example of the same thing is Skryabin's Fifth Sonata. I think that this single-movement sonata should be regarded as being in D♯ minor. At

Fig. 102   Skryabin, Fifth Sonata, opening

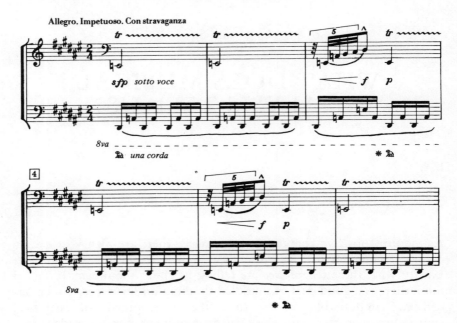

Fig. 103   Skryabin, Fifth Sonata, first subject

first sight this may seem perverse. The opening is in no real key at all but emerges from tonal obscurity (Fig. 102), and the first subject sounds distinctly like B major (Fig. 103). But my reasons for saying that the sonata is in D# minor are not so much to do with the sound of the music as with what I think Skryabin's intentions were. Consider the following facts: the piece ends in an emphatic E♭ major (there is bar upon bar of tonic pedals from 388 to the end). The second subject, at bar 120, is in an equally explicit B♭ major (Fig. 104). If we see the opening as in D# minor – and notice those low D#s with which the work begins – then we have quite a conventional Romantic tonal plan of tonic minor, dominant, tonic major. To be sure, the thematic plan and the plan of

Fig. 104   Skryabin, Fifth Sonata, second subject

keys are out of kilter in conventional terms (that is, the first subject is
recapitulated in a non–tonic key), but then this is also true of the first
movement of Chopin's B♭ minor Sonata which Skryabin would pre-
sumably have known well. Seeing the sonata as in D♯, then, makes
sense of its tonal plan and, as the clinching factor, makes sense of the
six-sharp key signature that is otherwise incomprehensible. But all of
this could, in principle, be refuted by the discovery of an autograph
score headed 'Sonata in B major': this would show that Skryabin did not
intend the sonata to be in D♯ and that therefore my analytical interpretation was simply wrong.

However, all these instances in which an analysis can be unambiguously shown to be right or wrong are a bit exceptional.
Normally this is not the case in musical analysis. Let us take as an
example one of the great analytical conundrums of the past century, the
opening of Wagner's *Tristan* Prelude (Fig. 105). A whole literature has
been devoted to the interpretation of the 'Tristan chord' (I have marked
it with asterisks). Some people have argued that it should not really be
considered as a functional harmonic unit at all, but as the outcome of
motivic structures (Fig. 106). Others have argued that it is really a
diminished seventh chord altered chromatically – that is, that it does not
particularly belong to any key. Still others have argued that it has a tonal
function – so that at its first appearance it is either an altered II⁷ or VI⁷ of

Fig. 105 Wagner, opening of the *Tristan* Prelude

Fig. 106 Motivic derivation of the 'Tristan chord'

A minor (but they do not agree which). Now, none of these interpretations is wrong in the same sense that it is wrong to say a serial transform is P–2 when it's in fact I–4. Nor could any of them be shown to be wrong by historical evidence. Admittedly an early sketch of the *Tristan* Prelude might always come to light, and if it took one of the following three forms (Fig. 107) then the advocates of the diminished seventh, II⁷ and VI⁷ respectively, might claim that they had been proved right. But their opponents could reply that this only told us about Wagner's starting point, and that the important thing was to explain the chord that Wagner eventually evolved from that – that is, the Tristan chord as we know it. And this reply is surely correct, because when somebody analyzes the chord one way or the other we do not speculate on whether or not that is what Wagner intended: instead we listen carefully to the chord, perhaps playing it several times on the piano, and asking: Is that how it works? Is that how I hear it?

Normally, then, we expect an analysis to tell us something about the way we experience music: we judge whether it is good or bad according to whether it seems true to experience or not, and the objection to old–fashioned harmonic and formal labelling was precisely that they were not true to experience. At the same time, the various analytical approaches which grew out of this objection do not simply consist of descriptions of what we experience when we listen to music.

Fig. 107   Variants of the 'Tristan chord'

Motivic analysts, for instance, talk about patterns which they find equally in the tiny notes of pianistic figuration and on the largest scale of inter-movemental relations: but do people really hear either of these as motifs, let alone recognize the similarity between them, when they listen to music in the ordinary way? Again, Schenkerian analysis is based on the experience of large-scale tonal continuity and finality – but do people really experience these large-scale directed motions in the way Schenkerian analysis suggests they do? If we stopped a sonata movement half way through the development, would most listeners actually be able to sing out the home tonic at which the development is aiming? I doubt it: and analysts do not seem to be overly concerned with the facts of the matter, since they virtually never begin an analysis by making objective tests of audience response like this.

    There are two possible justifications for analysts talking about things of which most musical listeners are not, in practice, aware. I think I can show both of them to be inadequate; but I shall explain what they are, partly because many analysts do believe one or the other, and partly because what I consider a more satisfactory answer to the question 'what does musical analysis tell us' will emerge from the argument. The first possible justification, then, is a frankly elitist one. As I said in Chapter 2, Schenker did not see himself as explaining how the average listener experienced music; in fact he was dismissive of the average person's abilities to appreciate music at any serious level at all. What he was explaining was how the music demanded to be heard by a fully adequate listener – and he emphasized that hearing music correctly was no easy matter but required serious application. Now this is a perfectly coherent position – it involves no logical absurdity – but I think it narrows the purview of analysis to the point of irrelevance: isn't the really fascinating thing about music the immediate effect it makes on even the most untutored listener?

    The second possible justification has to be taken much more

seriously and it involves the characteristically twentieth-century concept of unconscious perception. I shall explain what this means before showing how it applies to music. Analysts of music in the first half of the century derived their concept of unconscious perception from Freud. Freud had made sense of the apparently random and meaningless behaviour of neurotics by showing how it derived from their unconscious wishes or intentions. The neurotics themselves had no idea of these wishes or intentions; they had repressed them from their conscious mind, which is why they could not explain their own behaviour. But these wishes and intentions still determined what they did. So Freud was making sense of the incoherent actions of neurotics by setting them in the context of the unconscious mind – an unconscious mind which could not be directly proved to exist, but whose existence could be deduced from its effect upon neurotic behaviour. In the same way, musical analysts saw it as their task to make sense of the fragmentary and incomplete perceptions of musical listeners by setting these in the context of underlying structures which listeners don't consciously perceive, such as motivic resemblances between tunes. Of course people aren't consciously aware of these motivic parallels, the motivic analysts said, but they are responsible for the experience of musical unity none the less. And therefore the point of an analysis is not to *describe* what people consciously perceive: it is to *explain* their experience in terms of the totality of their perceptions, conscious and unconscious. Although it has been the motivic analysts who have adopted Freudian concepts most explicitly – and Hans Keller most of all – I imagine that Freud's thinking had some influence on Schenker too. Certainly Schenker's talk of the 'daemonic forces' of the middleground, and of the fundamental structure being a secret hidden behind the foreground, has a Freudian ring. And his concept of analytical interpretation being a process of revealing the meaning of the obvious, by deriving it from what is hidden, is very comparable with psychoanalysis.

Since the middle of the twentieth century, however, musical analysts have also been influenced by a different concept of unconscious perception, this time deriving from psycholinguistics. Linguists had succeeded in breaking down the structure of speech into phonemes – that is, significant structural units which can be consciously heard and articulated (a, f, th and ng are examples of phonemes in English). But could these phonemes themselves be broken down into smaller structural units? It was discovered, principally by Roman Jakobson, that they could; the various phonemes were all made up of different combinations of a few 'distinctive features' (as Jakobson called them) which, try as they may, people cannot perceive consciously when listening to someone talk. Their conscious perceptions – their understanding of what the person is saying – depend on their unconscious perceptions. Now, linguistic models of explanation have had a considerable influence on musical analysis in the last thirty years; neo-Schenkerians in particular have been very fond of likening their hierarchical explanations of musical structures to the hierarchical schemes of linguistics. And it would seem to them no more reasonable for someone to challenge their theories on the grounds that people do not consciously perceive all the interval classes and structural relations they talk about, than it would if the linguists' theories were challenged on the grounds that people do not consciously perceive 'distinctive features'. In other words, just as in the Freudian model, the point of analysis is to explain what is obvious – the experience of musical unity or whatever – in terms of structures that are not obvious and can only be deduced from analytical study. In fact it makes little difference which model of unconscious perception an analyst adheres to: in either case he feels that he is doing something essentially scientific – explaining how it is that people experience what they do – even though much of the time he is talking about things of which listeners have no immediate awareness.

All this will become clearer if we illustrate it by returning to the Tristan chord. As I said, analysts explain this chord by deriving it from one prototype or another – a motivic formula, a II⁷ or whatever. Now what does such derivation mean? It could simply mean 'it is convenient to think of the Tristan chord as an elaboration of x', and, as a matter of fact, I consider this to be the correct way to understand such a derivation. But this is clearly not what analysts have thought, because if so, the controversy over the chord could not have raged all these years; there would have been nothing to argue about. As it was, analysts furiously rejected each other's interpretations because they were arguing over whether the chord was 'really' a diminished seventh or whatever. They were trying to explain the obvious thing – that people experienced the chord in the way they did – in terms of something that was not so obvious, namely the structure that gave rise to the experience. In other words, they saw the process of deriving the chord from one prototype or another as not simply being something an analyst does, as an act of classification, but as in some way representing what the listener does too – though only unconsciously, of course. This is explicit in Ernst Kurth's classic study of the harmony of *Tristan*, which was published in 1920. Kurth analyzed Wagner's harmony as an interplay of what he called 'constructive' and 'destructive' forces (he associated these with diatonicism and chromaticism respectively) and regarded these forces as in essence psychological. As Curt von Westernhagen puts it, Kurth saw music as deriving from 'psychic impulses in the depths of the unconscious, beneath the level of perceptible sound, which, after rising into the conscious mind, insist on breaking out in sound'. And so, in Kurth's own words, 'the essential function of all music theory is to observe the transformation of specific impulses into sounds'.[1] All this sounds old-fashioned today. But even a modern analysis of the harmony of *Tristan* like Benjamin Boretz's is psychological by implication. The analysis itself, to be sure, is purely formal (Boretz sees the Tristan chord as generated by an extended cycle of invariant intervals), but he still assumes it has significance for how people respond to the music. Some way of explaining the chord satisfactorily must exist, he argues, because if the music does not embody some kind of rationally coherent structure, then what grounds do we have for caring for it?

The belief that analysis explains the experience of music in an essentially scientific sense – in other words that it uncovers causes of which a listener's response is the effect – has been extremely influential in the twentieth century. I consider this belief to be misguided; but before going on to rebut it I want to show some of the consequences that follow if you hold it. The most important is the immediate association Boretz makes between analysis and the aesthetic value of music. After all, if analysis can explain how it is that we respond to masterpieces with aesthetic pleasure, then it stands to reason that it can be used as a criterion of whether music is masterly or not. This link between analysis and evaluation is assumed by analysts as otherwise diverse as Meyer, LaRue, Schenker and Keller, who writes 'I have come to the widely-tested conclusion that this is true of all good music: the looser the manifest integration, the stricter the demonstrable latent unification. I use this criterion as one of my tools for objective evaluation'.[2] The result is a somewhat narrow and pedagogical aesthetic which puts a great premium on the clarity with which structural functions are expressed in music, on the absence of unnecessary ornamentation, and in general upon unity and inevitability. To many analysts it is unthinkable that in any particular compositional situation a whole range of alternatives will serve equally well – or at least they would consider this a condemnation of the music. In this way analysis has become associated with a kind of aesthetic determinism: the aim is

[1] *The Forging of the Ring*, Cambridge University Press, 1976, p.7.

[2] Mitchell and Robbins Landon (eds.), *The Mozart Companion*, Faber, 1956, p. 97.

to deduce aesthetic properties directly from the musical structure – or, more specifically, from the musical score. You might call this the 'deletion of the listener' as a free agent; he is replaced by a theory which correlates the material properties of the music with the appropriate aesthetic response (much as the psycholinguists replace the listener with a theorem correlating certain auditory characteristics of speech sound with the units of linguistic structure). And in consequence of this it has come to be widely thought that the highest aim of musical analysis – and the thing that distinguishes it from mere description – is the formation of general theories capable of being applied to any particular instance of music, rather like the theories of general grammar developed by the structural linguists. Perhaps this is the natural result of analysis having become to a large extent the preserve of the universities – institutions which are primarily geared to laying down a store of knowledge rather than to developing practical skills in the individual.

II

Now it seems to me that the principal types of musical analysis current today do not have any real scientific validity, and that we therefore need to rethink what it is that they can tell us about music. It is surprisingly easy to demonstrate this. All the principal types of musical analysis discussed in Chapters 1 to 5 are expressed primarily in terms of interval classes such as minor seconds and perfect fifths, whether these are coded graphically, verbally or numerically. But do these interval classes have any psychological reality for the listener? It appears not. This is because, psychologically speaking, there are far more intervallic categories than musical analysts have terms for. Every half decent violinist or singer bends or stretches his minor seconds to different sizes according to the musical context, and all his other intervals too; and he does this not because he has some theory about them, but simply because if he does not do it, the music sounds wrong. A string quartet playing Beethoven or Bartók in strict equal temperament – if such a feat could be managed – would sound intolerable even to the most naive ear. What musicians play and what listeners respond to, then, is not 'minor seconds' but an indefinite number of varying intervals all of which we normally class either in a single pigeonhole (if we are thinking in terms of equal temperament) or in one of two pigeonholes (if we are respecting enharmonic distinctions, say between E – E♭ and E – D♯).[1]

Now there is nothing wrong with pigeonholes, but we have to remember they are of our own making. The one or two pigeonholes marked 'minor second' do not belong to the psychology of musical perception; they are artifices of musical notation. And useful though the pigeonholes of musical notation are for things like performance and memorization, they will not do as the basis of scientific research into how listeners perceive musical intervals. They are simply too broad: they muddle any number of different responses together, so that it would be quite impossible to work out what the factors governing these responses might be. Any meaningful work in this area would have to be done on the basis of a far more detailed way of representing musical sound than conventional notation allows. At the very least it would have to be based on something like the graphs produced by Charles Seeger's melograph, which is a machine that plots the fundamental frequency of a musical input against time. Fig. 108 shows a performance of *Barbara Allen* as the melograph transcribes it, with a transcription of the song into conventional notation aligned against it.[2] This makes it very obvious just how much our ordinary way of writing down musical sounds omits. Ordinary notation ruthlessly segments the flow of the singer's voice into separate notes, assigning a single overall value to these notes that is far less evident in the melographic chart; it strips away vibrato and portamenti, and rationalizes rhythmic values. It is a much simplified model of what the singer actually sings: an interpretation or, if you like, an analysis of it, rather than a neutral record of the sound.

Now ethnomusicologists are well aware of the fact that any transcription, especially a transcription as drastically simplified as conventional notation, constitutes an interpretation of what is heard. Pandora Hopkins, discussing transcriptions of Norwegian folk fiddling, points out how different notational systems involve different interpretations of the music: 'it is our impression that, if we had attempted to transcribe into one of the Chinese notations, we would have found a

---

[1] You may say, what about pianos? But the fact that pianos are tuned in equal temperament does not mean people actually hear each minor second as being the same size in a given musical context. The interval between C and F♯ on a piano, if you think of them as part of a dominant seventh on D, *sounds* quite different from the same notes as part of a dominant seventh on A♭; the physical sound is the same, but the psychological response is not.

[2] Charles Seeger, *Studies in Musicology 1935–1975*, pp. 298–9.

Fig. 108   Melographic analysis of *Barbara Allen*

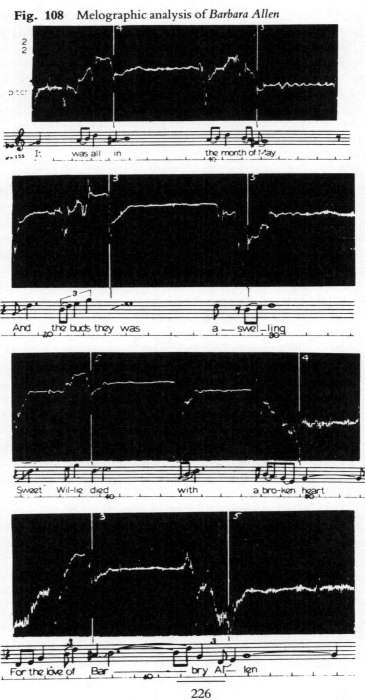

particular interest in melody waiting for us there. If we had sought a transcription into the old Byzantine neumes, matters of timbre would have been dissected. Our own notation . . . reflects an emphasis upon vertical relationships – the most characteristic feature of Western European music – and a disinterest in rhythmic complexity'.[1] Each system of notation, then, involves its own pattern of emphasis and omission. But the fact that the notation belonging to a given culture omits certain things does not mean that these things are not important for that culture's music. What it means is that when musicians use the notation for the purposes it is intended for – when, that is, they *read* it – they supply a great deal of information which is not actually in the score. For example a violinist does not play the notes of the score in the same way that a touch typist types what she (or he) sees. Instead he (or she) reads the notation as music, and his performance is an interpretation of the music as he understands it: an interpretation in which intervals, rhythms and dynamics are given what seem to the performer to be appropriate values. They are not simply executed as a series of instructions in terms of equal-tempered intervals, arithmetically-related durations, and a scale of eight dynamic levels from pianissimo to fortissimo. Consequently when a composer writes down music he is relying heavily on the reader's musical ear and imagination in supplying the precise intervallic, rhythmic and dynamic values that the notation omits, just as he has to contribute sonorous, dramatic and emotional values that cannot possibly be specified in the score.

But none of this happens if you make a strictly 'scientific' analysis of a score – analyzing the distribution of notated intervals in terms of set theory, say, or by means of statistical comparisons. When you do this, you are analyzing the score without actually *reading* it in the sense I have described. This is the musical equivalent of trying to analyze Shakespeare by counting the letters on the page and working out the principles governing their distribution. And whereas counting notes or letters can have some applications in the area of comparative stylistics (as I explained in the last chapter), it certainly does not allow you to make musical sense of pieces of music or literary sense of pieces of literature. Consequently, if you analyze a given composition this way, your analysis may be scientific in the sense of having an explicit methodology, but it will not be at all scientific in the sense of having any meaningful or predictable relationship to the music's physical or psychological reality – that is, to the noise it makes or the effect it has on

---

[1] 'The Purposes of Transcription', *Ethnomusicology*, 10, 1966, p. 313.

people. Indeed, the more strictly deductive your analysis of the score is, the more directly will it be conditioned by the particular cultural and pragmatic assumptions built into the notation and the less bearing it will have upon the music you actually wanted to find out about.

Now all this may sound like a wholesale indictment of musical analysis as it is generally practised: are not just about all the techniques of analysis I have discussed based on scores? Yes: but it does not necessarily follow from that that they are analyses *of* scores. It is true that a Schenkerian analysis, say, looks as if it were an analysis of the score. But in fact it is not. Rather it is using the score as a convenient, and tolerably adequate, way of talking about the real topic of musical analysis, which is the analyst's (and hopefully his reader's) experience of the music. And investigating the way you experience a piece of music is not something that can be done by means of formal deduction; nobody can prove your statements about what you experience to be right or wrong, true or untrue. However, this does not mean that self-interrogation, which is what I think analysis basically is, has to be an exercise in uncontrolled subjectivity in which anything goes and nothing is ever correct or incorrect, better or worse. Doing a Schenkerian analysis is like being asked a series of leading questions: at every point you have to say: 'Is this what I hear? Is it what I want to hear?' And though questions like this may have no scientific validity, the responses to which they give rise can certainly be musically valid or invalid. Doing a Schenkerian analysis is like composing in this sense, if no other: you actually have to be musical in order to understand what it is all about.

This is one way in which musical analysis is unscientific. There is another way, too. A precondition of successful scientific experimentation is that it should not perturb the phenomenon under investigation; if it does, the experimental data will be valueless. But this does not at all apply to musical analysis, one of whose characteristics is that it modifies the very experience of music that is being investigated. This is easily demonstrated if you think how listening casually to a piece of music can turn into an analytical experience of it. While you are 'just listening', images may pass through the mind but they are fragmentary and evanescent. As you begin to be analytically involved with the music, though, some kind of stable image builds up in the mind: an image which is in some way independent of your immediate reactions to the music (that is why it persists) and to which you assimilate what you hear. In other words, hearing music analytically means hearing it in terms of some kind of imagined structure, and this image is often visual: that is why one speaks of 'seeing' a structural relationship, and why pencil and paper are so necessary for analytical listening. Or else it is possible to use the score as a rough visual model of the music, flicking forwards or backwards through the pages as one theme or chord reminds you of another. In either case your experience of the music is analytical precisely to the extent that it is unlike ordinary listening: firstly in that you begin to become aware of things (like long-range tonal structures) that you do not normally perceive and that, without the mediation of some kind of analytical image, you perhaps could not perceive; and secondly – just as importantly – in that you begin to ignore things that are normally of overwhelming importance when listening to music. For example, as you develop a Schenkerian interpretation of a piece, so its rhythmic surface, dynamic ebb and flow and timbral coloration become so to speak transparent: you hear through them to the fundamental motion. The basic thing about an analysis, then, isn't what it manages to fit in (as the once-fashionable catch-phrase 'total analysis' implied), but what it manages to leave out. Schenkerian analysis for instance has been heavily criticized for omitting rhythm: but isn't the point of a Schenkerian analysis that it clarifies the music's pitch structure precisely through this and other omissions? So an analysis should not aim to be a carbon-copy of the listener's experience: rather it should simplify, clarify and illuminate it.

If musical analysis is a process whereby the analyst's experience of the music is modified, then the series of graphs or tables by means of which it is communicated should not really be thought of as 'the analysis'. What I mean by this is that these tables are not like tables of scientific data; they do not have any intrinsic meaning or validity. They only acquire meaning and validity by virtue of the musical experience that they engender. It is almost impossible to read a Schenkerian analysis with a radio playing some other music in earshot; the analytical process only happens as you 'hear' the music under investigation, which you cannot do under such conditions. In other words, a musical analysis has to be *read*, informally and imaginatively, just as a musical score does; it is on the basis of how satisfying a reading of the music an analysis embodies that you decide whether it is a good analysis, and not on the percentage of notes in the score that it can account for. Thus it is not even the conclusions an analysis reaches that necessarily make it good or bad, right or wrong; quite often it happens that diametrically opposed analytical interpretations are equally valuable. What makes an analysis good or bad under such circumstances obviously is not the conclusions as such but the way in which musical details are cited in defence of these conclusions, and the extent to which these conclusions clarify or illuminate the details. And an analysis which fails to stimulate its reader to such close reference to the music is unlikely to be a good analysis under any circumstances.

People who see musical analysis as some kind of scientific enterprise put a lot of effort into trying to prove the general superiority of one analytical method over another as a matter of theory. It seems to me that this is unfortunate because it leads people to adhere to one analytical method under all circumstances, and this can only blunt the analyst's sensibility to the individual qualities and variety of musical phenomena. Indeed, it can result in a kind of production-line mentality in which pieces are analyzed for no apparent reason except that they are there. In particular I am thinking of complex motivic and formal analyses that result in impressive tables and graphs whose actual significance nobody can quite figure out – especially when the music itself seems relatively simple and straightforward. This situation is the consequence of the emphasis laid on the theoretical component of analysis during the last twenty years or so. People such as Meyer and Alan Walker (who is one of the British motivic analysts) have repeatedly stressed the need for interpretative theories if analysis is to be anything more than 'mere description', as they put it, and which they disparage as being without any explanatory substance. For example, Alan Walker writes that 'you do not solve problems by describing them' (*A Study in Musical Analysis*, p. 23).[1] But it is everyday experience that this is just how problems are constantly solved; indeed without such careful description it is usually difficult to be sure just what the problem is, or indeed whether there really is a problem at all. So in analyzing music: reading the score several times, describing the details of the music in ordinary language, perhaps parsing the more complex chords – these simple procedures are usually more productive than immediately launching into some complex, theory-laden analysis. And in any case the difficulty two analysts can have in even agreeing what the facts of the matter are shows that the simplest description is not really neutral, but already involves interpretative criteria of some sort.

Whatever its theoretical shortcomings, a simple verbal description of the musical experience is a practical starting point for an analysis. And if there are drawbacks to such verbal description, these are more practical than theoretical: for instance, a symbolic tabulation of thematic sections, period-lengths, keys and chordal types allows you to see the structure at a glance (in a way that a prose description does not) and also

[1] London, 1962.

forces you to make rather more definite categorizations since such symbols on the whole have more precise meanings than words – though there is also a danger in this, in that such symbols may lead to a premature precision which your understanding of the music does not actually warrant. And even at a more advanced level it seems to me that the advantages and disadvantages of different analytical techniques are practical rather than theoretical. For instance Schenkerian analysis seems to me a much more useful technique in general than set-theoretical analysis, even though its theoretical foundation is manifestly spurious. The reason is that it is better adapted for the kind of practical self-experimentation I talked about earlier. In set-theoretical analysis you first decide on the segmentation (as I said in Chapter 4, this is where all the actual analytical *decisions* take place) and then you laboriously and mechanically deduce the results; it is not possible to see the consequences of any particular decision straight away, so that the set-theoretical deductions do not really help with the initial segmentation. But in Schenkerian analysis there is a constant give-and-take between informal decision and formal consequence; even the symbols of the analysis are fluid, floating half way between musical note and analytical abstraction.[1] The Schenkerian analyst may start (as analysts frequently do) with a hunch about some connection; as he tries it out graphically it will almost immediately become clear whether the connection makes sense or not. Conversely a graph-in-progress may suggest a certain connection and the analyst can immediately turn to the score, asking himself: is that a good way to hear the music? In this way a Schenkerian analysis allows a great deal of interaction between the aural experience on the one hand and the analytical rationalization on the other; and this is why (when it works, which is of course not always) it seems a more *musical* technique of analysis than others. Besides, it provides reasonably quick results.

---

[1] This isn't however true of Lerdahl and Jackendoff's adaptation of Schenkerian analysis. Their 'tree' notation is more explicit than Schenker's note-heads and beams; it is always possible to see exactly what it means. On the other hand this very precision can be a problem: like Meyer and Cooper's strong and weak beats, it forces you into a series of binary choices when your response to the music may just not be that definite, and it becomes unmanageably complicated if contrapuntal structure is taken into account. Which is better, Schenker's fluid and suggestive notation, or the precision of Lerdahl and Jackendoff's? It depends what you want the analysis for. For the purposes this book is mainly concerned with, I think Schenker's is the more useful. But, as Burton Rosner says in his review of *A Generative Theory of Tonal Music*, Lerdahl and Jackendoff's notation, together with the theory on which it is based, 'can perform an important function by providing psychologists with a systematic framework for empirical studies of the perception of rhythmic and harmonic properties of real music. At the moment, Lerdahl and Jackendoff have no competition in that arena' (*Music Perception*, 2, 1984, p. 290).

III

If there are not theoretical, scientific criteria for deciding whether the Tristan chord is 'really' a II^7, a motivic formation or whatever, then the century of controversy about it has been something of a waste of time; each interpretation highlights a particular aspect of the formation but none has a monopoly of the truth. But if a misplaced belief in the scientific validity of their work has been a hindrance to musical analysts, I think this is not so much because it has led them to do the wrong things but because it has led them to make the wrong claims for what they do. These claims have been both too ambitious and too modest. I think that the claim that analysis can produce reliable criteria for aesthetic evaluation is over-ambitious. Certainly the analytical process may clarify one's ideas about a piece; quite possibly it will show evidence of a certain kind of craftmanship; but there are too many fine pieces and even repertoires that cannot be satisfactorily analyzed for this to be a convincing criterion of aesthetic quality. Nor am I convinced that analysis is of that much significance as a means of creating an aesthetic appreciation where it previously did not exist. True, it encourages attentive listening, but anyone who only liked music because he could analyze it would be a crushing musical bore.

Inappropriate claims like these not only encourage a narrow-mindedness of musical response; they also deflect emphasis from the claims that can justifiably be made for analysis as it is practised. It is at undergraduate and college level, not as an instrument of advanced research, that analysis seems to me to have its most vital role to play in today's musical culture. It has this role because the ability to set aside details and 'see' large-scale connections appropriate to the particular musical context, which is what analysis encourages, is an essential part of the musician's way of perceiving musical sound. For the performer, it is obvious that analysis has a role to play in the memorization of extended scores, and to some extent in the judgment of large-scale dynamic and rhythmic relationships (although some of the claims that Schenkerian analysis, in particular, is indispensable for performers and conductors have surely been overstated). But it has a still more direct link with composition. To analyze a piece of music is to weigh alternatives, to judge how it would have been if the composer had done this instead of that – it is, in a sense, to recompose the music in a way that normal, concert-hall listening is not. In this way today's composers serve their apprenticeship with the masters of the past through analysis of their works; and it is obvious that the preoccupations of musical analysts are closely related to those of composers. For instance, a central aim of both Schenkerian and motivic analysts is to demonstrate the unity of musical form and musical content; and this is just what composers have been trying to achieve since the invention of serialism, by deriving the formal schemes of their compositions from the structure of their materials in one way or another.

Now, if we accept that the value of an analysis consists in what it does for the analyst, then it is plain that what would be a bad analysis under one set of circumstances can be precisely what is wanted under another. I am thinking especially of the serial composers of post-war Europe – Boulez, Stockhausen and the rest – who published a number of analyses of works by composers such as Webern, Stravinsky and Debussy. By and large these analyses were speculative to the point of irresponsibility and, in comparison with any remotely competent Schenkerian analysis, they were frequently downright unmusical. But at that particular time and place conventional musical sensibilities were not what was needed. Their analyses were good, not because they had any generally applicable validity, but because they stimulated an out-burst of creative innovation in musical style. Brilliant, partisan and hopelessly prejudiced, they were anything but the dispassionate commentary on musical culture that a scientifically-minded investigator might have attempted. But they were something much more important: they were a vital part of that culture.

Part Two

WORKED EXAMPLES OF ANALYSIS

CHAPTER SEVEN

STARTING AN ANALYSIS

I

There is not any one fixed way of starting an analysis. It depends on the music, as well as on the analyst and the reason the analysis is being done. But there is a prerequisite to any sensible analysis, and this is familiarity with the music. This does not just mean familiarity with the score. It is possible to know your way around a score without having any very clear idea of how the music sounds, and even when you do know how the music sounds – say in the case of a piano piece you play – it is easy to forget how knowledge of the score alters your perception of the music. Large-scale relationships of key are obvious in the score but they may not be so to a listener; forms which look concise and closed in the score may seem extended and open when you hear the music. Since the point of Western art music is the way listeners experience it rather than the way it looks in the score, it is important to begin analyzing it with as clear an image of the musical sound as possible. Ideally you should be able to look at any passage in the score and know just how it sounds – though in some music this is hardly possible, and in such cases the analytical process may help to clarify your image of the musical sound.

The important thing is not to start analyzing too soon. Of course some analytical observations will occur to you as you play the music or listen to it or read it: large-scale repetitions, motivic connections, points of high tension or release, structural breaks and so on. These are worth noting down, and so are any other immediate responses to the music, however fragmentary or subjective. The reason for this is that in some ways people's ears seem freshest the first few times they hear a piece of music. As they get to know it better, their perception of details increases but the immediacy of the music's effect can be blunted. If you write

Fig. 109 Schumann, *Auf einer Burg*

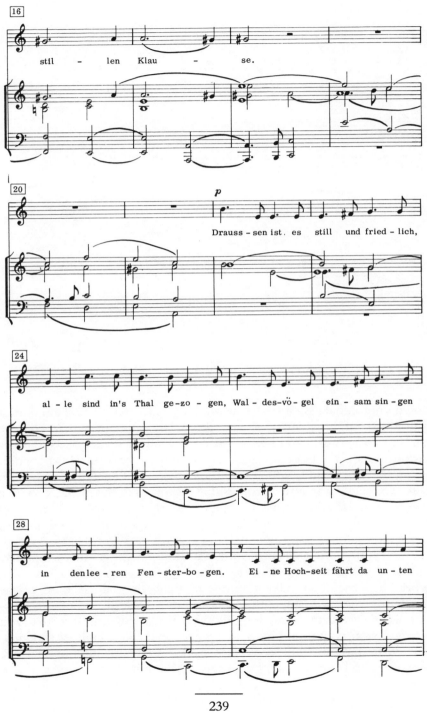

stil – len Klau – se.

Drauss – sen ist es still und fried – lich,

al – le sind in's Thal ge–zo – gen, Wal – des–vö – gel ein – sam sin – gen

in den lee – ren Fen – ster–bo – gen. Ei – ne Hoch–seit fährt da un – ten

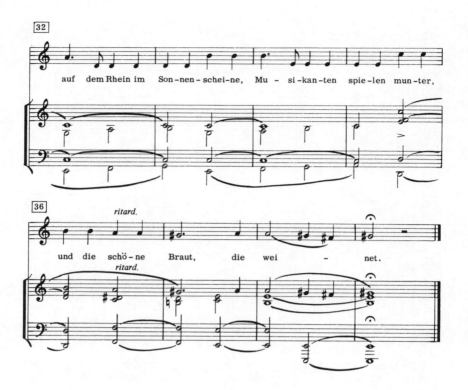

down your initial responses to the music, you can return to them during the course of your analysis, and this is the guarantee that you are analyzing the music you heard and not a kind of shadow-piece that is visible in the score but bears little relationship to the musical experience. If, on the other hand, you rush into some kind of analytical reduction before having made sure of your initial responses to the music, then in a real sense your analysis has nothing to work on. It will end up as an analysis of the score and not of the musical experience. It will not, in short, be a *musical* analysis.

Very often the analysis proper will emerge, almost imperceptibly, out of this initial stage of familiarization. For example, in extended works it is useful to make a simple table of the main sections of the music together with repetitions, key-centres and any other such distinguishing features. Something like this is needed simply so that you can find your way round the score; it functions like a table of contents. But what starts out as a convenience may well turn into an analysis, because it leads you to say: but is this a section in its own right or is it really part of a larger section? What defines it as a section, then? And is it a new one or a modified version of this previous one? Again, suppose you are analyzing Stravinsky's *Symphonies of Wind Instruments*. The published score is so full of different transposing instruments that most people will want to prepare a short score, or at any rate a harmonic reduction, if they are to grasp the unfamiliar harmonic combinations clearly. And the very process of doing this, and of associating the look and the sound of the harmonies, will bring certain repeated intervallic cells and linear motions into prominence; so that here simply trying to *read* the music properly initiates the process of analysis. In these cases, then, the music suggests its own means of analysis, and this means that there is no difficulty in getting the analysis started.

But what about pieces of music which are short and present no great difficulties of musical language, so that it is easy to become familiar with them without any particular analytical process being initiated? Let us take as an example Schumann's song 'Auf einer Burg' from the Eichendorff *Liederkreis* (Fig. 109). We could begin by making a descriptive tabulation of some kind. We could say, for instance, that there is a large-scale repeat (there are four verses grouped in pairs) and that each half is made up of two contrasted sections; that gives us an A – B – A – B form, such as countless other songs share. We could say that there are two motifs, one of a falling fifth (this appears somewhere in each of the first nine bars) and the other an ascent through a third (transformed into its inversion, a sixth, from bar 10 on). But how does this distinguish the piece from any number of others in which such motifs appear? Again, we could make a harmonic reduction; the first eight bars come out as in Fig. 110. This makes the sequential plan of these bars explicit; they consist of four groups of two bars in the form A – B – A – B1, where B1 means a transposed version of B. But we still have not learnt much about what gives Schumann's song its individual quality, since the same progression occurs at the beginning of Chopin's C minor Prelude, and here the effect is completely different (Fig. 111)!

If you are interested in the individual quality of 'Auf einer Burg', rather than the stylistic characteristics it shares with other nineteenth-

Fig. 110

bar:	1	3	4		7		8	
I:	I	IV⁷	V	I	VI			
VI:				III	I	IV	V	I

Fig. 111

```
I:    I  IV⁷  V   I    VI
VI:              III  I  IV  V⁷  I
```

century compositions, then a better approach is to ask yourself a few questions about the way it is experienced. At this early stage of an analysis it is best if such questions are posed in general terms rather than in terms of a specific musical style or analytical technique. Probably the two most useful questions are: what is the most striking feature of the piece? and, does it create a sense of moving towards some goal? Often these questions are in fact bound up with one another, and 'Auf einer Burg' illustrates this.

To me the single most striking feature of the song is the process of intensification that begins at bar 9 and reaches a climax at the dissonant chord halfway through bar 14 – the only chord in the whole song that Schumann marks with an accent. This chord is clearly the high point of the piece (or rather of each half of the piece). But what makes it so effective? It is not a specially striking chord in itself, so the answer must lie in its context – in what leads up to it and what comes of it. Fig. 112 shows what comes of it. The C and the E are treated as dissonances, resolving downwards while the D and F are held, so that the chord functions as a II leading to a cadential V of A minor. (The V does not literally appear at 17, owing to an elision, but it does at 38.) Again nothing could be more normal,[1] which means that if there is something extraordinary about this chord it must lie in what leads up to it – what 'prepares' it, to borrow a term from contrapuntal theory. And it is at this point that the piece falls analytically into shape, as Fig. 113 shows. The C and the E are indeed 'prepared' in the manner of strict counterpoint, only on a larger scale. The E is the outcome of the singer's ascent from C, beginning at bar 9. The C in the chord at bar 14 is not only the outcome of a parallel ascent from G, but has also appeared in the piano as a double pedal-note

---

[1] Compare, for instance, the opening of the Sarabande from Bach's English Suite No. 2.

sustained continuously from bar 8, where its beginning was highlighted by the low C (the lowest note of the piece up to that point). Fig. 113 (a) illustrates all this, besides showing how the low C of bar 8 leads directly to the D at 14 and the E at 16. And Fig. 113 (b) summarizes the preparation and resolution of our problem chord, simplifying the registration for the sake of clarity.

Fig. 112

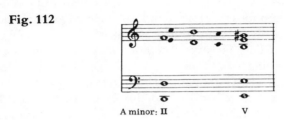

A minor: II   V

Fig. 113

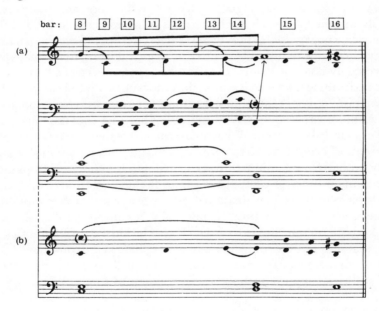

Considered by itself, Fig. 113 (b) is a rather boring phrase of counterpoint. But that is not the point. Considered in relation to 'Auf einer Burg', it shows how the dissonant notes of the chord at 14:3 are prepared – or, as Cooper and Meyer would put it, 'marked for consciousness' – over a number of bars. And the more detailed reduction shows how the various linear motions that lead up to it are set on a kind of collision course; hence the feeling of tension rising steadily to a breaking point. So we have explained how it is that a perfectly ordinary dissonant chord acquires a unique quality in this particular context. And we have done so simply by means of conventional musical skills and common sense, rather than by adopting one analytical method or another.

But the analysis does rather resemble a Schenkerian one, which is not surprising since the music is tonal and since the striking quality of the chord results from the linear motions that lead to it. Can we learn more about the music by turning our analysis into a proper Schenkerian one, then? Let us consider the fundamental line. The overall contour of the voice suggests that the fundamental line is going to be C – B – A (as $\hat{3}$ – $\hat{2}$ – $\hat{1}$). Then where does it start? With the C in bar 3? This C is supported by an A in the bass, which rises through C (bar 8) to the E at bar 16; and this gives the standard bass arpeggiation pattern shown in Fig. 114. This *looks* perfectly convincing. But actually it is quite untenable as a Schenkerian analysis. The reason is that the chord at bar 3 sounds unambiguously like a IV of E minor, and in any case the C resolves immediately to B. Only at bar 8 is a C heard as anything other than a dissonance, a note poised to move somewhere else. So, in Schenkerian terms, we have to see the whole of bars 1 to 8 as an introduction to the main piece. And certainly it is true that by the time the C major is reached it no longer sounds as if the piece were in E minor; the C does not sound like a VI (as the A♭ in Chopin's C minor Prelude does). On the other hand, it does not sound like a III of A minor either; only with the chord of bar 14:3 does the music really begin to sound like A minor. What this means is that the song is not 'in a key', in the sense of being directed towards a destination that is known all along; it simply evolves from E minor through C major to A minor, and stops there – rather in the manner of Chopin's A minor Prelude. (You may or may not consider it significant that this tonal plan arpeggiates an A minor triad.) Consequently 'Auf einer Burg' is not really 'a composition' at all, in the Schenkerian sense; and this is a reasonable conclusion since it is part of a larger work, that is to say, the song cycle as a whole. Indeed the consonant A with which the fundamental line must end does not actually appear with 'Auf einer Burg' at all; it is supplied by the beginning of the next song.[1]

---

[1] Possibly some readers will look askance at analysis of a Schumann song that makes no reference to the text. In the case of this song it doesn't seem to me that the text has a lot to do with the details of the music – it's only a general mood that text and music have in common. But if you want to see a song where a similar Schenkerian approach ties closely in with the text, turn to *Wenn ich in deine Augen seh*, the fourth song of *Dichterliebe*. The emotional climax – on the words 'Ich liebe dich', I love you – derives its musical intensity from the suspension with which the structural $\hat{3}$, prolonged up to this point, falls to $\hat{2}$ and thence to $\hat{1}$; harmonically it coincides with the first non-tonic structural harmony.

Fig. 114

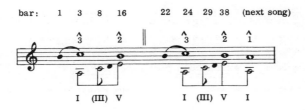

II

In this instance we are able to 'plug into' existing analytical techniques in order to refine our analytical observations and to set the piece under analysis within the context of other comparable pieces. Simply by using Roman-letter labels and Schenkerian graphing, we assumed such things as triadic formations, standard patterns of chordal progression and so on. When dealing with a style as familiar as Schumann's, there is no need to go back to first principles. But if you are dealing with a less familiar musical style, then it is important not to make inappropriate stylistic assumptions in your analysis. Again the answer is a simple, inductive approach.

Suppose you have a tape recording of a piece of choral music which you want to analyze, but which you know nothing about – not even where and when it was composed. So you begin by transcribing it: Fig. 115 shows the transcription. The first step towards simplifying the music analytically is obvious: you pick out the sections defined by a long final note, and the pattern of repetitions these sections make. That is what Fig. 116 does. And already something important about the music has become clear: the music consists of two different components – a fixed component (phrases 1–2), which is sung by the whole choir, and a changing component (phrases 3–4), which is sung by the cantor. Why does this second component change each time? Because whereas the words of the first component are the same each time, those of the second component are not; the music has to accommodate a varying number of syllables.

So far, then, the musical structure is simply a consequence of the textual pattern. However, both components of the music – the cantor's

Fig. 115 *Song of Simeon*: transcription

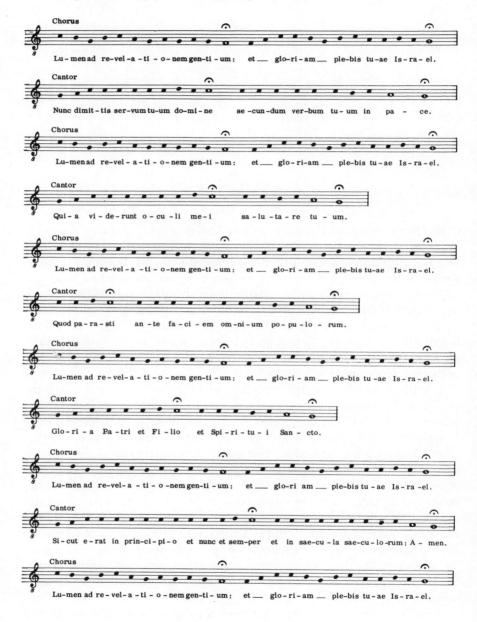

Fig. 116 *Song of Simeon*: analysis (1)

Distribution

1	2	3(ii)	4(iii)
1	2	3(iii)	4(v)
1	2	3(v)	4(i)
1	2	3(iv)	4(iv)
1	2	3(i)	4(ii)
1	2		

and the one sung by the chorus – end with the same two notes (A – G), which gives the music a rhyming scheme the text does not possess. Furthermore the first phrase of each component – that is, phrases 1 and 3

– ends on a note other than G. This means there is a cadential pattern: not–G, G; not–G, G. Clearly, then, G functions as the 'home' note: the cadences on G have a finality those on F and C do not. (To test this, sing the four phrases in the order 2, 1, 4, 3.)

But why does the G function this way? It is tempting to say: because the chant is in the Hypomixolydian mode (that is the name of the white-note mode that has G as its finalis). But saying this is like saying someone can't read because they are illiterate: it is a label, not an explanation. The chant is Hypomixolydian because it ends on G, not the other way round; if we want to know why it ends on G we have to ask what there is about its structure that gives G a special quality in it – that of finality.

How are we going to answer this? A useful first step is to narrow down the field of investigation by discounting factors that are irrelevant. Obviously, things like timbre, dynamics and articulation play no part since they are either constant or undefined; we are dealing with a two-dimensional structure whose variables are pitch and time. Furthermore, the structure that gives the G its quality of finality is based purely on diatonic scale steps and not on the particular intervallic relations that exist within the Hypomixolydian mode as against other modes. How do we know this? Because if you sing the chant in any other diatonic mode (imagine different key-signatures) you will find that the G still retains its air of finality. So we can make a further simplification of the score, in the knowledge that it still embodies whatever it is that gives the G this quality. Fig. 117 represents this simplified score in two different ways, both of which contain the same information. In the rest of this analysis I shall use conventional notation (though without clefs) simply because I find it easy to read – the analysis could just as well have been done numerically.

This is a much more straightforward pattern than was the case in 'Auf einer Burg' and for this reason it is possible simply to play around with the pattern and see what structural characteristics emerge. For instance, what patterns of recurrence are there within the various phrases? If you write out the pattern, beginning at the beginning and aligning repetitions under what they repeat, you will end up with something like Fig. 118 (a). Is there some kind of underlying pattern to these recurrences? Look at the way they intersect. Only one note appears four times between recurrent patterns: it is G, the finalis. Five notes appear three or more times: Fig. 118 (b) picks them out. And the interesting thing is that these five notes are identical to the fourth phrase of the hymn. This fourth phrase, then, summarizes the rest of the chant;

Fig. 117 *Song of Simeon*: two notations

5 4 2 4 5 3 2 3 2 3 2 1   1 3 5 5 4 2 4 5 3 3 4 3 2

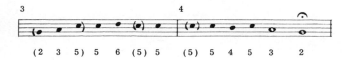

(2 3 5) 5 6 (5) 5   (5) 5 4 5 3   2

as Fig. 118 shows, the first two phrases are elaborated versions of it. That is one reason why the fourth phrase has a conclusive effect. But another lies in the nature of the phrase itself. It consists of a stepwise fall elaborated only by the repetition of one note. And if we write out the chant again, this time aligning it with a stepwise fall from the highest to the lowest note, we can see how this falling motion permeates the chant as a whole (Fig. 119).

Playing around with the pattern of the music like this is a useful heuristic device: it brings things to the attention that might not otherwise have been noticed. But how do we know these things are actually relevant to the way the music is experienced? We do not: and so we have to test them against experience. Is there, then, a sense of downward scalar motion in the first phrase? There is, and Fig. 120 explains how. The phrase is made up of cells of falling notes. In the first two cells the outer notes (the C and G) remain constant while the middle one falls from B to A; in the third cell all the notes shift down. So there is a constant process of downward movement, and the repetition of the As and Gs emphasizes this by delaying the completion of the process: you can hear the G changing from a stable note (as it is in the first two cells) to the unstable note it is in the third cell. In the second phrase, on the other hand, this does not happen: structurally it begins like the first phrase, as Fig. 121 shows, but this time the G is at first withheld so as to underline its conclusive role when it eventually does appear. What about the third and fourth phrases? Fig. 119 suggests that they are really a single, composite phrase, in·that they share a single scalar descent, and again this is confirmed by experience. Try singing the third phrase by itself: it sounds somehow incomplete, whereas the

Fig. 118 *Song of Simeon*: analysis (2)

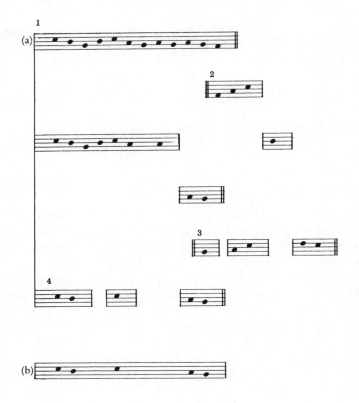

finality of the fourth phrase is increased by its forming the conclusion of the third. Notice also that the notes of the underlying scalar fall always appear however much these final phrases are abbreviated – it is the elaborating motions, not the structural ones, that are omitted when there are not enough syllables to go round. All this confirms that the falling scalar patterns on which the analysis was based are important musically: we really do hear the music as held together by them.

Now in this analysis we have been treating the music as if it had come from Mars; we have been talking about the music's structure and the effect it has when we listen to it, while completely ignoring its provenance – where it came from and when, the uses for which it was intended, and so on. Viewing this piece historically would have given us quite a different outlook on it. It is in fact a piece of antiphonal

Fig. 119   *Song of Simeon*: analysis (3)

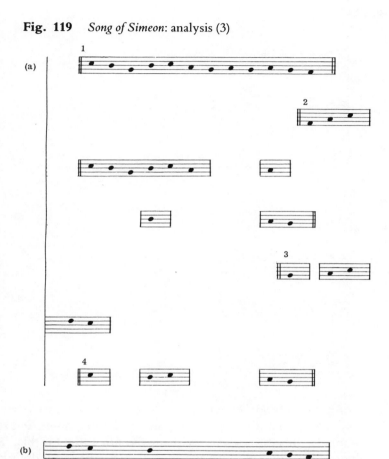

psalmody, and it consists of two entirely different things. One is what is sung by the cantor, though it could equally well have been sung by another choir: this is called a canticle, and the text is the 'Song of Simeon' (otherwise known as the *Nunc Dimittis*). The other is the unchanging component sung by the choir, and this is what is known as an antiphon – a short piece of chant sung in association with a canticle. Now what is important about this is that the association between these two components – the canticle and its attendant antiphon – is a loose one. This particular canticle does not necessarily have to be sung with this particular antiphon; some other antiphon could just as well have been chosen, as long as it was in the right mode. And it is actually rather

Fig. 120

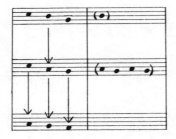

Fig. 121

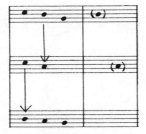

unusual to sing the antiphon between all the verses of the canticle, as is done here; normally an antiphon is sung only at the beginning and the end of the canticle. But the analysis we made did not allow for this. We analyzed the music as if each verse and its antiphon were an indivisible musical entity; in fact we showed how the two components were tied together to form a single, fixed musical structure. Doesn't the historical evidence invalidate our analysis, then? No, it does not: how could it, when the analysis was based on what we heard? But it does show that what we analyzed was a particular performance of the piece, and not the piece itself. Actually it is not at all clear just what it might mean to talk about 'the piece' in a case like this. If you sang the antiphon only at the beginning and the end, then you would be making a rather different 'piece' out of the same music (or I suppose it would be equally logical to say that you were making different music out of the same 'piece'). And if you sang a different antiphon, then the music itself would be different – so would this be 'the same piece' or another one? Should we really be talking about two pieces that are combined with each other, rather than a single piece at all (in which case, were we wrong to hear it as a single piece when we first listened to it?) Or should we stop thinking about 'pieces' altogether, and instead think in terms of a repertoire of possibilities from which the performer chooses? This last alternative stresses the compositional role of the performer in music of this sort: he 'puts together' the available materials as he sees fit, which is what 'composing' means literally, and our analysis suggests possible reasons why the performers on this recording may have chosen to 'compose' the music the way they did.

III

Approaching music unhistorically, in terms of its formal patterns and one's own responses to them, has a particular advantage in that it leads directly to illuminating parallels betwen pieces of music that come from very different historical contexts. To demonstrate this, we shall move from the Middle Ages to the present century, and specifically to 'Pan', the first of Benjamin Britten's *Six Metamorphoses after Ovid* for oboe solo (Fig. 122). This is a very different piece in its aesthetic style and in its techniques from the canticle we have just discussed, though both are constructed from a series of cadential phrases each ending on a pause. But it is at a deeper level that we shall find the most striking parallels between the two: each works by means of musical processes which, once initiated, tend towards completion, so that the whole piece is in essence a single elaborated cadence – just as was 'Auf einer Burg', in fact. However, we cannot adopt quite the same methods as we used before to show this. In 'Auf einer Burg' there was a particularly striking passage and this served as the starting-point for the analysis. The canticle was so simple that it was possible to analyze it as an abstract pattern and then test this against experience. 'Pan', on the other hand, is not quite so simple, nor does it have any one particularly striking moment. Consequently the best way to begin analyzing it is by means of a straightforward bar-by-bar commentary. We can still focus on cadential structure in doing this, but because the music consists of a large number of brief cadential phrases the important questions take on a more specific form: which are the more and which the less important cadential phrases? How far do groups of cadences

Fig. 122 Britten, 'Pan'

become associated into larger cadential motions? To what extent is the very end of the piece an outcome of cadential processes that begin earlier in the piece?

Before beginning a bar-by-bar description of a piece of music it is always a good idea to think what preconceptions or expectations you are starting off with when you listen to it. The title of Britten's set – *Six Metamorphoses after Ovid* – does two things: it creates an expectation that there will be some kind of process of change within each piece; and it associates this expectation with figures from classical mythology. The inscription at the head of 'Pan', which is usually reproduced in programme notes, says 'Pan, who played upon the reed pipe which was Syrinx, his beloved'. So this invites the audience to hear the oboe as a panpipe (hence the legato, stepwise motion that prevails in this piece) and to imagine the music being improvized in a classical landscape. All this is important for the overall nature of the musical experience, but because these are expectations of a very general kind they do not really affect the way in which the internal structure of the piece is experienced. We can carry out more detailed analysis in purely musical terms.

Bar 1 (which means the first phrase – the bar-lines are being used simply to indicate phrases) constitutes a single motion. Admittedly it is notated as a rhythmic pattern ♫. which is stated twice, but that is not how it is heard. Much more relevant to the listener's experience of the music is the asymmetrical pattern of the contour: a hook-like motif connecting A, D and E. This is shown in Fig. 122.

Bar 2 is an elaborated repeat of the first bar, and the hook-like motif again appears – only this time it is inverted so that it links C$^\sharp$, F$^\sharp$ and E. But in each case it is a specifically cadential pattern, in that it links an earlier starting note or change in contour with the final two notes of the phrase. This will be one of our criteria in picking out further appearances of this motif.

Bar 3 begins with a scalar fall to low A. Is this implied in what has come before? Yes: it carries on the motion from D to C$^\sharp$ in bars 1–2, as well as balancing and completing the fall from A to E in the first bar (which it resembles rhythmically). But is it a possible stopping point, then? (Try playing up to it and then stopping.) No: the music needs to go on – perhaps simply because it is too early to be stopping. And the A becomes part of a series of three hook-like motifs that are linked to each other and drive the music up by superimposed thirds from A to C$^\sharp$ to E to G$^\sharp$.

Bar 4. A further rise of a third (to B) lifts the music out of the A – A tessitura that has contained it up to now. (Hence the peculiar significance this note seems to have in performance – oboists tend to lengthen it beyond its notated value.) With a final hook-like motive the music cadences on an F# : the first cadence which is not part of the same series of superimposed thirds.

Bar 5. The music has up till now consisted of a series of waves of gradually increasing speed, with the sixth as the largest interval between a peak and the next trough. Now this contour is extended to give the traditionally tense interval of a major seventh between its highest and lowest notes (C# and D). This accentuates the fact that the C# is left hanging – the upper register is now abandoned. What is implied at this point? Try playing from the beginning and stopping at the end of bar 5. A scalar resolution down to low A seems to be required to complete the motion.

Bar 6. Here the resolution to low A is supplied – but the music cannot now end on it. (Play up to the end of bar 6 and stop there.) Clearly the reason is that a new idea has been interpolated. Four things distinguish this idea as new: it is not diatonic to A major; it contains a leap (from A# to C#) whereas everything has been stepwise until now; it contains tongued repeated notes whereas everything has been slurred; and it is pianissimo. Bar 6 is therefore a structural overlap: it completes the process of bars 1–5, but in doing so it initiates a new process.

Fig. 123 summarizes the cadential structure of bars 1–6.

Fig. 123

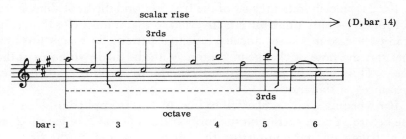

Bars 6–8 have a much simpler contour than bars 1–6. The D of bar 6 (the same D as in bar 5) leads through D# to the E of bar 7. The progression is repeated more concisely in bar 8 and then the E rises through F to G♭, and after that by whole-tones to B♭ (or A#). This gives a rise of an octave from the A# of bar 6, balancing the fall of an octave in bars 1–6. (Is the fact that it rises an octave actually important for the way

the section is experienced as a whole? Test it by extending the whole-tone pattern as in Fig. 124.) At the same time the low A♯ itself rises through whole-tones to high A♯, though this motion only begins as the other one ends. This means that whereas bars 1–6 consist of a single moving line, like an arabesque, the shape outlined by bars 6–8 is a solid one. It has a leading edge and a trailing edge, the two meeting on the upper A♯ (notice how the final G♯ is not just a twiddle but the completion of this process). And when this happens, the melodic individuality of the section has been completely 'worked out': nothing remains but sporadic single notes. Fig. 125 notates bar 8 in such a way as to make this shape easy to see. Incidentally these bars would be rather hard to play on a panpipe!

Fig. 124   Variant of 'Pan', bar 8

Fig. 125   Analysis of 'Pan', bar 8

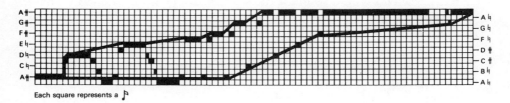

Each square represents a ♪

Bars 9–12 return to the diatonic, stepwise, slurred material of the first six bars. In fact they restate the main cadential pattern of bars 1–6 but more or less in reversed order, as Fig. 126 shows. However, whereas bars 9 and 10 are a more or less literal restatement of bars 5 and 4, bars 11–12 are separated from them by a change of tempo and also of character. Instead of a free melisma, the phrase loses its individual

257

contour by becoming stuck on a scalar pattern that is repeated with increasing frequency until it is torn off on a trill – something quite different from the controlled cadence with which every previous phrase has ended. This is followed by the longest pause of the piece – a tense one, in that there is a heavy implication that the piece is about to reach its final climax. (Imagine what it would be like if the piece ended here, or if there were now a repeat *da capo*!)

Fig. 126

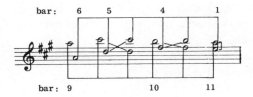

Bars 13–15 begin with a brief recollection of the A♯ idea from bars 6 and 8. (It is too brief to be a 'restatement', which refers to a formal balance. 'Recollection' refers to a psychological balance, which is what we have here – just enough to remind the listener of what came before, but no more.) Bar 14 is also modelled on bar 6 – on the A♯–C♯–D (this also recurs in bar 15) and C♯–B–A♮ figures, now extended down to low D.

Why is this a satisfying conclusion? The last four bars contain the sharpest dynamic contrasts of the piece; the longest pauses; the most rapid melodic motions; and its highest and lowest notes (imagine how feeble the end would sound if the scale in bar 14 stopped on A). These bars *sound* like an ending: what could possibly follow such a strong gesture? At the same time there are at least two ways in which we can see these bars as completing processes started earlier in the piece. One is large-scale pitch structure. The high D is not just the highest note of the piece; it is also the completion of a scalar rise from the very first note of the music, A, through B (bar 4) and C♯ (bar 5 – remember how this was left hanging at the time). The other is thematic structure. As we've seen, the piece clearly falls into sections defined by thematic content. The first two are plain enough: bars 1–6 (call this A) and bars 6–8 (call this B). Where the third section ends is not quite so plain. Clearly we could call bars 9–10 A1, where A1 means an abbreviated version of A. But we could also think of bars 11–12 as being part of A1, since they share the same notes as the first bar of the piece. Alternatively we might think of bars 11–12 as something new – new partly because of the change of tempo, and partly because of the way it liquidates the A-material. ('Liquidation' is a term Schoenberg used, meaning the fragmentation of a thematic idea so that it loses its individuality.) And what about bars 13–15? Clearly they contain elements of B; but equally they are an expansion of the final cadence of A in bar 6. (Hence they supply the cadence that A1 so markedly lacked.) What makes it possible for this section to combine attributes of A and B like this is that bar 6, on which it is modelled, was itself an overlap between the two thematic types. Consequently these final bars serve several functions at once. They serve as a highly abbreviated reference to the B-material, thereby suggesting a kind of vestigial A – B – A – B form. They complete the process of liquidation – nothing remains of either A or B by the end except a rapid scale and a hurried three-note twiddle. And they function as a formal cadence, playing the same role in the piece as a whole that bar 6 played in terms of the first six bars. In other words, however we may choose to classify them in terms of formal labels, the last six bars are to a high degree implicit in what has come before; they must be, for they would sound silly played by themselves – imagine a piece *beginning* with bars 11–15! In the context of 'Pan' as a whole, however, these bars form a satisfactory conclusion.

The three compositions examined in this chapter have been different in style and so they have required different analytical procedures. But in each case the basic approach was the same: we concentrated on the sense of completion created by the music. We discovered that in each case the sense of completion did not derive so much from the end in itself, but from the way the rest of the piece implied the ending – in some respects at least. Obviously you cannot explain everything about a piece of music by approaching it in this manner. But it is not a precondition of useful analysis that it should explain everything in a piece; in fact it is not even a practical possibility in most music, at least if the explanations are to have any very direct connection with what listeners experience. Though the approach did set limits on what could be discovered, it showed that the way we experience a given section of a piece of music depends on the role that section has within the piece as a whole. And that makes a useful definition of what musical analysis is.

CHAPTER EIGHT

ANALYZING MUSIC
IN SONATA FORM

I

If you look up 'form' in a musical dictionary you will be told about things like binary form, da capo form, sonata form, expositions, first subjects, closing groups and codettas. Terms like these refer to the surface patterning of music – they either designate a pattern or identify a particular element within the pattern. In the last chapter we did not focus on such patterns. Instead we tried in each case to look *through* the surface pattern so as to see some general process underlying it. We showed how the various constituents of the music – a chord, a melodic phrase or whatever – derived their effect from the structural process. So in a way we were making an analysis of the musical form. But this is 'form' in a different sense from the dictionary one. There are, then, two aspects of musical form: the surface pattern and the underlying process. And when we analyze traditional forms like sonata, we are not simply talking about the one aspect or the other, but rather about the way in which the two interact.

Now, you can have music in which there really is not any inter-action between the surface pattern and the underlying process. In some music the form derives solely from the process; Bach's C major Prelude, for instance, has very little surface patterning above the level of the single bar. But this is usually the case only in miniatures: imagine trying to turn the C major Prelude into a piece lasting ten minutes without introducing surface contrast! Conversely, baroque dance suites consist of a pattern of contrasted movements with hardly any underlying process tying them together – you can play the movements in more or less any order you like and it will not really matter. The same may apply within movements, too. A typical Vivaldi concerto movement consists of a more-or-less symmetrical pattern of more-or-less independent sections, and there is often no obvious reason why the sections need to be in that particular order. It is easy to analyze the form of sectional music like this – you simply call the first section A and anything else B, C, D and so on – but discovering that a movement is in ABACDA form does not actually tell you very much if, musically speaking, it might just as well have been ABBCDB. In other words form is not a very significant aspect of this kind of music.

On the other hand, everyone agrees that form is important in music of the classical period. Although there are frequently passages of anonymous material in classical music – cadential passages that could easily be transferred to other pieces in the same key, for instance – you generally cannot swap around entire sections in the way you sometimes can in a Vivaldi concerto; the form is too organic for that.[1] But, as I said in Chapter 1, this is not because there is anything very special about the surface patterns found in classical music. It is because of the way in which these patterns reflect underlying processes, and this is particularly easy to see in the case of opera, because in opera the words can make these processes explicit whereas in instrumental music they are only implicit. Let us briefly consider the first number of Mozart's *Marriage of Figaro*, the duet between Figaro and Suzanna. At the beginning of the duet each is engaged in a different activity – Figaro is measuring up their room, Suzanna is trying on her bridal hat (they are to be married that afternoon). Suzanna wants Figaro to admire her hat, and tries to attract his attention. Figaro wants to get the measuring done, and tries to palm her off with a few perfunctory compliments. But Suzanna won't have it, and in due course Figaro has to capitulate to her. So there is a psychological process going on through the number – Suzanna establishing her dominance – and at the end of it we know something about Figaro and Suzanna's relationship that we did not know at the beginning. The words tell us all this, of course. But so does the music. Figaro has one tune (actually his tune is only heard complete in the orchestra) and Suzanna another. Both are in the tonic, G major, but as

---

[1] Organic at the level of movements, anyhow. But you could probably interchange movements between many classical works – swapping one minuet with another and so on – without most listeners being too disturbed. So perhaps the apparently absurd habit of analyzing movements as if they were independent pieces – which is what most analysts do – is in fact perfectly reasonable. Reti would not have agreed, though.

Suzanna tries to attract Figaro's attention the music edges towards the dominant, D major. The point where Figaro stops measuring and compliments her on her hat is marked by his singing her tune in the dominant. He then makes repeated attempts to get back to his work (these are marked by very definite cadences) before giving up – and his capitulation is symbolized by his singing Suzanna's tune in imitation with her over a dominant pedal (she leads, of course). There is a cadential pause, and after it there is a recapitulation (a particularly happy term here!) with Suzanna's tune in the tonic, Figaro and Suzanna both singing it in parallel tenths. The number ends with a cadential extension of her tune. His has completely disappeared, reflecting the development of the dramatic situation in the course of the number.

The underlying form of this number is given by the developing dramatic situation. The text makes this form explicit; the music, while perfectly coherent as music, is primarily designed to project or comment on this situation. Forms in classical operas are not on the whole stereotyped as they were in baroque operas; they are as variable as the dramatic situations they are expressing. But in instrumental music there is no text to explain what is going on. And it is to make good this lack that more-or-less stereotyped formal patterns were adopted in classical symphonies, quartets and piano music. A traditional form, like the sonata, consists essentially of a set of expectations listeners have when hearing a piece. In a sonata the listener expects there to be a move away from the opening tonality to another, and later on a return to the opening tonality. He expects these tonalities to be presented as opposed forces, the opposition between them creating a tension that is resolved in the final return to the home key. And he expects this tonal drama to be projected and clarified by the musical surface with its themes, cadential passages, repetitions and caesuras. In other words a sonata is a kind of plot, functioning rather analogously to the stories on which ancient Greek plays were based – stories that the audience knew beforehand, so that what they were interested in was not *what* the play presented but *how* it was presented. Analyzing a sonata as a sonata, then, means analyzing it in the light of the expectations a contemporary listener might have been assumed to have.

There is more than this to the analogy between sonata form and opera. In opera a text can only explain the situation if it is audible. For this reason in his operatic ensembles Mozart likes to introduce each character separately, normally with a separate theme identifying each character. Once the themes have been introduced in this manner, they can be superimposed on one another – which makes the words unintelligible – while still being understood as symbols of the dramatic situation; in this way themes function as the vital link between the dramatic form and the purely musical patterning. Consequently any Mozart ensemble is likely to begin with an expository section, in which readily identifiable themes are presented, and to continue more developmentally with the themes being used freely as symbols of the 'working out' of the dramatic process. Or thematic and developmental passages may alternate. (No. 7 of the *Marriage of Figaro*, the trio between Suzanna, Basilio and the Count, is a good example.) And it is likely to end by recapitulating some or all of the themes – a recapitulation that is not simply a repetition (as in a baroque dance form) but that reinterprets the themes in the light of the changed dramatic situation. With its exposition, development and recapitulation, the instrumental sonata is really a special type of operatic ensemble in which the explicit drama of the opera is replaced by an implied one based on a traditional set of expectations: and this means that analyzing a sonata as if it was not a sonata is like analyzing an operatic number as if it was not about a dramatic situation.

However, there is a subtle difference between the function of a theme in opera and in the instrumental sonata. In opera the themes simply highlight the situation; when we call something a 'theme' we do not mean anything more than that it is readily identifiable. But in a sonata the themes actually define the situation. Hence if we call something in a sonata a 'theme', we are not just talking about how it sounds, but saying that it has a certain function in relation to the form as a whole. For instance, a tune may at first hearing sound thematic, but turn out not to be – say if it never recurs, not even in the recapitulation. And in order for something to function thematically, as a symbol of a structural tonality, it does not actually need to be a tune at all; as I said in Chapter 1, it merely needs to be something that will be easily identified when heard again, and which can be worked into a variety of musical contexts while remaining identifiable. So in the case of sonata form, calling something a 'theme' represents an act of analytical judgment; it is not a description but an analytical term.

But complications of this sort are the exception rather than the rule in classical music. On the whole classical composers wanted their sonatas to be readily intelligible as sonatas (something that is by no means so true of all Romantic composers). So they made their themes sound thematic, their cadences sound cadential, and their developments sound developmental. And, except in concertos, they adhered to the textbook 'sonata' pattern more frequently than it has been fashionable to admit.[1] So I do not think it is true, as has frequently been maintained, that 'sonata form' is no more than an analytical fiction. But even if it were true, that would not really be the point. The point would be, how useful an analytical fiction is sonata form? And the answer would depend entirely on how it is used. If one thinks that the purpose of analyzing a sonata is to show that it is a sonata, then little is gained by the exercise. But if one shows *how* a piece is a sonata, then 'sonata form' functions as a short cut to all sorts of useful analytical results. Because the interesting thing is not the conformity but the variety of sonata forms, the rest of this chapter will contrast two pairs of sonata forms – one pair that is rather close to the textbook model and one pair that is more remote from it.

II

If a piece of music is in sonata form, then it must somehow fall into the segments shown in Fig. 127. All the segments shown in brackets are optional, so that the only really obligatory ones are exposition and recapitulation, and within the exposition the division into first and second thematic areas (these correspond to A and B in Fig. 127)[2]. The recapitulation is by definition modelled more or less closely on the exposition (it restates all the thematic material previously stated in keys other than the tonic, plus some or all of what was stated in the tonic), so that it is the exposition that is crucial to the analysis of sonata form: if you analyze the exposition correctly, most of the rest should more or less fall into place.

Normally in classical music the entire exposition is repeated, which makes it obvious where the exposition ends. This is the case in each of our first pair of works, the first movements of Beethoven's Sonata Op. 49/2 and his G major Quartet Op. 18/2. Nor is it difficult to decide where the first thematic area of the exposition ends and the second one begins; in each case this point is marked by a rest – at bar 20 in Op. 49/2 and at bar 35 in Op. 18/2. However, it is not these rests that are definitive – there are longer rests at bars 8, 16, 20 and 24 of Op. 18/2.

---

[1] Why are concertos different? Because in them a more basic opposition still, that of soloist and orchestra, cuts across the normal sonata oppositions of tonality and thematic materials. No standardized method of dealing with this ever emerged.

[2] Sometimes the term *sonatina form* is used for a sonata form that lacks the development.

Nor is the fact that in each case the rest is followed by a tune definitive in itself; the tune at bar 21 of Op. 18/2 is just as tuneful as the one at bar 35. What is definitive is the fact that there is a striking event that marks the cadence into the new tonality (in both these works the new tonality is the dominant, D major, which is normal in major-mode works but not obligatory). For this reason the quickest way to find the beginning of the second thematic area is not to look at the top line of the music but to scan the bass, searching for dominant, or dominant-of-dominant, pedals – sometimes, as in both of these examples, coupled with cadential fragmentation. It is because tonality rather than melody is the crucial factor that some people avoid talking about 'themes' altogether and instead refer to the 'second tonal area' or simply to the 'dominant area'. However, it is not just the tonality but the way it is presented that matters, so perhaps it is better to retain the term 'theme' – while remembering that this means not a tune as such, but whatever it is that identifies a structural tonality. The important thing is not the term you use but what you mean by it.

Fig. 127

(Introduction)			
Exposition	A	B	(Codetta)
	1st key	2nd key	....
(Repeat of exposition)			
(Development)			
Recapitulation	A	B	(Coda)
	1st key	....	

What next? It would be possible to continue the process of segmentation by distinguishing the various parts of each thematic area and labelling them according to the traditional categories of 'thematic' (A1, A2, B . . .),[1] 'transitional' (Tr1, Tr2 . . .) and 'cadential' (Cad1, Cad2 . . .). This is fine for quick reference but it should not be taken too seriously as a statement of musical function. The idea is that 'transitional' refers to material that makes a new tonality intelligible in relation to an old one, and that 'cadential' refers to the consolidation and conclusion of a tonal shift. So bars 21–35 of Op. 18/2, for instance have a transitional function; they cannot be omitted without making

---

[1] There is a minor terminological muddle here. When people say 'the second theme' they may mean B (the second thematic area) or A2 (the second strain of the first thematic area). Usually the context makes it clear which is intended.

265

nonsense of the tonal progression. On the other hand bars 50:2 – 80:1 merely prolong a single tonality: so they are cadential. But it is not always so easy to distinguish the two functions. And in any case, if you think about it, you will see that the idea that something must be either thematic *or* transitional *or* cadential does not really make sense. The function of a theme is to mark a tonality, as I said. And it can do this in various ways. Sometimes a theme coincides with the move towards the new tonality; in which case, as well as being thematic, it has a transitional function. At other times a theme can clinch a tonality, in which case, as well as being thematic, it has a cadential function. In any case it can be very difficult to decide where a theme ends, since it is often only the beginning of the theme that is really distinctive. It is easy to waste a lot of time over meaningless boundary disputes if you insist on assigning a functional label to everything at this stage. Often it is better simply to divide the exposition into its two thematic areas – these are what matter structurally – and then look at the rest of the movement to see how the various components of these areas take on particular functions within the context of the piece in question. And a convenient way to do this is to answer a more or less standardized set of questions that pose general analytical issues in a manner specifically adapted to sonata forms.[1] Here is such a list.

Q. 1 *How unified is the material presented in the exposition? Are there obvious contrasts of thematic and non-thematic materials? Are the themes strongly contrasted with one another?* The materials that mark the two thematic areas of Op. 49/2 are not only similar texturally (that is obvious) but melodically too: Fig. 128 shows this. And there is also a rhythmic similarity between the upper parts of bars 3 and 27. On the other hand the two themes are distinct harmonically in that the A theme is quite discursive with its implied V^7 of IV, whereas the B theme hugs its tonic closely (everything is either a D major chord or resolves directly to one). It is conventional for first and second subjects to be distinguished in this way, but this is not only a matter of convention – Fig. 129 is a practical demonstration that the two themes do actually function differently. However the contrast between the themes is much less than the contrast between them and the non-thematic material, which *sounds* non-thematic because it is made up of shorter, repeated

---

[1] Lists of questions adapted to a large number of stereotyped forms, plus a sophisticated set of symbols for labelling them, will be found in Chapter 7 of Jan LaRue's *Guidelines for Style Analysis* (Norton 1970).

Fig. 128 Op. 49/2, I, comparison of first and second themes

patterns and scalar or harmonic clichés. All the non-thematic material is
linked together by virtue of sharing the triplet pattern (which comes
from A's opening arpeggio but doesn't recur in either of the themes).

Op. 18/2 is more complicated. The first twenty bars are a closed
unit that you might confidently label 'first theme'. But it does not
function so much as a theme as a boxed set of independent thematic
ideas all marking the first thematic area. The phrases at bars 1–4 and 9–
12, though clearly variants of each other, remain distinct throughout:
you only get bars 1–2 coupled with bars 3–4, never coupled with bars
11–12 or even by themselves. So they function as independent thematic
elements. Similarly the phrase at bars 5–8 recurs by itself as the codetta.
On the other hand, the closing phrase, at bars 17–20, never recurs – so
that you could maintain that, like bars 21–35, it is not really thematic at
all. In any case much of the material of the first fifty bars shares a
number of common features that cut across any distinction you might
make between thematic and non-thematic materials, or even between
first and second themes (Fig. 130). By contrast, the materials of the
remaining 31 bars of the exposition, though distinctive enough, are
more repetitive and have no specially significant links either with one
another or with earlier material. This is the only reason you might have
for calling them non-thematic, since the pattern of their recurrence is
identical to that of the second theme proper: both recur bar-for-bar in
the recapitulation but nowhere else.

Fig. 129 Variant of Op. 49/2, I, bars 1–35

Fig. 130 Recurrent patterns in Op. 18/2, I

Q. 2 *How is the transition between the structurally opposed areas of the exposition achieved? Does the modulation serve more to link or to separate the structural keys? Does the second thematic area simply coincide with the move to the new key or does it serve to clinch a move that has already been made?* In Op. 49/2 D major was reached very easily by the chromatic alteration in the bass at bars 13–14, turning a II of G major into a V of D major. But this is not enough to establish the new key very strongly, and anyhow the cadential passage following it (bars 15–20) reintroduces C♮s so that it is not clear whether the D is a tonic or a dominant pedal (that is how

Beethoven can use the same passage in the recapitulation, without transposing it, as a cadence back into G). In other words there is not a very strong implication of D major when the second theme starts, and the extensive circlings round D major during the rest of the exposition – approaching it from different directions – serve an important function in consolidating D major as the new tonal area.

There is a more extensive process of harmonic reinterpretation in Op. 18/2 (Fig. 131). This means that D major is more strongly established when the second theme starts: this time it would sound very odd to continue in G major. So it would be boring and pointless if the rest of the exposition – and more than half of it is still to come – simply circled round D in the manner of Op. 49/2. Instead, Beethoven makes the second subject cadence, with no warning at all, into D's submediant (that is, B minor). Two cadential passages follow, each made up of repeated V–Is – again in B minor. Each passage in fact closes, via a diminished seventh chord, in D major but the effect is none the less that the D major is seriously destabilized. Hence the remainder of the exposition consists of a much more intensive series of encirclings of D than was found in Op. 49/2 (note in particular the cello's line at bars 72–5, which magnifies its line at bars 36–9 and throws a lot of weight onto the V–chord at bar 75). At the end of this the sense of D major is very secure, and the contrast between the two structural keys of G and D is thrown into relief when the exposition is repeated – especially since bar 5, second time round, directly echoes the codetta but in G major. (Analysts have no more justification than performers for ignoring repeat marks at the end of classical expositions.)

Fig 131

Bar number	22	24	26	34	36
Chords	G	D	e	A	D
G major:	I	V	VI		
D major:	IV	I	II	V	I

Q. 3 *What is the tonal and thematic plan of the development? Does it fall into clearly-marked sections? When does the home key begin to be clearly implied? Is the tonic used in the development and if so, how? Is there new* *material?* In keeping with its miniature dimensions, Op. 49/2's development is little more than a decorated structural break between exposition and recapitulation – a symbol of development rather than the real thing. (Actually the same is really true of the sonata as a whole; it is clearly a beginner's piece rather than a 'real' one, whatever that means.) There are a few obvious links between the development and what has come before; bar 53 echoes the rhythm of bar 1, bar 54 recalls bar 21, and 64 is a shadowy reflection of bar 9 (Fig. 132 explains this). As for the tonal plan, it is an excursion and return by conjunct fifths framed within a D-minor/major relationship and avoiding G altogether. When does G begin to be implied as the destination? – during the V–of–E–minor pedal, whose very length creates an anticipation of structural resolution, so that the rapid motion through chords on E, A and D is heard as VI, II and V of G (unlike the initial D minor and A minor, which are not heard as related to G but as independent, if purely local, tonics). Fig. 133 shows all this.

Fig 132

Fig. 133   Analysis of Op. 49/2, I, bars 53–67

Bar   53   57   65   67
d (I)   a (V–I) e (V–I–VI#⁶–V–I)
G: VI (V–I) – II – V – I

The development of Op. 18/2 also uses A materials (from bars 5–8 and 9–12), but in addition it uses some 'transitional' material from bar 21, so that the amount of totally new material is proportionally smaller than in Op. 49/2 (examples include the second violin's off-beat grace note figure in bar 88 and the first violin's motif at bar 107; the former does not recur at all, the latter persists for some twenty bars and then disappears). Like Op. 49/2, it begins in D minor, but it moves in a much stronger progression through B♭ major to E♭ major. The B♭ behaves as a V to the E♭, complete with cadential fragmentation (note the patterns of repetition shrinking from two bars at 94 through one bar at 98 to half a bar at 99); so that when the A theme is stated at bar 101, in its version from bar 13, it sounds highly structural – except that it is in altogether the wrong key. The rest of the development compensates for this premature rise of tension and false reprise. Beginning at bar 105 there is a prolonged tensional low-point, so to speak, in which the double-dotted material of bars 103–4 is worked out in a more or less aimless manner. There is hardly a downbeat anywhere (even the pattern of transposition in bars 116:2 – 121:1 cuts across the barlines). Nor is there any sense of tonal direction; the music wanders from E♭ through A♭ to B♭ major, B♭ minor, and F minor before getting lost in a welter of diminished seventh chords. From time to time the diminished sevenths condense into a tonal region (there is some sense of B♭ minor, G minor, C minor and D minor at bars 119, 121, 124 and 126 respectively) but there is no impression of a connected tonal or harmonic progression. Nothing, except the knowledge that the development cannot go on for ever, implies the return of the home key. What happens is simply that at bar 134 a V⁷ of G emerges from the diminished sevenths and remains there while increasingly fragmented repetitions of the 'transitional' motif prepare for a structural cadence. If what happened at bar 145 were a literal repetition of the opening of the movement then the effect would be quite amazingly banal – and that brings us to the next question.

Q 4 *Is there a caesura reflecting the beginning of the recapitulation? Is this projected as a point of structural resolution? Where is the point of highest tension?* Bar 145 of Op. 18/2 is a false reprise, and a much more convincing one than that at bar 101; harmonically it functions not as a I but as a I♮ resolving to V at bars 147–8. Bar 149, not bar 145, is the real parallel to the opening of the piece, as its continuation makes clear. But bars 149–156 are greatly intensified as against bars 1–8. In part this is a matter of the viola's syncopations and the moving bass, but mainly it is the second violin's imitation of the first violin at one bar's distance. And this imitation prompts the viola to an even tighter imitation at bars 153–4, where it repeats the second violin's syncopated phrase a step higher and at the distance of a quaver. The result is a grinding discord (look at the chord half-way through bar 154) which is clearly the tensional high point of the entire movement. The point of structural resolution, then, is not the beginning of the recapitulation but the cadence at bar 156, after which the recapitulation continues in an almost unaltered form (though only for four bars). Why does the structural crisis occur *after* the beginning of the recapitulation? Because of the perfunctory and unconvincing manner in which the return to the home key was accomplished. Something had to be done to turn the G major into a real tonic, that is, into a point of structural resolution. Possibly the alterations that occur from bar 74 of Op. 49/2, which bring the music for the first time into the subdominant region, have a comparable function.

Q 5 *How is the recapitulation altered as against the exposition and why? Is there any important material which is not finally stated in the tonic?* Since a recapitulation stays in the tonic where the exposition went into another key, the point of transition between the two keys always has to be rewritten. But the alterations are not always exactly where you would expect to find them. This is particularly clear in Op. 49/2, where the passage that immediately preceded the new key in the exposition is literally repeated, without transposition, in the re-capitulation (bars 82–7); the second theme simply takes off in G where before it took off in D. At the same time, if you play from the beginning of the recapitulation up to bar 87, and then continue with the second theme in D, you will find that it does not sound quite right this time. Why is this? It is because the section preceding the literally repeated passage has been altered and now goes to the subdominant. This alters the centre of gravity of the entire first thematic area and it seems to be this that requires a continuation in G, not D, at bar 87. The purpose of the alterations, then, was tonal rather than having to do with the particular material introduced – it is one of the cadential ideas (from bar 40) but there is no special reason why it had to be. Apart from this, and of course the transposition of the entire second thematic area, the differences between exposition and recapitulation are cosmetic: the F#s at 100–1, the chromatic passing-note at 108 (why these changes? why not?), and the rewriting of the end which extends the final cadential phrase with an extra repetition and expands the chords of bar 52. There are three aspects to this expansion. First, the chords are expanded dynamically (*ff* in contrast to the preceding *p*)[1]. Second, they are expanded registrally, the low D of the penultimate chord picking up the D of bar 52, and the G of the final chord being much the lowest note of the

---

[1] This *ff* doesn't appear in the Urtext; however, it appears in most other editions, and certainly represents normal performance practice.

movement and eliciting a type of piano sonority that has not been previously heard at all. And thirdly, they are a rhythmic augmentation of bar 52 – crotchet attacks being converted into minim attacks. The effect of all this is to create a sense of finality otherwise lacking in what is tensionally a rather homogeneous sonata structure.

The alterations as between exposition and recapitulation in Op. 18/2 are more complicated and it helps if we divide them into two categories: structural and local. An example of what I mean by local alterations is the whole of the second thematic area, that is to say bars 187–232. These correspond bar-by-bar with 36–81, and the changes are mainly registral. When you transpose a passage from the dominant to the tonic, you can either transpose it a fourth up (or an eleventh or whatever) or you can transpose it down by a fifth (or twelfth or whatever). Or you can alter the relative tessitura of the lines, transposing some up and others down. Beethoven does all these things here, and where there is a reason (does there always have to be?) it is a purely local one – for instance, his alterations at bars 216–9 make the first violin's emergence at the top of the texture that much more climactic than it was in the exposition. On the other hand the differences between the exposition and recapitulation of the first thematic area have a more-than-local significance – a structural significance, that is to say. Bars 157–60 are in fact the only passage that is not significantly altered. Where they were immediately and literally repeated in the exposition, they are developed by sequence in the recapitulation, passing through a series of chords by fifths (G major, D minor, A minor, E minor) and cadencing strongly in E major. Here, at bar 170, the first six bars of the movement are for the first time restated in their original form – but in the wrong key, just like the false reprise early in the development. From here the ubiquitous figure from bars 5–8 is used by sequence and fragmentation to form a transition back to G, thus replacing bars 21–33 of the exposition. What is the point of all these alterations? Again we are anticipating the next question.

Q 6 *If there is a coda, what brings it about? Does it seriously affect the tensional shape of the movement?* In local terms, the tonic is strongly re-established by the time the second thematic area of Op. 18/2 comes round in the recapitulation. But in larger terms the E major has disrupted the recapitulation's tonal stability – especially since it ties in with the submediant inflections of the second thematic area's cadential material. In the exposition there were B minor inflections (submediant of D); now, transposed, they are E minor inflections, and the result is that E major/minor is established as a significant rival centre of gravity in the recapitulation. And this instability is highlighted by means of the strongest symbol of structural incompletion sonata form possesses: the fact that by bar 232 (which, by analogy with the exposition, ought to be the end of the movement) the statement of the opening material in E major still has not been counterbalanced by a final statement in the tonic. We have to think of this as a structural dissonance that needs resolving – and the principal function of the coda that is added after bar 232 is to provide this resolution. It does so both thematically and harmonically. The diminished seventh chords at bars 238 and 240 represent pivot points between G and E. Bar 238 stresses the E minor aspect (hence the D$^\sharp$). Bar 240 is written with an E$^\flat$ but the note is heard as ambiguous: will the first violin's scalar rise continue to E$^\natural$, or will it fall to D and so support the overall G major tonality? If this sort of analytical interpretation seems far-fetched, note how it ties in with an otherwise pointless detail: the harmonic alteration of bar 188 as against bar 37. If bar 37 had simply been transposed, the first violin would be playing E$^\flat$ – D. But it plays D$^\sharp$—E instead, inflecting the E$^\flat$/D$^\sharp$ towards E minor instead of G. Bars 240–1, where the E$^\flat$ finally falls to D, are therefore more than a diminished chord resolving to a G chord: they are a symbol of the movement's structural resolution. And the completion of the tonal process is highlighted by the D being the first note of the postponed, and required, statement of the opening theme in the tonic.

There are a few little alterations in these final bars as against 1–8, all of which support the sense of completion. The cello's B, instead of G, at bar 241 gives a first inversion triad and this throws relatively greater weight on the final, root-position chords. The two-octave registral displacement between the first violin at bars 245–6 and the viola at bars 247–8 expands the one-octave displacement at the end of the exposition, which was itself an expansion of bars 5–8 (where there was no displacement at all, the phrase being repeated at the same pitch). And the pizzicati introduce a hitherto unused sonority as a final symbol of conclusion, just like the low G of Op. 49/2.

What is the main thing that we have learnt about this coda? That it is not something tacked on *after* the end of the movement proper, as a framing device; structurally it *is* the end of the piece. Everything is directed towards it.

Q 7 *How do phrase-lengths tie in with the sonata plan? What are the movement's overall proportions?* Op. 18/2 is a more directed and more dramatic piece than Op. 49/2 and this shows up if we compare their overall proportions (Fig. 134). Op. 49/2 consists of two nearly equal sections with the development being the point of balance (the repetition of the exposition does not really seem to affect this sense of symmetry). In other words it is essentially binary, so that apart from the final chords it would be conceivable for the second half to be repeated as well as the first, as in a Scarlatti sonata. You might chart the movement's tonal plan as G – (D) – G. By constrast Op. 18/2 is not such a symmetrical movement: the addition of the coda – as an integral part of the re-capitulation – puts the centre of gravity later in the piece (the halfway point is in fact somewhere in the tonal limbo that precedes the re-capitulation). The lack of symmetry reflects the fact that at any given point Op. 18/2 is normally moving *towards* a key, whereas Op. 49/2 is simply *in* a key. So you might think of Op. 18/2's tonal plan as being (G) – D – G. In other words, whereas the form of Op. 49/2 is based on the *statement* of keys, in Op. 18/2 it is their *establishment* that matters. And it is because of this large-scale directionality, and the sense of dramatic tension and resolution associated with it, that a repeat of bars 82–248 of Op. 18/2 would be absurd.

Fig 134

	Exposition	Development	Recapitulation	Coda
Op 49/2	52 (× 2)	14	56	—
Op 18/2	81 (× 2)	67	84	16

100

Op. 49/2 gives the impression of being very regular in its phrase construction. Actually it is not. Although downbeats are easy to locate, the phrases are sometimes three bars long and sometimes four – and there is something of a pattern governing their distribution. The first explicit three-bar phrase is at 33–5 and results from the almost im-perceptible truncation of a four-bar phrase (compare bar 35 with 27–8). Precisely the same thing happens again at bar 42. And the following passage simply consists of two three-bar phrases (bars 43–5, 46–8). So there is a simple process whereby three-bar phrases emerge from the initial four-bar phrases and become established in their own right. In fact the seeds of this development can be found in the very opening of the piece. We have been thinking of bars 1–4 as a single, four-bar theme – which it is, structurally speaking, since it is consistently repeated as a unit. But in a way the opening bar is simply a flourish, a kind of upbeat to bar 2; so that we could divide the theme into (1 + 3) bars. In other words the theme carries within it an implied three-bar phrase length (Fig. 135), and this becomes explicit in the development at bars 53–5 and 56–8. All this is significant musically but does not particularly tie in with the sonata plan.

Fig. 135 Variant of Op. 49/2, I, opening

Op. 18/2 presents a more typical picture in that regular powers-of-two phrasing is characteristic of the thematic materials but less so of transitional and cadential passages, and of the development as a whole. The second theme is totally regular in this respect, consisting of (2 x 2 x 4) bars. The first theme is made up of four-bar groups but there are five of them; you could link this with the recurrence of five-bar groupings later in the movement (at bars 51–5, 116:2–126:1 which is a pair of five-bar sequences, and 165–9) but groups of five are not really so uncommon in classical music as to warrant special explanations. On the other hand from bars 51–77 and 105–30 there is no clear overall metre; there are groups of two or four bars but they are set in metreless contexts. So phrase-lengths do reflect, or contribute to, the distinction between thematic and non-thematic materials in Op. 18/2. At the same time there is a prevailing metric ambiguity in this movement, as compared with Op. 49/2. This does not have to do with the length of the phrases but with where the downbeat is situated within them. If you parse the opening into four-bar phrases, the obvious thing is to start the first phrase with bar 1; the whole look of the music changes with each succeeding four-bar unit (that is, at bars 5, 9 and so on). But is the opening bar actually a downbeat? Doesn't it rather lead to the D in bar 2? and isn't the arpeggio in bar 3 really an upbeat to the D at bar 4? What's more, this sense of accentuation on the second bar of the four-bar units sometimes surfaces into the notation – see the *forte* marking at bar 18, and the *sforzandi* at bars 22 and 37. So should we begin our parsing with the second bar rather than the first? There is not a yes/no answer to this: the music is simply ambiguous. On a local level it is this ambiguity which leads to the just about indecipherable metrical situation from bar 51 on (is bar 51 a metrical overlap? is 54:2–55:1 an interpolation into a basically four-bar phrase? is 56 a downbeat?). And at the level of large-scale form it is tempting to see the movement's crisis-point at the beginning of the recapitulation, where the violins are in imitation at the distance of one bar, as a surfacing of this underlying metrical tension.

III

Sonata form is classical in origin. But it retained its prestige as a compositional model throughout the Romantic period and hence remains useful as an analytical approach to nineteenth-century music. So our second pair of sonata forms consists of one transitional, and one fully Romantic example: the first movements of Beethoven's Fifth Symphony and of Berlioz' *Symphonie Fantastique*. We can use the same list of questions as before, but we shall find that this time they are not always so answerable. When this happens, we can at least work out what it is that makes them unanswerable. And this does make it clear just in what ways these movements are, and are not, sonata forms.

Q 1 In both examples the distinction of the two structural areas within the exposition is projected less clearly than it might be. In the Beethoven all the transitional and cadential material is so closely modelled on the first theme, with its three-quaver upbeat pattern, that the second thematic area is projected as a closed passage where this pattern is absent (bars 63–109) rather than as the second half of the exposition as a whole: bars 110–24 are almost like a return to first-theme material. The mottos which introduce each thematic area (bars 1–5, 59–62) also confuse the issue. The mottos are obviously similar to each other, but at the same time each summarizes the theme it precedes (Fig. 136) and the result is that it is the continuity, rather than the contrast, of the themes that is stressed. How should we label all this? It does not seem right to run the first 21 bars into one and call it a single theme when the pauses clearly cut off the first five as a separate unit; but equally you cannot call bars 1–5 one theme and 6–21 another because the motto is not a theme, rather it is a kind of symbol of the theme. On the other hand the second motto (at bars 59–62) is more integrated into what is generally called the second theme, at bar 63, which is a sort of consequent to the motto; taken by itself it would be very slight. There is no point getting bogged down in terminological complications over this: the fact is that there is something unclassical about these mottos, and the sensible thing to do is to find a way of labelling them that admits this. So I shall call the mottos MA, MB and the main themes 1A, 1B (this makes it possible to use 2A, 2B for successive strains in each thematic area, and 1A1, 1B1 for variants). And when, as in the development and coda, there are variants of the mottos that could equally well be MA or MB, I shall simply call them M.

Fig 136

The *Symphonie Fantastique* also creates labelling problems. The first theme is of course the *Idée Fixe* (bars 72–111). The difficulty is that really it is the only theme. It is conventional to call the three-bar cadential phrase at bars 152, 156 and 162 the second theme, simply because it coincides with the shift to the dominant (first as VI, and then as I, of G). But it does not sound like a theme; it is not strongly contrasted to the first theme since it is on each occasion introduced by a variant of the *Idée Fixe*; and, most importantly, calling it a 'second theme' implies a kind of structural balance that is notably lacking in this exposition – which, viewed this way, has a 15–bar second thematic area as against a first one that lasts 80 bars. This seems to me a good reason for avoiding the usual 'A' and 'B' tags altogether. Instead I shall simply label the *Idée Fixe* as such, and use 'x' and 'y' to refer to the other materials in the exposition that recur in the remainder of the movement. These are the derivative of the *Idée Fixe* at bars 119–25, and the cadential phrase otherwise known as the second subject. Nothing else recurs and therefore no further labels are necessary. It is better to risk saying too little rather than too much in your choice of labels, because it is always easier to add to an analytical interpretation than to subtract from it.

Q 2 The harmonic progression of Beethoven's exposition works mainly from the bass and is of a stunning simplicity (Fig. 137). C is converted from a consonance into a note of tension by means of a long pedal (bars 33–47) that culminates in a diminished seventh (bars 52–6); though the C clearly has to resolve, the direction of its resolution is not yet defined, and it simply slips up through D to E♭. Tonally this is perfunctory, and so the entire section based on 1B (bars 63–93) repeats the process of intensification and leads to another, and this time more structural, V of E♭ at bar 94; this is marked by a characteristic melodic idea (should we call it thematic or cadential?) and resolves to I at bar 110. The same kind of tonal postponement also occurs with the initial C minor. The opening motto is simply ambiguous; C minor emerges through the first subject, but its first emphatic I does not arrive until bar 33 – the beginning of the pedal that drives it to the new key. The result of this is that neither of the main themes (nor of course their mottos) actually coincides with the structural statement of a tonality. The brackets in Fig. 137 show this dislocation between what might be called the thematic and tonal downbeats.

Fig. 137 Tonal and thematic plan of Beethoven's Fifth Symphony, I, exposition

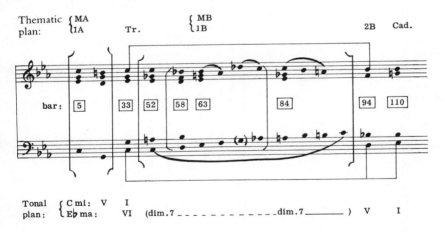

The fact that Beethoven never presents C minor as a strong structural consonance means that his exposition's centre of gravity is E♭. In the *Symphonie Fantastique*, on the other hand, the exposition is so heavily weighted towards C that the G is hardly more than a big

Fig. 138 Tonal and thematic plan of Beethoven's Fifth
Symphony, I, development

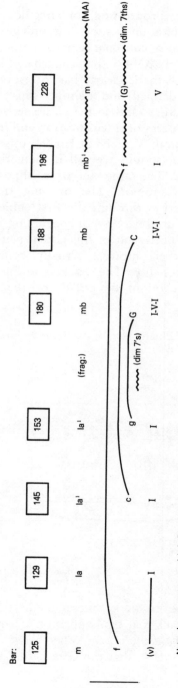

Note: Lower-case materials indicate non-structural statements of them.
Lower-case keys indicate minor mode.

imperfect cadence. The actual means of getting from one key to the other is similar, except that Berlioz' dissonance is not a vertical one, like Beethoven's, but a horizontal one: the rapid series of fifth-related chords in bars 143–5. Just as in the Beethoven, a tonal resolution is strongly implied but its particular direction is not. The difference is that whereas Beethoven then devotes half his exposition to strengthening this modulation, Berlioz simply cadences. When the repeat of the *Symphonie Fantastique*'s exposition is played (often it is not) the return to C does not feel like a structural jolt at all, which shows that the G never had time to become properly established as a new key. Really there is no modulation in the exposition of the *Symphonie Fantastique*; hence, nothing for a second theme to project; hence, no second theme.

The next three questions on the list were about the development and recapitulation. These are easy to locate in Beethoven's symphony but not in Berlioz's. So it's more convenient this time to run the three questions together and consider each work in turn.

Q 3–5 The tonal plan of Beethoven's development is again very simple, consisting of a symmetrical pattern of keys by fifths (Fig. 138).[1] The tonic occurs twice but each time it is presented as part of an ongoing motion and not as a destination, so that its overall function as the home key is not affected. Although the tonal plan is symmetrical – as in Op. 49/2 – the effect of the development is strongly directional. It falls into two halves, each of which works towards a climax. However, whereas the first climax (bars 168–179) leads clearly to the G major of bar 180, the second one involves a complete loss of tonal direction. Fig. 139 is a reduction of this passage, which leads from F minor (bar 196) through a succession of parallel $^6_3$ chords to D major (bars 221–232). What is this loss of tonal direction, then? Isn't the D major simply the V of the incomplete dominant minor ninth at bars 233–40, which is itself the V of C minor?[2] It

---

[1] Why does Fig. 138 simply show thematic and tonal labels whereas Fig. 137 gave a full harmonic and linear reduction? Because the development works by large tonal blocks rather than by means of harmonic or linear progressions. In his analysis of this symphony Schenker reduced the entire development to a single scalar fall (see his Ex. 6 and 10, reprinted in the Norton Critical Score of the Fifth Symphony, pp. 168 and 176). But these notes are not harmonically 'active' in the way a Schenkerian analysis normally implies (see p. 52 above). This analysis is interesting as an early example in which Schenker's conception of linear motions is essentially motivic rather than harmonic; his reduction is in fact quite similar to Reti's (in *The Thematic Process in Music*). I do not find Schenker's reduction convincing, though. Where music falls strongly into tonal blocks, as it does here, there is no particular need for large-scale linear coherence as well.

[2] Schenker reads a structural V beginning at bar 229 (see his chart, p. 181 of the Norton Critical Score).

may *look* that way, but that is not the effect when you listen to the music. Bar 233 does not actually sound in the least like an incomplete dominant minor ninth. It sounds simply like a diminished seventh chord, with no real relationship to any key; so that when the opening motto in its A♭ – F form (as at bars 22–3) bursts out of the diminished seventh and brings the recapitulation with it, the effect is of a violent structural jolt resembling, but much surpassing, the corresponding point in Op. 18/2. The immediate result is the same as in Op. 18/2: a structural caesura shortly after the beginning of the recapitulation, this time in the form of the long oboe cadenza (it looks short but sounds long) which prolongs the curiously held violin G of bar 21 and replaces the original half-statement of the motto at bars 22–3. (Why is it replaced? Because this motto has been used up in bars 240–7: it would sound very tame now.)

This cadenza is of course a point of structural intensification. But in no sense is it *the* climax of the movement, as was the polyphonic intensification at this point in Op. 18/2. Instead the long-term result of the recapitulation's sudden irruption in the first movement of the Fifth Symphony is to push the recapitulation's centre of gravity even later than was the case in the exposition. The structural alterations in the recapitulation tie in with this as well. As in Op. 49/2, what was originally the point of tonal transition is hardly altered at all (the main difference is that the diminished seventh chord at bars 296–300 is re-registered in the winds so that its highest note is an F♯ that rises to G: compare this with the flute's G♭ at bar 56, which was left hanging). However, there are extensive alterations *after* this point, that is in bars 315–46 as against 71–93. The changes both prolong and intensify the second theme. The four repetitions at bars 307–22 are organized by register and orchestration into two groups of two as against the original single group of three; bars 323–45 contain similar re-registrations as well as transpositions that heighten the passage's harmonic dissonance. All this intensifies the structural dominant at bar 346, and so confirms the interpretation of bar 94, and not 58, as being the important structural chord. The alterations after this point are confined to rhythmic underlining (compare the brass at bar 365 as against 113).

Fig. 139

Like Beethoven, Berlioz uses the overall tonic in his development but this time the effect is very different. In fact it so confuses the situation, formally speaking, that it is not clear where the development ends and the recapitulation begins; in other words the movement begins to be not really in sonata form at all. The first tonic key-area is only twenty-two bars into the development and consists of four bars of emphatic V⁷ followed by the cadential figure 'y' (the so-called second subject) stated twice in C. What are we to make of this? One possibility is to regard the C not as a tonic but as IV of G, which is what Edward T. Cone does in his analysis. This deals with the formal problem but unfortunately it bears no resemblence to the way the music is actually experienced. Cone explains that the C is 'immediately vitiated by the onset of the chromatic sixths. Moreover, it enters as a sixth (first inversion) and leaves as a sixth – the first of an episode. So the root position of the cadence is only an accident of detail'¹. But it is none the less audible for that! It seems much simpler to accept that it *is* heard as C, and not as IV of G, and that if the effect is not one of structural anti-climax, then this is because the G was never properly established as a key in the first place. It is only *after* the following episode that there is a sustained block of G (the only such block in the movement): bars 241–305, which incorporate a complete thematic statement of the *Idée Fixe* with extensions and new cadential material. This is quitted through parallel diminished sevenths (bars 306–312), leading oddly to E minor and so, through more diminished sevenths, back to C – which is again marked by 'y', the cadential figure. An extensive block of C follows (bars 324–53) and for this reason Cone, following Schumann – on whom his analysis is based – regards this second return to C as the structural one; he sees it as initiating a recapitulation in which the three thematic ideas – the *Idée Fixe*, 'x' and 'y' – appear in reversed order (at bars 412, 331 and 324 respectively). This means seeing the long chromatic passage from 360 to 411, beginning with A major and ending with Vs of C, as an altered and intensified transition: one that heightens the structural resolution represented by the appearance of the *Idée Fixe* at bar 412, at double speed and with the first orchestral tutti of the movement. All this again seems analytically sensible except that it does not correspond to the music we hear. Though it is easy to *see* the motives from the *Idée Fixe* in the bass from bar 362 on (that is why Cone labels it as a development of the first subject, p. 252), the aural effect of

---

¹ Norton Critical Score of the *Symphonie Fantastique*, p.258. The original has 'accent' in place of 'accident', which I assume is a misprint.

the cadence into A major and the oboe tune is of an important structural break initiating something new; the fact that the cadence is marked by a change of speed underlines this. How many listeners, if you asked them at this point, would tell you this was halfway through the recapitulation? Should we not then forget about 'x' and 'y' as thematic elements and simply call bar 412, which any listener will surely recognize, the beginning of the recapitulation? Yes, if we have got to locate the recapitulation somewhere; but the term does not seem terribly appropriate when each statement of the *Idée Fixe* modifies it in a new way, and this time quite drastically. It is an *Idée Fixe* now integrated into a fully symphonic texture, with its characteristic irregularities of metre and tempo all ironed out.

Q 6 The *Symphonie Fantastique* really has two codas. The coda proper begins at bar 493 and consists of two halves, each of which recalls and liquidates elements of the *Idée Fixe*.[1] All this is structurally quite inessential; the movement could easily have ended at bar 493, and in fact it originally did. Berlioz added this coda as an afterthought, so it is quite reasonable (though analytically unfashionable) to see it as being demanded by the 'religious consolations' the programme refers to, and not by any strictly musical logic. The other coda-like point is bar 453, an interruption which anticipates both the melodic character and the religious sentiments of the coda proper. Structurally it, too, is an interpolation: you can easily imagine the whole of bars 441–62 being cut.

By analogy with its exposition, Beethoven's movement would end at bar 374. But this is actually just under three-quarters of the way through the movement. What would have been the final tonic chord is expanded into a 129-bar coda rooted in the tonic (though returning to the minor mode). The material at the beginning and end of the coda is familiar enough; bars 374–95 consist of climactic chords 'thematized' with the semi-quaver motif, while the final bars mimic the end of the development. As before there is an irruption of the opening motto (even more powerful this time because the semiquaver motif is now completely liquidated: bars 477–8 are the first in which the entire orchestra has played repeated semiquavers all on the same note) and a second recapitulation begins – except that it is abandoned after a few bars and terminated with chords on the model of bars 369–74.[2] However, the

---

[1] Cf. Cone, p. 261, Ex. 10. The coda is a throwback to the original, vocalistic character of the *Idée Fixe* as against the symphonically integrated version of bar 412.

[2] Why does the repeated four-bar phrase at 483 work so well as a conclusion? Fig. 140 suggests a reason.

main body of the coda is by no means familiar. Admittedly it can be seen as a liquidation of the motto: this appears, with pitches as in bars 1–5 and rhythm as in bars 59–62, at the head of this section (bar 398), and is reduced to a stepped scalar pattern in the lower strings at bars 407–8. Meanwhile the counter-melody in the upper strings at bars 407–8 reappears as the main melody at bar 423 – only in contrary motion and rhythmic augmentation! What this shows is not the complexity of Beethoven's compositional technique so much as the fact that everything has been broken down to elementary scalar patterns which, by this stage in the movement, have acquired strong thematic or motivic associations. Similarly the A♭ – Gs that become increasingly prominent from bar 455 to 466, while they have the immediate purpose of strengthening the cadential G, are also pregnant with thematic associations (the oboe at bars 486–7 explicitly links them with the first theme, and perhaps there is an implicit link with the A♮ – Gs of the second theme in the recapitulation).

But having said all this, the main body of the coda does not actually sound in the least like anything that has been heard before; the downbeat march-like mood solidifies at bars 423 and 439 into what can only be called a new theme. And having a new theme at this point, however unclassical, makes sense because this coda is not the resolution of the movement's structural process but its climax. Although it is not the sort of thing you can really prove or disprove, it seems appropriate to think of this as a consequence of the tonal postponement I talked about before. The movement's centre of gravity, being shifted further and further back, has broken out beyond what would, in classical terms, have been the end of the piece. The basic symmetry that underlies the classical conception of sonata form has disappeared. In its place is a single motion towards a final climax – something which is much more characteristic of the Romantic than the classical sonata.

Fig 140

Q 7 Beethoven's movement falls into four almost equal sections: the exposition, development, recapitulation and coda consist of 124, 123, 126 and 129 bars respectively. Looking at these figures we could interpret them as outlining a symmetrical, though unconventional, form: the repeat of the exposition balancing the recapitulation and coda (which can normally be regarded as a single structural unit in classical sonata forms) and so giving a three-part construction of 248, 123 and 255 bars. But the music does not project such a grouping. Even repeated, the exposition does not seem to balance the recapitulation and coda combined (as I said before, literal repetition does not double structural weight). And in any case, do we really hear recapitulation and coda as a single unit? With its long-range intensification of the motto, the coda functions as a kind of second development, and the suggestion of a second recapitulation just before the music stops strengthens the analogy between the coda and the development. So perhaps we should symbolize the form as A B A B1 (A), with the final bracketed A being merely suggested. Obviously it is not a matter of one symbolical coding being right and all others wrong: the music is too complicated, too multifarious in its implications, to be packaged so neatly. But it does seem reasonable to say that here sonata form – the first ABA, with all its internal complexities – has become just part of a larger form of a rather simple, potentially rondo-like nature. Actually there is a general principle here. The bigger a musical form is, the more straightforward its basic structure generally needs to be. If it is not, chaos ensues; Schoenberg's First Chamber Symphony is an example of what happens.

Although there is plenty of clear four- or eight-bar phrasing in the Beethoven movement, the placing of the downbeats is persistently ambiguous. (You remember this was also the case in Op. 18/2.) If we were to regard the three quavers of the motto as an upbeat, then we would read bar 7, and similarly bar 26, as downbeats. Since everything at this point is in four- or eight-bar phrases, that makes bar 34 a downbeat. But is it? Don't the winds and lower strings mark bar 33 as the downbeat? And surely by bar 44 the opening iambic pattern ($\smile$ $-$) has changed to a trochaic one ($-$ $\smile$)? But then when did the change happen? With the second theme the ambiguity increases. In line with the eight-bar phrasing of the previous bars, we could read bar 60 as the downbeat, and after all E♭ is the note implied by the cadence; but it is difficult to read what follows on this basis.[1] Alternatively, we could regard the whole section from bars 60–93 as prolonging V and not I of E♭, and so read 62 as the downbeat, which gives a thirty-two bar section up to bar 93; this falls nicely into four-bar phrases until 81, but thereafter Beethoven's phrasing contradicts any regular patterning. And in any case I suspect that many people, if you asked them to write out this passage, would say it went like Fig. 141 – hearing everything a crotchet out. If this is correct, it explains the metrical jolt you feel at bar 94: a jolt similar to but exceeding that at bar 44, and which serves to underline the structural V of E♭ just as bar 44 underlined the structural tonic.

Fig 141

In these cases there is at least a sense of metre, though an ambiguous one. But in the prolonged passage preceding the recapitulation there is no overall metre at all. Even the five-bar statement of the motto at bars 228–32 – ambiguous at the best of times – is metreless because it is set into a metreless context. The lack of metre parallels the lack of harmonic direction in the same passage: both prepare for the irruption of the recapitulation and so project the sectional form. In fact, absence of metre and absence of harmonic direction are really the same thing. Phrase structure can result from patterns of repetition, changes of texture and other such things, but the most important thing that creates downbeats (and therefore metre) is harmonic progression. At whatever level, motion towards a goal constitutes an upbeat and the achievement of a goal constitutes a downbeat. In bars 196–239 of the

[1] It is tempting, though, since the result is a neat scheme coinciding with every important structural point of the exposition. Ignoring the statements of the motto at bars 1–5 and 22–5, which are metric interpolations, and discounting bar 6 as an upbeat, the exposition falls into groups of

$$(34 + 16) + (34 + 16) + 16 \text{ bars}$$

coinciding with the first structural tonic (bar 44); the beginning of the second thematic area (bar 60); the structural V of E♭ (bar 94); and the structural I of E♭ (bar 110) where the three-quaver motif emerges in a kind of codetta. In other words the first and second groups of (34 + 16) bars are the first and second thematic areas, and the final 16 is the codetta. But obviously nobody hears such a neat plan, and I am doubtful that Beethoven planned things like this on purpose; so I suppose it is all coincidence.

Beethoven (the passage summarized in Fig. 139) there is no perceptible goal and hence no metre.

Now, the *Symphonie Fantastique* is full of passages constructed in just this way. Bars 200–24, 372–407 and 442–50 all consist of parallel $\frac{6}{3}$s rising by step, the only structural differences as against the Beethoven being that the first two Berlioz passages consist of a wave-like motion of chords rather than a straight ascent, and that the last two are lightly disguised by counterpoint. All these passages (and others where chords are linked by other intervals or by linear motions) are atonal, and hence metreless. You cannot assign Roman letters to them because there is no tonic to relate them to; they go by too fast to create tonal implications. Just as in Chopin's E minor Prelude, which exhibits the same compositional technique only on a much smaller scale, there is simply a series of chords suspended between one functional harmony and another – rather like lines between electricity pylons. The chord-series implies neither a destination – that is, what the next functional harmony will be – nor when it will arrive; you can step off such a progression at any point you like (compare bars 451–2 with 474–5).

Furthermore the passages of the *Symphonie Fantastique* which *do* project a functional harmony tend to be themselves very static. The *Idée Fixe*, for instance, is definite enough tonally (you always know what key it is in) but harmonically it is vague, and the way Berlioz uses diminished seventh chords and pedal notes or ostinati to accompany it makes it all the more so; it simply comes across as a static, closed block of I. Furthermore, this movement almost completely lacks any kind of transition between one tonal block and another. Bar 313 is the only point where a pivot chord is used (E minor as VI of G and III of C); otherwise every tonal block is cut off from the next by means of an atonal passage. There are different keys, then, but no modulations between them. In fact, since they are never opposed to each other in the manner of a classical modulation, it might be more appropriate not to think of C and G as being structurally distinct tonalities at all. Perhaps it is better to think of G as being simply an intensification of C: C raised to a higher level.

Essentially the form of Berlioz' movement is very simple. It consists of static blocks of C or G major, mainly associated with the three recurring melodic ideas, which alternate with atonal passages – passages which do not generally recur and so function as more or less free episodes. Fig. 142 omits the introduction but otherwise it is an attempt to represent the form of this movement in the simplest and most direct manner; for this reason it is scaled by bar numbers (duration being a factor that the usual alphabetic charts of form suppress). Does this look

Fig. 142 Plan of Berlioz' *Symphonie Fantastique*, I (Introduction omitted)

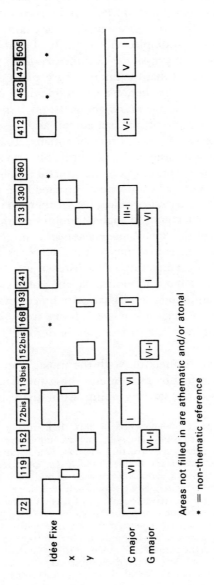

like a sonata form? Obviously there is a superficial resemblance; but it would be possible to make some quite minor changes – changes which would not devastate the music, in fact might even be an improvement – that would make this resemblance vanish. (For example, imagine that the repeat of the exposition took place not at bar 167 but at bar 200.) Our study of Berlioz' harmonic progressions, perfunctory though it has necessarily been, is enough to tell us that the underlying process that gives rise to the surface form is very different here from that on which the classical sonata is based. Let us review what we know about the process underlying classical sonata form. It consists of the statement and resolution of a tonal opposition, projected by means of thematic materials associated with each tonal area. There will be athematic, and probably also atonal, passages but these will serve to define and project the structural points – points that are critical in terms of the tonal drama being enacted. We will not understand the significance of such passages unless we see them in relation to this tonal drama: it would be like trying to analyze a representational painting as if it were an abstract. But the *Symphonie Fantastique* is not like this at all. It is a work of moments, a kaleidoscopic series of episodes each creating some immediate psychological effect upon the listener. As the programme indicates, it is not a drama but a monodrama, the portrayal of an individual's changing moods and fantasies. That is why it makes sense for the movement to have one real theme (though one from which almost all the episodic material can be more or less loosely derived[1]) and, perhaps, only one structural tonality.

If it has so little connection with the music's underlying structure, why did Berlioz give his movement the superficial resemblance to sonata form that was the starting point of our analysis? Because in 1830

---

[1] See Cone's analysis for evidence of this. Individually his derivations seem sometimes far-fetched, but collectively they are impressive – even if all they really show is that, with its scalar structure, the *Idée Fixe* is capable of making almost anything sound thematically derived (which is a good reason for the *Idée Fixe* being the way it is). But perhaps if we want to find the common factor between the various different materials we should not look for precise motivic links but rather at the recurrent wave-like patterns of tension that are frequently visible in pitch, dynamics and time – and sometimes in several of these at once. The *Idée Fixe*'s contour outlines a stepped ascent with intermediate falls. Among the most prominent recurrences of this contour are bars 200–30 and 360–407; this last is interesting because the pattern is fragmented from four bars to two bars to one bar (see the oboe at bars 360, 382 and 399 respectively). And the final, simplified version at 399 establishes a link with the stepped-scale pattern that recurs throughout the movement: at bars 123 (flute), 204–23 (winds), 280–2 (oboe – a variant of 123), 284–5 (cello and bassoon), 487–8 (strings) – and perhaps even in the final plagal cadences, in which the figure of 123 seems everywhere audible though nobody actually plays it.

sonata form was something a composer took for granted when planning a symphony; it was part of the definition of what a symphony was. But if the sonata plan is no more than a conditioned habit of mind in the *Symphonie Fantastique*, is it a sensible starting point for analyzing the work? Yes, provided you remember that it is only the starting point; after all, no sonata is just a sonata. Approaching any piece of music from the point of view of sonata form is simply an analytical method, and no analytical method can tell you everything about a piece of music. The most it can do is to bring you as quickly as possible to the point where you have a sufficiently clear perception of the work's unique properties to be able to formulate the detailed questions appropriate to that particular piece. And although sonata form casts rather an oblique light on the *Symphonie Fantastique*, this does throw into relief a great deal of what is striking and characteristic about the music. What I have said about it may be no more than the beginning of an analysis: after all, I have hardly touched on its chordal vocabulary, its use of linear formations and pedals, or the role register and orchestration play in it – not to mention the introduction, which lasts nearly as long as the main body of the movement (and in my opinion is the best part of it). But it ought to be much clearer now just what there is to analyze.

CHAPTER NINE

ANALYZING SERIAL MUSIC

I

How far is analyzing serial music the same as analyzing any other music?

According to Allen Forte, the kind of reduction technique that Schenkerian analysis exemplifies 'is not suitable for the analysis of 12-tone music, nor is it required there in order to explain structure. The 12-tone system has its own history, its own terminology and analytic technique.'[1] Now the kind of analytic technique which Forte has in mind involves identifying the series present in a composition together with the various transformations in which it appears, which is sometimes called doing a *note count*; and it involves deducing the formal properties that hold between the various transformations of the series, so that they can be correlated with those aspects of the musical design that are not directly determined by the serial structure – things like rhythms, textures, thematic design and so forth. And procedures like this are basically different from the kind of analytical techniques I was setting out in the first part of this book. They are different on two counts. First, they are explicit; they require the application of precisely stated rules, so that they could well be carried out by a computer. Admittedly this is also true, to some degree at least, of the kind of formal techniques (such as Forte's own set-theoretical technique) which I discussed in Chapter 4, as well as the comparative techniques I described in Chapter 5; but even these are unlike the techniques of serial analysis, because (and this is the second point of difference) serial

---

[1] In Maury Yeston (ed.), *Readings in Schenker Analysis and other approaches*, Yale University Press, 1977, p. 33.

techniques relate directly to compositional procedures. That is to say, more or less any piece can be analyzed by Schenkerian, formal or comparative methods, if with varying degrees of success; it is in no way a precondition that the composer himself should have been consciously aware of Schenkerian or formal principles. Indeed, you can analyze a piece in terms of sonata form without being sure that the composer was consciously thinking of his music in terms of sonata form, because (as I explained in the last chapter) the basic principles underlying sonata form became a habit of mind for composers – something that they took for granted in writing music. But serial structures do not occur except through a conscious decision on the composer's part to construct them; and where they do not occur, serial analysis is simply a non-starter. Serial analysis, then, is more tightly bound to a specific repertoire than other analytical techniques.[1]

But even when a piece is composed by serial methods, are specifically serial techniques of analysis all that is required to 'explain structure', as Forte put it? The answer to this is certainly no, because the techniques of serialism – at least of classical serialism, meaning Schoenberg, Berg and Webern – leave so many crucial aspects of the music undetermined: rhythm, texture, patterns of consonance and dissonance, form and so on. All these free aspects of the music play a crucial role in determining what effect, if any, the series makes on the listener. In fact, it is only when there is an unusually direct association between these free aspects and the serial structure that it becomes possible for a listener to perceive the serial structure as such.

An example of this is Webern's Symphony. Everything here is designed to make the series audible. The series is presented melodically rather than harmonically. The texture is sparse and the tempo very moderate. Each statement of the series is divided from the next by a caesura and a change of texture. Under these circumstances it is, if not easy, then at least possible for a listener to pick out the occurrences of the series – in a way it is not when, as is more often the case in serial music, the series is used harmonically, split up texturally, staggered against the phrase structure, or used at faster tempi. But there is a further point. The fact that listeners *can*, if they try, pick out the series does not mean that they *do* so in the normal way; I have carried out tests

---

[1] I mentioned in Chapter 3 that motivic analysis arose partly through attempts by some of Schoenberg's pupils to discover more-or-less serial patterns in non-serial music, particularly that of the classical era. I do not find these demonstrations convincing or musically interesting, but for another opinion see Hans Keller's 'Strict Serial Technique in Classical Music', *Tempo*, No. 37, Autumn 1955, p. 12.

in which musically qualified listeners made detailed observations of the first movement of Webern's Symphony without becoming aware of its being serially structured at all – simply because they had not been asked to listen out for a serial structure! And the observations these listeners did make were the sort of observations that could have been made about many non-serial pieces – of tensional shapes, developmental processes, effects of finality and so forth. It is clear that basic categories of musical experience such as these are as applicable to serial as to non-serial music. And this means that if what you are interested in is how a given piece of serial music is experienced, then its serial structure can only be the starting point for your analysis. As with sonata form, the important thing is not the structure as such, but the use the particular piece you are analyzing makes of that structure.

This chapter includes brief expositions of the techniques of serialism, interspersed between the analyses. But its main topic is the relationship between these techniques and the wider concerns of musical analysis as a whole.

II

A piece of music is serial if in some respect it is determined by a strict pattern of recurrence. In classical serialism it is pitch classes that are ordered this way, and the series states every note of the chromatic scale once and once only. It is possible to use series that contain only a selection of the twelve chromatic notes, but when this is done the effect of the music tends to depend more on the harmonic properties of the set of notes as a whole, and less on the order in which they come. In twelve-tone serialism (also called 'dodecaphony' – a term which in practice implies serial organization, as opposed to 'atonality' which implies the lack of it) it is only the order in which the pitches come that distinguishes one series from any other. As the analytical techniques specific to serialism are based on ordering as their structural principle, it is twelve-tone serialism that I shall talk about in this chapter.

About the simplest possible example of twelve-tone serialism is the twenty-bar piece from Webern's sketchbook of 1925, the first half of which is shown in Fig. 143; it would be sensible to play it through before reading further.

Fig. 143 Webern, Piano piece, bars 1–19

Fig. 144

Apart from a couple of minor reorderings, the music simply consists of the same pattern of pitch classes repeated over and over again, only at different registers and in different rhythms (Fig. 144).[1] The registral, dynamic and rhythmic variations, however, are inventive enough that the rather banal means of pitch organization is effectively disguised; the piece is best seen as an exercise in variation technique. This puts the analytical emphasis on the free rather than strictly organized aspects of the music, and a practical demonstration will confirm that the serial structure as such has a comparatively small part to play in the music's effect. Fig. 145 shows some of a recomposed version of the music which uses an entirely different series (it is in fact that of Stravinsky's *Movements* for piano and orchestra) while preserving the rhythms, repetitions and, as far as possible, the registers of the original. I think the effect is really quite similar, apart from a few obvious defects in the recomposed version – defects which are of a purely surface nature, such as the excessively disjunct left hand of my bar 3 in comparison to Webern's, or the excessive leaps from low B to high C# at the beginning of bar 4. (Why are these excessive? Obviously the answer cannot be a strictly serial one.) What this indicates is that it is the negative qualities common to most twelve-tone series, such as the lack of tonal weighting, rather than the positive qualities of this series in particular, that matter for the musical effect; and it follows from this that the registral, dynamic and rhythmic structure is what matters most from the analytical point of view.

Register, dynamics and rhythm work together in this piece to create a quite traditional pattern of musical motion in triple time – Webern marks it as a minuet, but the rubato indications reveal its affinity with the waltz. In other words, the bar lines indicate genuine downbeats, and in the absence of harmonic rhythm these are established primarily by means of surface rhythm – by the recurrent use of the opening ♫♩ figure to mark downbeats (bars 1, 4, 5, 6) and by the semiquaver upbeats to bars 3, 4, 6 and 7. Associated with this downbeat

---

[1] How do you decide what register to write down the notes of the series in, as in Fig. 144? There is no general rule: simply choose registers that make clusters of adjacent notes or motivic patterns easy to see.

Fig. 145

pattern is the division of the piece into distinct phrases which could be characterized as rhythmic statement (bars 1–2), counterstatement (bars 3–5) and development (bars 6–9). The last of these constitutes the climax of the first half. It does so rhythmically, through a kind of hemiola at bars 7–8, texturally (the thickening of the texture automatically means a quicker statement of the series), and registrally: the G♯ in the right hand at bar 7 is not only the highest note so far, but is the terminus of an upper registral line that starts at the beginning of the piece and moves upwards through B♭, C, D, E♭ and G♯ – a formation that has no function in relation to the series.

All this, then, constitutes a rhythmic and formal structure independent of the piece's serial construction. How do the two relate? The answer is given in the otherwise odd lack of alignment between the phrase structure and the rubato indications in the first half. In each case the ritardando is associated with B♭, the first note of the series, and the fact that the B♭ occurs at the same register each time helps confirm that it is not just an accident. These rubato indications, then, advertise an underlying pattern of temporal recurrence – the recurrence of the series – which is coordinated with the rhythm of the musical surface only at the beginning (the two rhythmic cycles start off together) and with the cadence at the end of bar 9, where they terminate together. In other words the coincidence of the surface rhythm and the serial pattern at the double bar seems to have a cadential function. At the same time it looks as if Webern had no great faith in the audibility of the series as a means of creating a cadential effect, because he reinforces it by a number of non-serial devices: the hemiola already mentioned, the spread chord in the right hand at bar 9, the triplet (a new formation to be developed in the second half) and, most of all, the unprecedented repetition of a motif in bar 8.

III

The piece discussed in the last section is an unusually primitive example of serialism. More representative is Webern's Piano Variations of 1935–6. Technically, the main difference has to do with the series being treated as a unit. In the 1925 exercise, the series functions simply as an indefinite stream of recurrences, without any particular beginning or end. In the Piano Variations, however, and in all classical serialism, the series is treated as a structural unit which can be modified, as a unit, in a number of ways. The basic ways in which a *prime set* (P) can be modified, or *transformed*, are *transposition* (T), *retrogression* (R) and *inversion* (I); these operations can be combined, as in inverse retrogression, and they are explained in Fig. 146.[1] In the case of most series these operations generate a possible repertoire of 48 different transforms: 12 (one transposition at each semitone within the octave) x 2 (prime or inverse) x 2 (stated forwards or in retrogression). In the case of certain series however – those that are symmetrical or made up of repeated intervallic cells – some of these 48 transforms are identical to others so that the repertoire of distinct transforms is smaller: like most of the formal properties of a series, this is something a composer can choose to exploit or to ignore.

In fact it is worth realizing that, though when set out like this the serial system seems so self-evident, a definite compositional decision is involved in looking at these operations this way. In classical serialism

[1] In Fig. 146 and elsewhere I use the American terminology for serial transforms, in which 'P' refers to prime, and set members and transpositions are both numbered from 0 to 11 (or terms 10 and 11 can be written as T and E to avoid confusion). Schoenberg and his followers, however, used 'O' (for original) instead of 'P' and numbered set members and transpositions from 1 to 12; this may seem more intuitive but it can cause problems in computation. A third, and less common, convention defines P–0 not as the first transpositional level at which the series happened to be stated in the piece, but as the statement of it that begins with a C; so that the transform marked P–0 in Fig. 146 would become P–4. It does not matter which convention you use as long as you are consistent; deciding what to call P–0 is just a matter of defining your terms, not a musical decision like deciding what key a piece is in. There is a further complication, which is that when the operations of inversion, retrogression and transposition are combined, the order in which they are carried out makes a difference. IR–0 in Fig. 146 means the inverse of R–0; really it should be written I(R–0), because the series is first put backwards and only then inverted. If the series is first inverted and then put backwards, it comes out at a different transposition; in this case you can see that IR–0 is the same as RI–2, but the transposition depends on the relationship between the series' first and last notes. Many people do not bother to distinguish RI and IR like this, however.

Fig. 146 Transposition, inversion, retrogression

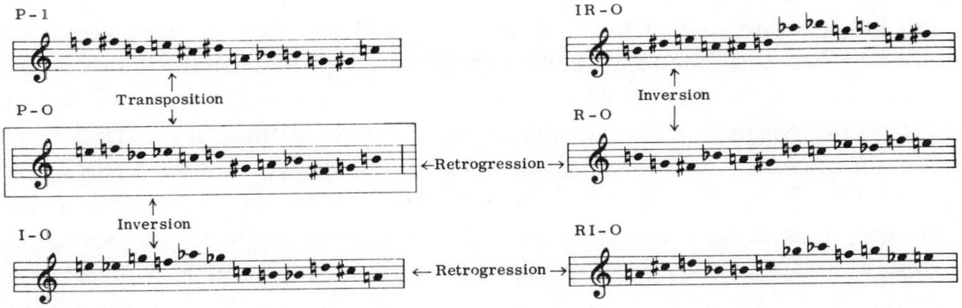

pitch classes were ordered systematically, in order to maintain a constant equality of weighting between the notes of the chromatic scale; the intervals between them were not systematized, so that certain intervals could be freely given prominence and others suppressed in any given series. But it would have been equally possible to serialize the intervals and leave the pitch classes free. Again, operations on pitch such as transposition and inversion result in permutations of the original ordering of the pitch classes. For example, if the members of P–0 in Fig. 146 are numbered as 0, 1, 2 . . . 11 then P–1 can be written as 1, 9, 5, 0, 2, 3, 7, 8, 11, 10, 4. This does not make much sense regarded as a permutation. Schoenberg and Webern chose to control relationships between different transforms in terms of pitch without making any very serious attempt to produce intelligible relationships of permutation between them; but logically speaking they could equally well have done the opposite. So the serial techniques I have been talking about are not a direct reflection of the formal possibilities inherent in the system as such. They take into account only a small fraction of those possibilities, the ones the composers actually exploited. Classical serialism, in other words, is not a system but a style.

All the serial structure of Webern's Piano Variations can be explained in terms of the T, I and R relations, but to do this it is necessary first to identify the series and its transformations. Now, note-counting is fairly straightforward in Webern's music because there are few deviations and because the musical surface is so designed as to project the serial transformations clearly, so that it is essentially a mechanical trial-and-error search such as a computer could carry out, rather than one that requires musical understanding – though a musically-trained eye can pick out emphasized intervals or segments in the music, and these are sometimes a short cut to deciphering the serial structure; familiarity with a given composer's style can also speed up the process. For example, you might find it difficult to work out what is happening in the left hand at bars 7–8 of the first movement of the Variations, if you were not familiar with Webern's habit of using a single statement of a note as a pivot for two statements of the series: you can see this in Fig. 147, which shows the whole of the first movement. Another complication arises from the use of chords. Obviously bars 1–4 could be derived from a series F E B G F♯ C♯ B♭ A E♭ D C G♯; it is only later, when the juxtapositions are altered, that it becomes clear that this is the wrong way of looking at things, and that they are a composite result of P–0 and R–0 statements being made simultaneously (and it is worth noting that the distinction between the two is not textural or registral but is made purely in terms of the distribution between the hands – that is to say, it is not an audible distinction). But even given this distribution, the set of the right hand could be F E C♯ E♭ D C . . . or E F C♯ E♭ D C . . . or E F C♯ E♭ C D . . . and so on; again deciding which of these is the correct interpretation involves looking ahead, and in fact since terms (0, 1), (4, 5), (7, 8) and (9, 10) are coupled throughout the first and last sections of the movement (bars 1–18, 37–54) it is only the middle section that shows which is the intended order. And since the middle section uses other couplings – for, instance, terms 3 and 4 always occur together – the whole series is never in use as a fully ordered set at any single point of the movement; there are works, such as late Schoenberg, where this is taken further, so that there is no single definitive statement of the series (this is sometimes referred to as serial 'troping').

Now once the series has been established the analysis can go in either of two directions. One is to look at the formal properties of the series – such as the recurrence of intervals or sets of intervals between different segments of the series – which not only give the series an individual character but govern ways in which different transformations of the series can be associated with one another. These properties vary from one series to another, in a way the different keys of tonal music do not; so that you have to determine them for each individual piece. Perle calls this 'precompositional structure', as opposed to 'compositional structure', which (as I said in Chapter 4) refers to the ways in which formal properties are actually applied or exploited in the music; and this is a useful analytical distinction, though it does not really correspond to distinct stages of the compositional process. The second analytical direction I mentioned is the opposite: that is to say, concentrating on what the composer actually does and only after that going on to consider the

Fig. 147 Webern, *Piano Variations*, I

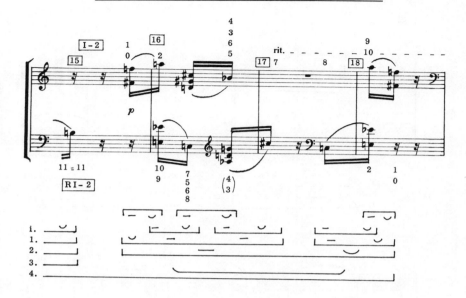

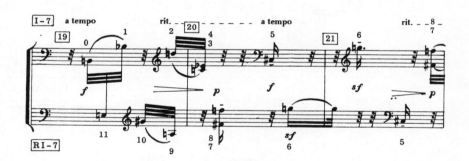

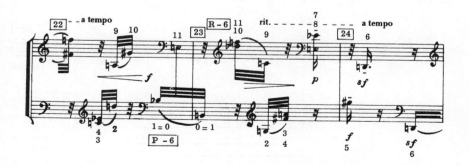

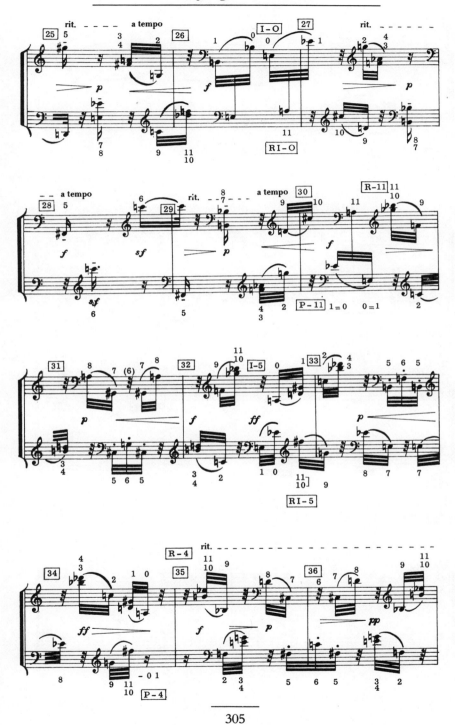

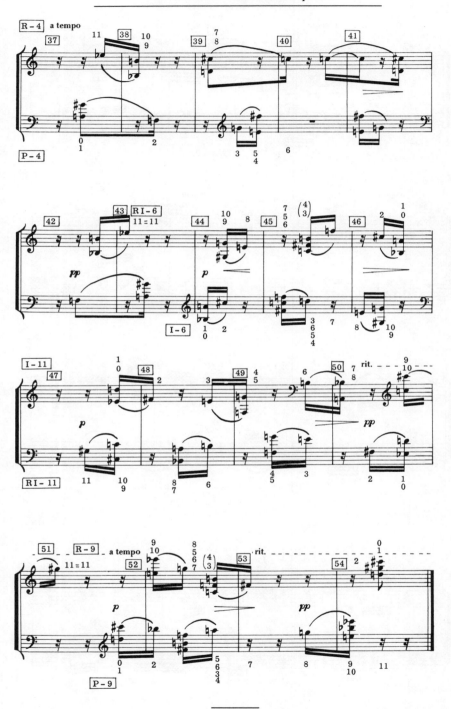

formal implications. In classical serial music this is usually a more sensible approach, simply because Schoenberg, Berg and Webern on the whole took advantage of only a small proportion of the structural possibilities inherent in the series. Fig. 148 illustrates this in the case of Webern's Piano Variations. It shows, first, that the series falls into two halves separated by a tritone, which does not appear anywhere else; and that the same tritone is a common feature between P–0, P–6, I–2 and I–8. Secondly, it shows that each half of the series (or *hexachord*) consists of a chromatic wedge, which is a common trait in Webern, and this means that the first hexachord of P–0 has the same content as the first half of the series I–9 or the second hexachord of P–6. Thirdly, it shows that one particular three-note cell or *trichord* (if we number it in semitones we can call it [0, 3, 4]) crops up several times in different transformations – for example, as D♭ – E – F it occurs as terms 0–2 of P–0, terms 7–9 of P–7 and terms 8–10 of I–3. Webern could have exploited all of these as neat ways to join different versions of the series by means of common segments between them, but in fact he does not take advantage of any of them. However, if instead of analyzing the precompositional structure you simply make a table of the transformations Webern actually *does* use, as in Fig. 149, then you can see that surface formations are employed as a way of linking serial transformations, but that these links are of a rather simpler nature. They are marked by the boxes and they consist of, first, shared final notes (but never first notes) and, second, shared but reordered pairs of first notes (but never final notes). And you can also see that the first relationship is used exclusively in the outer sections (bars 1–18, 37–54) and the second in the central section (bars 19–36). The rather casual nature of these serial relationships suggests that Webern saw them as more or less surface links between sections rather than as the basic structural principles governing the musical form. In other words, his approach to serial transformations seems to have been empirical rather than formalistic. For this reason the main analytical interest of his music, and that of his contemporaries, does not lie in the serial structure *per se* so much as the manner in which the serial structure is associated with the non-serial and often traditional aspects of the music.

The serial plan of the first movement of the Piano Variations corresponds quite closely to the main sections of the movement's form. This is an ABA structure in which the beginnings and ends of the sections coincide with statements of the series. Furthermore, although the serial structure as a whole is open or chain-like, there are recurrent relationships between pairs of series within each section and these are

Fig. 148 Transformational invariants in the set of Webern's *Piano Variations*

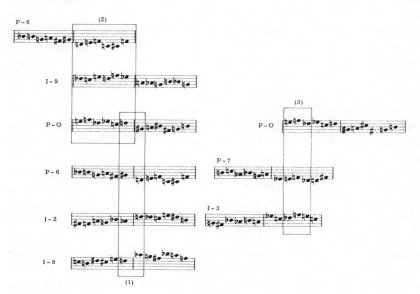

marked at the right of Fig. 149. However this ABA form is primarily distinguished not by the serial structure but by the rhythms and the chords used in the various sections: the middle section is in more or less constant semi-demi-quavers as against the semi-quavers of the outer sections, and major and minor thirds predominate in the middle section as against the major sevenths and minor ninths of the outer sections. So much for the relationship of serial and non-serial structure at the level of form. There is also a close association between the serial and the non-serial structure at phrase level, particularly in the frequent palindromes that occur throughout, sometimes with their central axes prominent, as at bars 4 or 21, and sometimes with them lightly concealed, as at bar 9.[1] These palindromes create a kind of rhythmic rippling through the local recurrence of notes within the overall chromatic sonority. It is possibly because of this close association of the series and the phrase structure that it is relatively easy to hear the series in this piece, at least in the

---

[1] The palindromes are basically literal (apart from the structural though inaudible swapping of the hands) but there are some deviations, normally in register: the transfer of G – F$^\sharp$ to the lower register at 14:3 (as against 11:3) is an obvious example, the inversion at 14:1 of the minor ninth A – B$^\flat$ at 12:2 is less so. Similarly there are minor rhythmic deviations.

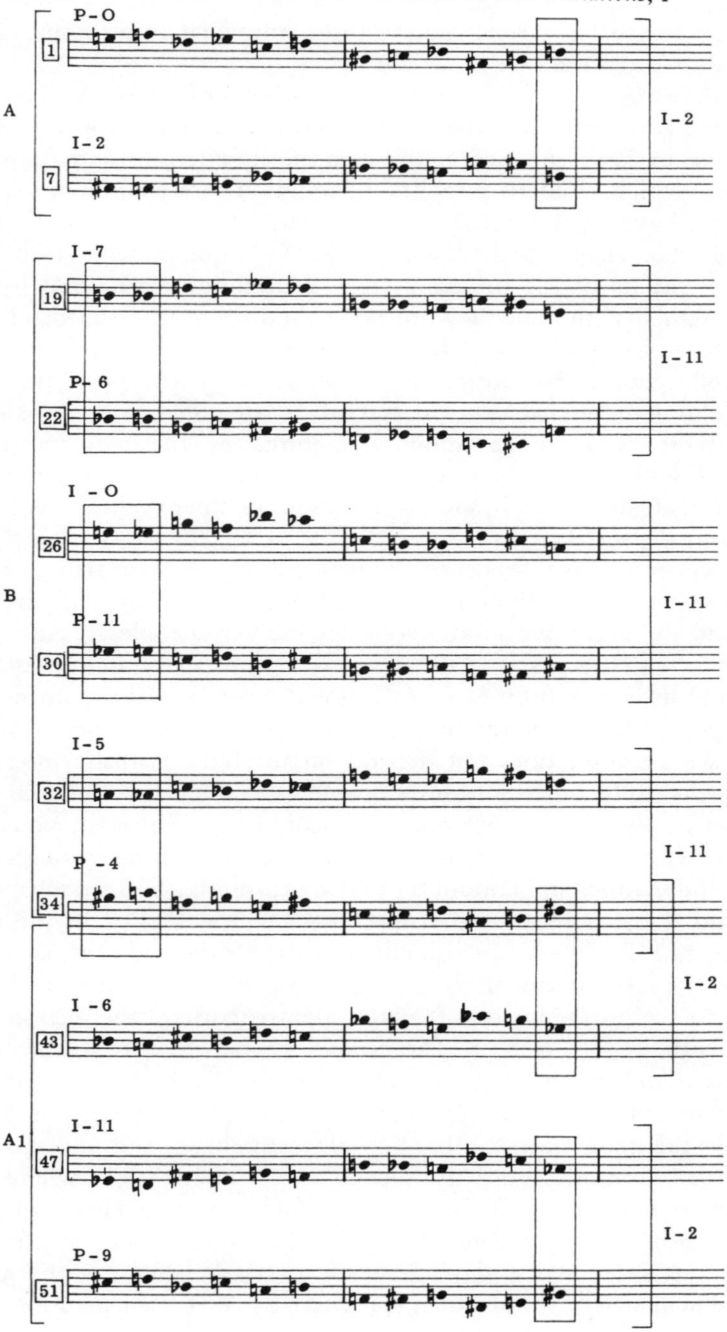

Fig. 149 Serial transforms in Webern's *Piano Variations*, I

negative sense that a 'wrong' note is more immediately recognizable as such than is often the case in serial music.

At the same time, there are important aspects of phrasing which cut across the palindromes and the serial structure in general. Some of these are visible in Webern's score: for example the tempo and dynamic markings which Webern supplies liberally. The dynamic markings sometimes have a palindromic structure paralleling that of the rhythm and pitch, as in all except the last two bars of the middle section; and the tempo markings of the middle section sometimes correspond to the serial statements, though they are not palindromic (the ritardandi are not mirrored by accelerandi). But at other points neither dynamics nor tempi follow the serial structure: the dynamic markings in the first section show the arch-like form typical of late tonal or freely atonal music (there is a climax about two-thirds of the way through, coinciding with the highest note of the section), while the only notated ritardando, at bar 17, has a cadential function. Neither of these has much to do with the serial structure.

However, if we want to understand the phrase-structure of Webern's music, we should not simply look at what Webern has marked in the score: we should consider the way people actually play the music, which is just as valid a source of information as the score. You could listen carefully to a professional recording of the music for this purpose. Or you might simply play it yourself. The sort of information we are after does not depend on masterly pianistic interpretation: it is simply a matter of how people naturally phrase the music as they play it. Even if you are not a particularly good pianist, you will find that, without thinking about it, you phrase the music through fine control of dynamics and tempo: try playing through it and see what you do. I find that, though no dynamic changes are marked in the first phrase (bars 1–7), I make a small climax towards the end of it, slowing down to the last bar and slightly lengthening the rest after it; and this means that the phrase mirrors the arch-like structure of the section as a whole, with its late climax. The second phrase (bars 8–10) is more compressed and urgent, with its climax coming perhaps as late as bar 10:2; there should be no rallentando or lengthening of the rest, otherwise the main climax at bar 11 will seem abrupt and unprepared. This climax continues until the second C—D at bar 13:2, where the diminuendo marked by Webern comes out as quite a rapid collapse coupled with a slight rallentando and a lengthy rest at bar 15. All through this section my playing seems to be shaped by a rhythmic structure which is no more than hinted at by Webern's notation and which is based on rhythmic groups or cells. I have shown these in Fig. 147, using Cooper and Meyer's notation,[1] although there are so many ways of hearing relations of accent and non-accent in this music that it is hard to be absolutely definite about this. You can see that at the beginning there are rhythmic groups of three (unequal) beats whereas during the remainder of the section groups of two predominate; however, these are staggered against each other in such a manner that the latent metre of the time signature is constantly on the brink of establishing itself. (It actually does so in bars 8–10, and although it then becomes submerged again it remains as a latent force – hence the cadential rest in bar 17, which compensates for the elision at bar 16.) What is it that creates these relations of accent and non-accent? Partly, of course, the dynamic stresses resulting from both hands' patterns of one note succeeded by a chord, or the other way around; partly, no doubt, from intervallic patterns; but also from registration, since the rhythmic effect seems to be much weaker in the final section, which is the same apart from registral layout. In fact the final section strikes me as altogether less successful than the first; and yet its serial structure is just the same.[2] And this goes to show that what matters is not the serial structure *per se* but the way it interacts with the rhythmic structure; particularly striking is the way in which the palindromes highlight the juxtaposition of rhythmic groups by creating what Cooper and Meyer call 'rhythmic reversals' (two accented beats directly following each other, as in bar 4).

At all events it seems ,clear that there are musically important aspects of Webern's Piano Variations that have nothing to do with the formal properties of its serial structure. (Webern apparently thought so too, for Peter Stadlen, who gave the first performance under the composer's supervision, has recounted how insistent Webern was on just the small factors of dynamic shaping and rubato that I have been discussing.[3]) In spite of the close association between serial structure and phrase structure, the form of the movement is not essentially a serial one at all; so it would be instructive to compare it with a movement whose

---

[1] See p. 76 ff. above.

[2] Even less successful is the inverted version of the opening 7 bars Cone presented in his article 'Beyond Analysis' in Boretz and Cone (eds.), *Perspectives on Contemporary Music Theory*, Norton, 1972, p. 72. The interesting analytical question this raises is: why does this music work better in the one version than the other? and the answer – whether to do with registration, harmonic formations, or strictly acoustical factors – obviously lies outside serial theory as such.

[3] 'Serialism Reconsidered', *The Score*, No. 22, 1958, pp. 12–14.

form is essentially conditioned by the serial structure, and in particular
by the use of pairs of notes that are shared by different transformations
of the series.

IV

The fourth of Stravinsky's *Movements* for piano and orchestra, then,
uses a similar means of relating transformations as Webern does in his
Piano Variations, but does so in a form-building manner. A glance at
the score (Fig. 150) shows that it consists of three closely similar
sections. Each of these sections has more or less the same dynamic
markings and follows the same plan: an introductory phrase for two
flutes (or flute and piccolo) of which four notes are prolonged in string
harmonics; an interjection from another group of instruments which is
variable; an extended phrase on the piano; another interjection from
four cello or double bass soli; and a short, final piano phrase. However,
in terms of pitch structure the most striking link between the three
sections is the string harmonics chord which is in each case made up of
two superimposed fifths. Fig. 151 summarizes the relations of these
chords: each includes A and C$^{\sharp}$ at the same register, but whereas the
third of these chords is simply a re-registration of the first, the second is
a pitch class transposition at the fifth. These chords are so designed as to
project the relationship between the informal aspects of musical design I have been talking about and the serial structure of the movement.
Fig. 150 shows that the series is laid out in quite a straightforward
manner; the movement is built on two transforms, P–0 and IR–0,
together with their retrogrades, plus a single occurrence of I–0.[1] This
means that transpositions are not used at all, so instead of talking about
P–0, IR–0 and I–0 we might as well simply say P, IR and I. These
transforms are shown in Fig. 152.

Now if you compare P and IR, you will see that the chord at bar 111
serves the same function within P as the chords at bars 98 and 125 serve
within IR; that is to say, each has the same serial derivation (from terms

---

[1] Many people would refer to IR–0 as RI–2, or even IR–2 (see p. 300 above). But this
is not appropriate here, as Fig. 152 shows, because the design is not based on
transposition but on inversion round the first and last notes of the series. The first
statement is labelled IR–0 and not P–0 because it is defined as such by the first
statement of the series in *Movements* as a whole.

Fig. 150 Stravinsky, *Movements*, IV, with note count

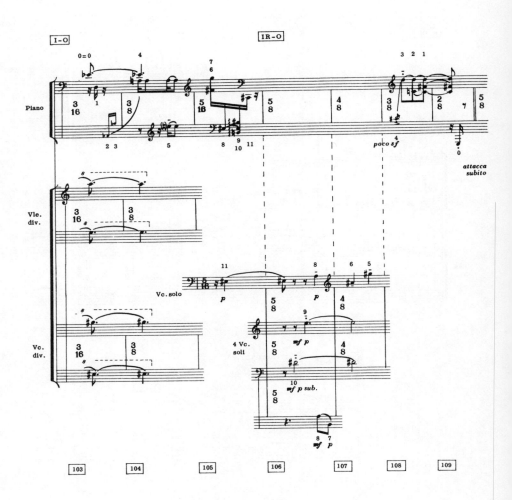

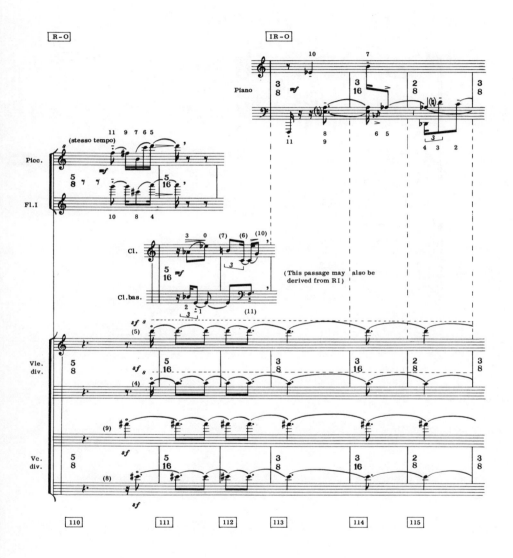

(This passage may also be derived from R I)

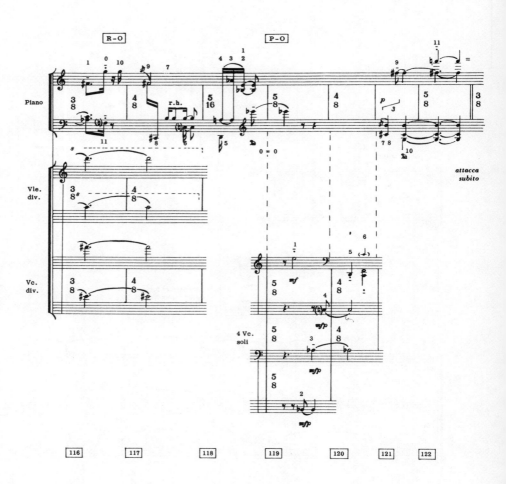

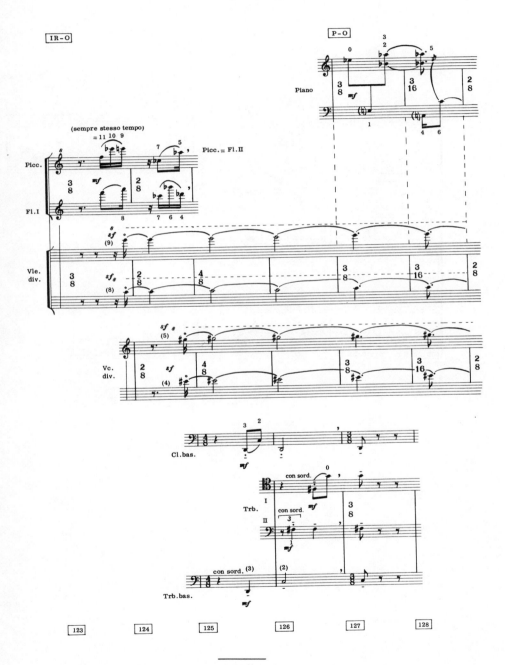

Fig. 151

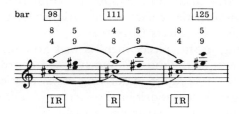

Fig. 152   Serial transforms in *Movements*, IV

4–5 and 8–9). The A and C♯ are common to both P and IR, providing an audible link between them;[1] but the other two notes are different (D and F♯, or E and G♯) and so these serve to identify the particular transform in use. Furthermore, if you examine the series closely, you will find that there are four other pairs of notes which are also common (or *invariant*) as between P and IR, namely D – C, E – E♭, A♯ – G♯, and G – F♯; the last two also appear in RI. As you might expect, then, all these pairs of notes play a disproportionately prominent role in the music – sometimes, as in the cello solo at bar 107 and in the bass clarinet and trombone at bars 125–6, being marked with accents or doubled. On the other hand there are other prominent two-note motifs, such as the minor seventh B–A in the fourth cello at 106, which do not recur as between the various serial

---

[1] Mathematically this is a perfectly trivial consequence of the fact that A and C♯ are equidistant from F, the axis of inversion between P and IR. But the important question is not why these formal relations hold: it is what use the composer makes of them.

319

transforms and which therefore serve to distinguish them from each other. In this way Stravinsky can choose to emphasize either the similarities or the dissimilarities between the various serial transforms, according to the motives he selects from them.

What is happening in this piece, then, is that Stravinsky is using informal, surface aspects of the music – motivic and chordal textures, register and dynamics – to project underlying serial relationships. To use Perle's terminology, the compositional structure is designed so as to present certain precompositional structures clearly. The principal technique Stravinsky uses to do this – the invariance of certain adjacent notes as between different transformations – is similar to that used by Webern in his Piano Variations. But Stravinsky uses the technique in a considerably tighter manner, employing a much smaller number of transforms than Webern. In a real sense the form of Stravinsky's movement, unlike that of Webern's, is most concisely expressed in the chart of its serial transformations. This is shown in Fig. 153. You can see that in nearly every case the series appears in a transformation inversely related to the corresponding point in the previous section. (Retrogression is irrelevant in this.) And since two inversions cancel each other out, the third section ends up more or less the same as the first; this means that the serial structure outlines an ABA plan roughly analogous to a tonal composition in ternary form, in which the same material appears successively in tonic, dominant and tonic.[1] This sectional pattern of identities and non-identities, repeats and transformations, is therefore a genuinely serial form, though a simple one; Fig. 154 shows the close association in each of the three sections between particular members of the series and the phrase structure outlined by orchestration, which is really the principal means of compositional articulation in this movement and in *Movements* as a whole.

Fig. 153

Bar				
96	IR	R	I	IR
110	R	IR	R	P
123	IR	P	IR	R

---

[1] Only the final appearance of the series – at bars 132–5 – deviates from this plan; it is altogether an eccentric statement, since the hexachords come in reversed order. I do not know whether Stravinsky is making some structural point here.

Fig. 154

2 flutes	4 –11			
Vle/vcl div.	4 –5, 8–9			
Variable group	0 –3			
Piano		0 –11	0 –11	} 0 –11
Vcl/cb soli				

However, this basically tight association between serial structure and musical surface is realized much more flexibly than was the case in Webern's Piano Variations. The rhythm of the piano part in bars 127–135 precisely repeats that of bars 100–109 (this, like the string harmonics chord previously discussed, advertises the ABA plan) but apart from this the links between the various statements of the series are quite loose and informal. Examples of these are the rhythmic link between the piano at bars 104–5 and 117–18, and the quasi-tonal C – D – F# – G formation that appears prominently three times – at bars 108–9 and 132 in the piano, and at bars 126–7 in the bass clarinet and trombones where the repeated chord not only draws attention to the formation but links up with a motif that runs throughout *Movements*.[1] In fact calling these surface formations 'statements' of the series, while of course correct, can be misleading in that it suggests that the only function of the surface is to project the series. It is undeniable that a rather pedagogical conception of music – as a projection of formal structures – is built into the serial method; but it is perhaps better to think of the musical surface of *Movements* (more so, paradoxically, than that of Webern's so-called Variations) as a series of fairly free variations on the series, because doing so puts the emphasis on the individual characteristics of each section of the music rather than on the underlying plan that is common to all of them; and, besides, the basically linear way in which each section varies the series is akin to the variation technique found in Stravinsky's non-serial music. After all, the surface of the music could not possibly be deduced from the serial plan, tight though the relationship between that plan and the musical form may be; everything I have said about *Movements* would apply equally if the entire piece were played upside down or backwards. The formal relationships

---

[1] Eric Walter White called 108–9 'a moment of ghostly allegiance to the tonality of G major', deriving it in a complicated and mistaken way from a reordered segment (6, 7, 8, 10, 9) of I–7 (*Stravinsky: the Composer and his Works*, 2nd edn., p. 506).

would still hold, even though the sound would be quite different. And if so little of the music we hear can be deduced purely from the serial plan, then equally little of the music's effect can be explained purely in terms of that plan.

V

The final piece of serial music that I am going to discuss is Schoenberg's Op. 33a, which also closely integrates the serial with the musical form, but which does so by means of a much more explicit analogy between serial and tonal structure than the one I made with regard to *Movements*: Op. 33a is quite simply a serial sonata movement. However, before this can be properly illustrated there is one further technique for associating serial transforms to be explained. The kind of invariant formations I have been talking about do not really involve the structure of the series as a unit – they merely consist of isolated pairs of notes which recur under transformation, or groups of notes which share the same intervals and thus exchange positions under certain transformations. The technique Schoenberg uses extends this in two ways. First, it is based on the overall content, rather than the specific ordering, of consistent segments of the series such as hexachords or tetrachords (sets of four notes); this means that these segments are functioning as structural units. Second, it does not depend on relations of identity but of complementation between these segments (though obviously these properties are linked).

To clarify, suppose we look at the series of Webern's Piano Variations again. If we take its first hexachord and couple it with its transposition at the augmented fourth, as in the first line of Fig. 155, we end up with a new twelve-note set, since no notes recur as between the two hexachords; and this means that the two transforms of the first hexachord p–0 and p–6 are complementary. The same applies when p–0 is coupled with i–3 instead of p–6, as in line (2); and the same relations naturally hold for the second hexachord of the series as for the first, as shown in lines 3 and 4. Furthermore, a twelve-note set can also be formed between the first and second hexachords of the series when one is inverted in relation to the other: lines (5 and 6) show this. Here, then, we have six varied twelve-note sets each of which is derived from the original series (and the number of distinct sets can of course be multiplied by retrogression), and which could be used as semi-inde-

pendent subsidiary series. Alternatively you could use two different transformations of the series at the same time while maintaining a consistent
chromatic sonority. It would have been easy for Webern to have done this
in his Piano Variations; instead of merely coupling statements of one
hexachord of the series with the other hexachord (which by definition
gives you all twelve chromatic notes), he could have coupled one
hexachord with a transformation of itself or a transformation of the other

Fig. 155 Combinatorial relations in the set of Webern's Piano
Variations

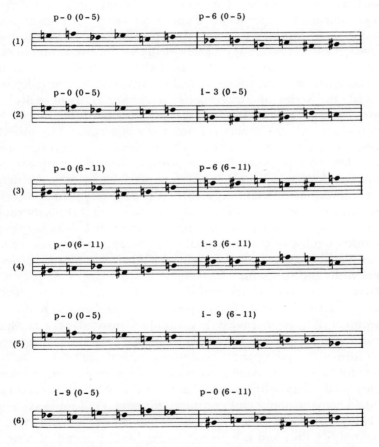

Lower case letters identify transformations of a segment, rather than of
the series as a whole.

hexachord, choosing the particular combinations that give a twelve-tone aggregate – that is, all twelve chromatic notes – in the case of this series. However, he didn't: and in fact Schoenberg was the only one of the Second Viennese School to exploit *combinatorial* relations, which is what this way of combining different segments of a series is called.

According to Milton Babbitt's terminology, which is widely used where a precise formulation is required,[1] a series is described as 'hexachordally combinatorial' when one hexachord forms a twelve-tone aggregate either with a transformation of itself or with a transformation of the other hexachord. And where there are multiple relationships of this sort, as in the set of Webern's Piano Variations, the set is referred to as 'all-combinatorial'. Hexachordal combinatoriality, though in practice much the most important, is not the only form of combinatoriality. You can get a twelve-tone aggregate equally well from combining three cells of four notes each, or four cells of three notes. Series that allow such combinations are called tetrachordally and trichordally com-binatorial; the series of Stravinsky's *Movements* is trichordally com-binatorial because either half of the second hexachord (but not the first, unless it is rotated) can generate a chromatic aggregate. The subsidiary twelve-note sets that result from such combinatorial relationships are termed 'derived sets' when they are formed from one segment under various transformations, and 'secondary sets' when they are derived from a number of different segments. It is probably worth using this terminology because it is explicit and consistent, but it is more complex than is actually necessary for an understanding of Schoenberg's rela-tively restricted use of combinatorial relationships; only when trying to account for the procedures of post-war American serialism does it become really indispensable.

Now it may have struck you that the combinatorial properties of the series I have discussed are really rather trivial, because in each case the segment I have discussed has simply consisted of a wedge of chromatic notes – so that it is quite obvious that a twelve-tone aggregate can be formed by piling these wedges on top of each other, and that inverted forms have the same properties as uninverted forms. However, combinatorial relationships are not generally so obvious, necessitating more deliberate planning on the composer's part – and more systematic unravelling on the analyst's. The series of Schoenberg's Piano Piece Op. 33a exemplifies this, and it is shown in Fig. 156. It could of course be

[1] 'Set Structure as a Compositional Determinant', *Journal of Music Theory*, V (1961), p. 72 ff. See also Perle's *Serial Composition and Atonality*, 5th edn (1981), pp. 96–104, for a concise explanation of combinatoriality.

calculated numerically, but possibly the easiest way of grasping the combinatorial relations of this set is by visualizing the first hexachord in the manner shown in Fig. 157. Seen like this, it is evident that it is made up of two chromatic wedges and that there are gaps between these wedges into which the wedges will fit when transposed (that is to say, shifted to the right in the diagram); but it is also clear that each wedge has to be transposed a different amount, so that the combinatorially equivalent transformation is not a straight transposition. It is, in fact, P–0 and I–5 that are combinatorially related (as Fig. 158 shows), and it is this particular combination of sets that Schoenberg uses in most of his mature serial works.[1] Apart from bars 1–2, 6–7, and 37–8 (in which these transformations, or their retrogrades, are used one after another) the whole of Op. 33a is made up of pairs of combinatorially-related sets used concurrently; while in the development section (bars 25–32:1) pairs of combinatorially-related hexachords are used. Consequently there is no particular reason to regard the single twelve-note series P–0 as the basic structural unit; really it would make just as much sense to regard the 24–note combined set P–0/I–5 as the basic unit, or to derive every-thing from a single hexachord.

Fig. 156   Series of Schoenberg's Op. 33a

Fig. 157

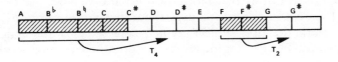

[1] In fact the specific hexachordal content we find here – chromatic wedges of four and two notes separated by a minor third – also recurs several times in Schoenberg's mature serial works: see the Variations for Orchestra and the String Trio. But of course the ordering is different.

Fig. 158

There are other significant features designed into the series of Op. 33a apart from combinatoriality. As Fig. 159 shows, all interval classes appear between adjacent notes; the series presents a much more balanced spread of interval classes than the other series we have discussed. Therefore what gives the series of Op. 33a its distinctive character is the way its component intervals are organized according to the different ways in which the series, as a unit, can be split into segments or *partitioned*.[1] What we are concerned with here is the totality of the intervals between the notes of a given segment regarded as a harmonic unit – in other words, with what Allen Forte calls their 'interval vectors' (p. 134 above). When you split the series into hexachords, each hexachord has the same interval vector; that is obvious, since the hexachords are transformationally equivalent. And each hexachord contains all interval classes in a balanced distribution; this is shown in Fig. 160 where the interval vectors of the different segments are compared. In the second subject (bars 14–18, 21–23:1, 35–6) Schoenberg stresses the hexachords, treating them in effect as antecedent and consequent; but because the hexachords contain every interval class within them, this theme does not have any very striking harmonic identity as a whole, and the clear association of these passages with each other depends more on texture and register. By contrast, segmenting the series into tetrachords produces much more distinctive harmonic formations; you can see this from Fig. 160. And Schoenberg uses these distinctive harmonic formations to mark the first subject, which consists of a succession of four-note chords. Finally, segmentation by threes characterizes the development and again this produces distinctive harmonic formations, such as the superimposed fourths of the first trichord and the [0, 2, 6] formation

---

[1] By 'as a unit' I mean that, for instance, the significant tetrachords are 0 – 3, 4 – 7, 8 – 11 and not 1 – 4, 2 – 5 and so on. Strictly speaking 'partitioning' means something different from 'segmentation': partitioning is a formal property belonging to the series, segmentation means the way the composer chooses to divide it up at any particular point.

found in both the third and fourth trichords: a formation which can either lend a momentary tonal coloration (as an incomplete dominant seventh) or be used to build up whole-tone harmonies. An important aspect of combinatorial serialism is that it allows you to magnify the particular intervallic characteristics of a segment while keeping all twelve pitch classes in circulation, by using the same segment simultaneously in two combinatorially-related statements of the series. This is what is happening at bars 5–6 and 27, where the fourths and whole-tone harmonies reach their respective peaks. This is what is meant by the statement you will sometimes come across to the effect that combinatorial serialism stresses the harmonic rather than the linear aspects of the series – a statement which is otherwise puzzling, since by definition combinatorial relations depend on all twelve notes being present as an aggregate, so that it is only the sequential patternings of the notes that distinguishes one transformation from another.

In his book *Serial Composition and Atonality* (p. 113) George Perle

Fig. 159

Interval class	1	2	3	4	5	6
Webern, Piano Piece	7	0	2	1	0	1
Webern, Piano Variations	4	2	1	3	0	1
Stravinsky, Movements	4	4	0	0	2	1
Schoenberg, Op. 33a	2	3	1	1	3	1

Fig. 160

Interval class	1	2	3	4	5	6
Hexachords (1,2)	4	2	2	2	3	2
Tetrachord (1)	2	1	0	0	2	1
(2)	0	1	2	1	1	1
(3)	1	1	1	1	1	1
Trichord (1)	0	1	0	0	2	0
(2)	0	1	1	0	1	0
(3)	0	1	0	1	0	1
(4)	0	1	0	1	0	1

gives a chart summarizing the precise associations between different segmentations of the series and the traditional sonata pattern of Op. 33a. The transpositions within which the P-0/I-5 combined set appears are also associated with the sonata form, although they are not quite equivalent to the traditional tonal plan since the first transposition occurs near the beginning of the development (bar 27) and not with the second subject; this might be better regarded as an attempt to recreate the tensional arch-shape typical of a sonata rather than as a direct substitute for tonal relations. Nevertheless, the return from the 'foreign' transposition of P-7/RI-0 to the 'home' combination of P-0/RI-5 at the point of recapitulation is clearly modelled on tonal practice; there is even a cadential pause preceding, so to speak, the final tonic. And the first 'modulation', at bar 27–8, is also similar to tonal practice – at least its

Fig. 161   Schoenberg, Op. 33a, bars 26–8

technique is comparable, even though the aural effect clearly is not. Fig. 161 shows the passage, and Fig. 162 represents the serial relations schematically; the circles represent twelve-tone aggregates between hexachords. Only the first hexachord of the series is used in the actual 'modulation' (the second does not appear until the very end of bar 28), and Schoenberg takes advantage of the way in which the fourths of this hexachord overlap as between the different serial transforms he is using. Fig. 163 explains this and it shows how each trichord appears once and once only. This means that the fourths have different functions each time they appear, and what these functions are is only made clear by the other notes of the hexachord. These vary between transformations and thus serve to identify the transformation in use (this is a bit like the role chromatic inflection has within a cycle of fifths). The most interesting example of this technique, however, occurs in the right hand of bar 27 – that is, just before the 'modulation' proper. This is the only time Schoenberg exploits a peculiar relationship that exists between certain trichords of P-0 and I-5 and which you can see if you turn back to Fig. 158: the first two trichords of I-5 are the same as the final two trichords of P-0 (which are themselves transpositionally related) except that the G and the G♯ swap positions. Schoenberg is making this relationship as plain as he can in bar 27 by keeping each note in the same register throughout the passage.

Fig. 162   Serial plan of Op. 33a, bars 26–8

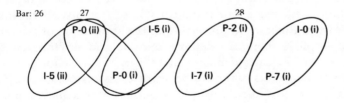

(i) and (ii) mean first and second hexachords. Primes are not distinguished from retrogrades.

But all this rather abstract discussion tells us more about Schoenberg's technical aims than it does about the effect of the music. As usual, this depends to a very large extent upon factors that have little or nothing to do with the abstract structure of the series, and this is true both at the local level and in terms of the large-scale form. It can best be illustrated by examining first the phrase structure of the music and then its texture.

Fig. 163   Invariant fourths in Op. 33a, bars 26 – 8

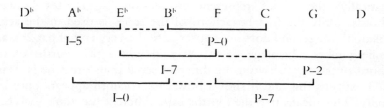

The series of Op. 33a is buried deeper beneath its surface than is the case either in Webern's Piano Variations or Stravinsky's *Movements*. This becomes particularly plain if you compare the final bars of Op. 33a, in which the serial structure is palindromic (Fig. 164), with similar passages in the Webern piece. Only in the development, round bar 28, are brief surface phrases found which are transformed more or less in accordance with the serial plan, and these are clearly modelled on the sequential working of tonal developments. Nevertheless, the beginnings and endings of serial statements do generally coincide with the beginning and ending of phrases; and though there is not any very definite association of particular formal elements with particular transformations, structurally important points in the form generally coincide with a new transformation. However it is non-serial elements that have the crucial role in defining phrases: the same arch-like contours can be seen in register, dynamics and tempo. There are even cadential patterns (bar 13 rhyming with bar 8, for instance) whose syncopated rhythms come straight from Richard Strauss. And, as the application of the term 'syncopation' implies, there are definite upbeats and downbeats; the rhythm of, say, bar 27 clearly demands that the right hand chords on the second and seventh quavers of the bar be heard as dissonances, resolving to the chords that follow them. And how is this to be achieved in the absence of tonal relationships? Partly through the superficial kind of dissonance that can be created by registration and intervallic content, but mainly by the performer: the result is the somewhat cloying style of performance that is practically impossible to avoid when playing this piece, in which downbeats and other aspects of phrasing are projected by exaggerated dynamic accents and rubato. The same applies on the formal level: the conventional characteristics of the various formal areas all have to be exaggerated if the sonata plan is to be made perceptible – the assertive quality of the 'masculine' first subject, the downright slushy quality of the 'feminine' second subject, the tempestuous and

Fig. 164 Palindromic pattern in Op. 33a, bars 35–40

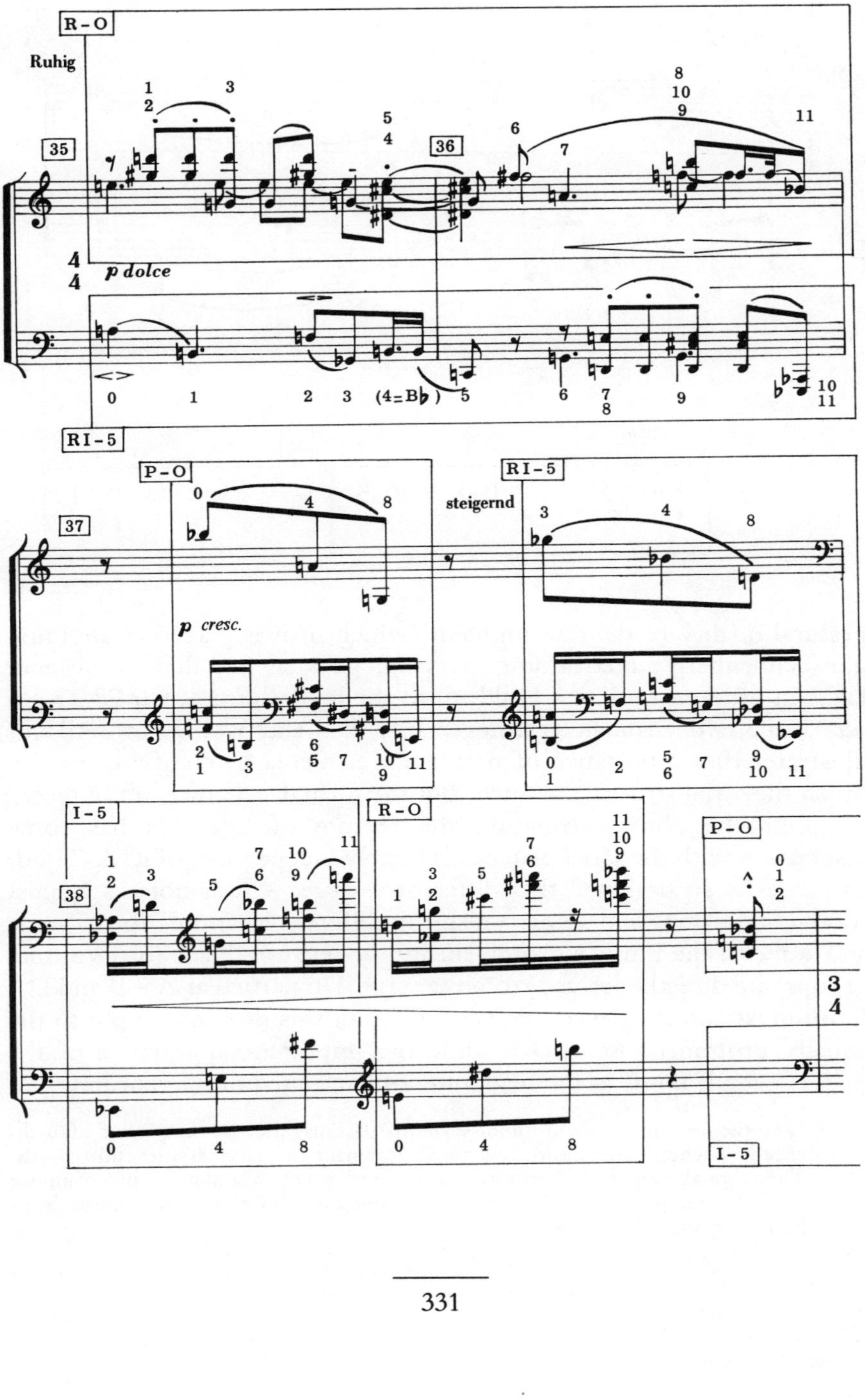

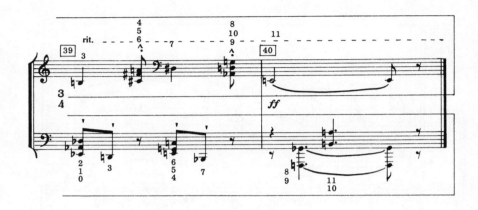

Bar	35		37		38		39
{ R–0		P–0	RI–5	I–5	R–0	P–0 }
{ RI–5						I–5 }

gestural quality of the development (which, if it is played at anything like Schoenberg's metronome marking, goes so fast that the listener takes in little more than a build-up to the high chord at bar 28:2 with which the two virtuosic gestures at bars 29:3 and 30:4 begin). All this illustrates the importance of non-serial elements in clarifying not so much the serial structure as such, but the formal structure of the piece.

Like the phrase structure, the texture of Op. 33a has some association with the serial plan but is largely independent of it. As I said, the series is so designed that different textures – four-note as against three-note groups and so on – result in different harmonic formations, and some of the music's prominent minor-seventh dyads (or two-note groups) are directly derived from the series.[1] In particular A – B and D – E are invariant as between P–0 and I–5; but this does not apply to the equally prominent E♭ – D♭, while the important appearance of the major seventh B – C at the beginning of bar 12 requires a reordering of

[1] Why the prominent use of minor sevenths? Because they can be part of a fourths chord, a whole-tone chord, and tonal dominant or secondary seventh chords. These are all important harmonic formations in Op. 33a and the use of minor sevenths not just as dyads but as the outer notes of three-note chords helps harmonic integration.

P–0 for its achievement. In any case there are important aspects of the handling of chords that are purely traditional. It is very noticeable that Schoenberg tends to use each of the more prominent chords in a consistent formation throughout, that is to say with the different notes registered in the same way relative to each other (though the absolute registration may vary, except in the case of immediate repetitions – of which Schoenberg makes a great deal of use here). This helps to delimit and structure the otherwise rather diffuse harmonic vocabulary of the music; the chords singled out in this way are in fact largely similar to those found in Schoenberg's pre-serial music. Indeed, there are moments in Op. 33a which are clearly tonal, not simply in that tonal formations appear, but in that there is a harmonic effect which would disappear if the music were turned upside down – an operation which is by definition neutral as far as purely serial structure is concerned. The clearest of these moments is the VI⁹ of A♭ in bars 17, 18 and 34. The first subject, too, has enough tonal coloration for the statement at bars 10–11, where the chord series is used forwards and backwards simultaneously, to sound distinctly bitonal. These tonal colorations function like the fourths and wholetones: as a play of light and shade, and as a recognizable sonority for highlighting important points, but without any deeper connection with the musical structure. In fact one could say that Schoenberg reverses tonal practice in that harmonic structures play a purely surface role in his sonata, while phrase structure and texture are the main means of formal articulation. This again emphasizes the importance of the compositional, rather than the purely precompositional, aspects of serial music – compositional aspects that vary widely between the three composers considered in this chapter, even though the serial technique they use is essentially the same.

VI

I began by saying that when they analyze serial music people tend to concentrate on the systematic, precompositional aspects: there seems to be a vague assumption that this must somehow explain the musical effect even when it is obvious that it does not relate to anything the listener is consciously aware of. It seems to me much more realistic to assume that twelve-tone series have very little perceptual identity and their transformations less, except under very constrained conditions such as those of Webern's compositions that have extremely clear textures and use series made up of a few simple trichords. (Even then, it is probably the motivic identity of the trichords rather than their systematic association into twelve-tone series that most listeners perceive.) By contrast, textural techniques such as registration, repetition, grouping notes into motifs or chords, and associating non-adjacent notes by retiring unwanted pitches into the background, have far more effect upon the listener's experience; indeed they can be used to 'derive' more or less any desired formation from more or less any series. (This is made obvious by extreme cases such as Berg's serial 'composition' of Bach's chorale *Es ist genug* in his Violin Concerto). Books of instruction in serial composition, like Rufer's and Perle's, mainly consist of illustrations of such techniques, even though these are not serial techniques at all but simply compositional techniques – more specifically, they are variation techniques. In fact, the relatively simple techniques based on invariance and combinatoriality that I have described in this chapter constitute practically all the specifically serial techniques that can be found in works of the Second Viennese School (apart from Berg at any rate).

There are of course much more complicated serial techniques in post-war works: but techniques such as rotation and other permutational devices, Boulez' 'proliferating series' and the extension of serialism to parameters other than pitch always seem to mean a decline in serial perceptibility so drastic that trying to work out serial structure in such cases becomes as musically pointless as it is difficult and tedious. If it is the music rather than the compositional process that you are interested in, then the first step required in analyzing pieces like Boulez' *Le Marteau sans Maître* is to repress the natural urge to discover ciphers and secret keys and instead to attend to what you hear. But even when discovering the serial structure is straightforward, you should not think of this as a substitute for other analytical techniques. It would be better to think of it as on a par with the analysis of compositional sketches: that is, as a means of reconstructing the process of composition, which now and then illuminates problematic aspects of the musical experience.

CHAPTER TEN

SOME PROBLEM PIECES

I

The pieces I talk about in this chapter are all difficult to analyze satisfactorily; that is to say, it is difficult to find any unified analytical approach that shows them to be coherent. This does not necessarily mean that there is anything wrong either with the music or with the analytical approach, as some people seem to think. They think this because they believe music to be a rational activity. If music were wholly rational, then it would always be possible to explain why a coherent piece of music was coherent; and if no such explanation could be found, that would mean the piece was not in fact coherent. But very little music is wholly rational. I am not saying it is wholly empirical either; that would mean that nobody could ever explain anything about music, which obviously is not true. Virtually all music lies somewhere between these two extremes. It is rational to the extent that it is constructed out of standardized sounds and combinations of sounds: musical cultures are in essence sets of standards for facilitating composition, performing and teaching. But practically any music of interest goes beyond such standards, exploring combinations or juxtapositions whose effects cannot be predicted but have to be determined through trial and error. Music, then, is partly rational and partly empirical. However, the balance between the rational and the empirical aspects varies from one style to another, and even from one piece to another. What is happening in the case of problem pieces is that the empirical aspect is outweighing the rational aspect. This is always an analytical problem; it may or may not be a musical one.

To some degree the two things go together in Chopin's *Polonaise-Fantaisie*. Like all fantasies, the *Polonaise-Fantaisie* has an abundance of contrasted materials, abrupt changes of key, and discontinuities of pitch and texture. Fantasies are meant to be loose and improvisatory, of course, but they are not meant to be simply a

335

hotch-potch of unrelated ideas coming in no apparent order. This is a definite danger in the case of the *Polonaise-Fantaisie*: pianists can easily turn it into a *Polonaise-Medley*. The introduction and the initial section up to bar 115 are usually safe enough; the improvisatory episodes at bars 37–43, 56–65 and 101–7 are held together by the repetitions of the main polonaise tune and the organization of the section as a whole round A♭.[1] The trouble starts with the new tune (what is it?) and key (where is it going?) at bar 116; and it intensifies at the end of the central section, where all sorts of different tunes and keys crop up in an apparently random sequence. There is then an unconvincing transition to the return of the main tune, and the work ends in an orgy of tub-thumping rhetoric.

Not all performances of the *Polonaise-Fantaisie* sound this way, of course, but the danger of incoherence does present the performer with very real difficulties of interpretation. How are these to be overcome? Essentially in the same way as you avoid rhythmic incoherence on the small scale in Chopin. As I mentioned in Chapter 3, the secret of Chopin rubato is that you maintain a steady metric continuity behind whatever rubato you introduce – for example, that the left hand remains steady while the right hand is flexible. In other words, you need to project the foreground rhythm of the rubato as an elaboration of the underlying metrical structure. The same principles operate in the *Polonaise-Fantaisie*, only transferred to the level of form. What you have to do is project the surface contrasts of tunes, keys, textures and the rest as an elaboration of the underlying formal structure. As it is principally control in time that is involved in this, it is useful to stick to the analogy of rubato and think of this underlying structure as a sort of 'formal metre'. This is not a technical term: I simply mean by it the temporal pattern created through the alternation of structural and transitional points in the music, through the alternation of points of departure and points of arrival, and so on. Now analysis is obviously useful in deciding what these various points are. And for this reason it should help to clarify precisely what the problems the music creates for the performer are; it may even suggest some guidelines for their solution. This is what the pianist Paul Hamburger attempts in his analysis of the *Polonaise-Fantaisie*. He employs two main approaches:

[1] Paul Hamburger's graph of the piece's tonal plan (Walker, *Frédéric Chopin: Profiles of the Man and the Musician*, p. 111) shows this section as moving from A♭ to E♭. But the E♭ at bar 94 is a V of A♭, leading through IV (bar 98) to I (bar 108). You cannot decide what key a section is in just by looking at its first bar.

Fig 165   A motif in Chopin's *Polonaise-Fantaisie*

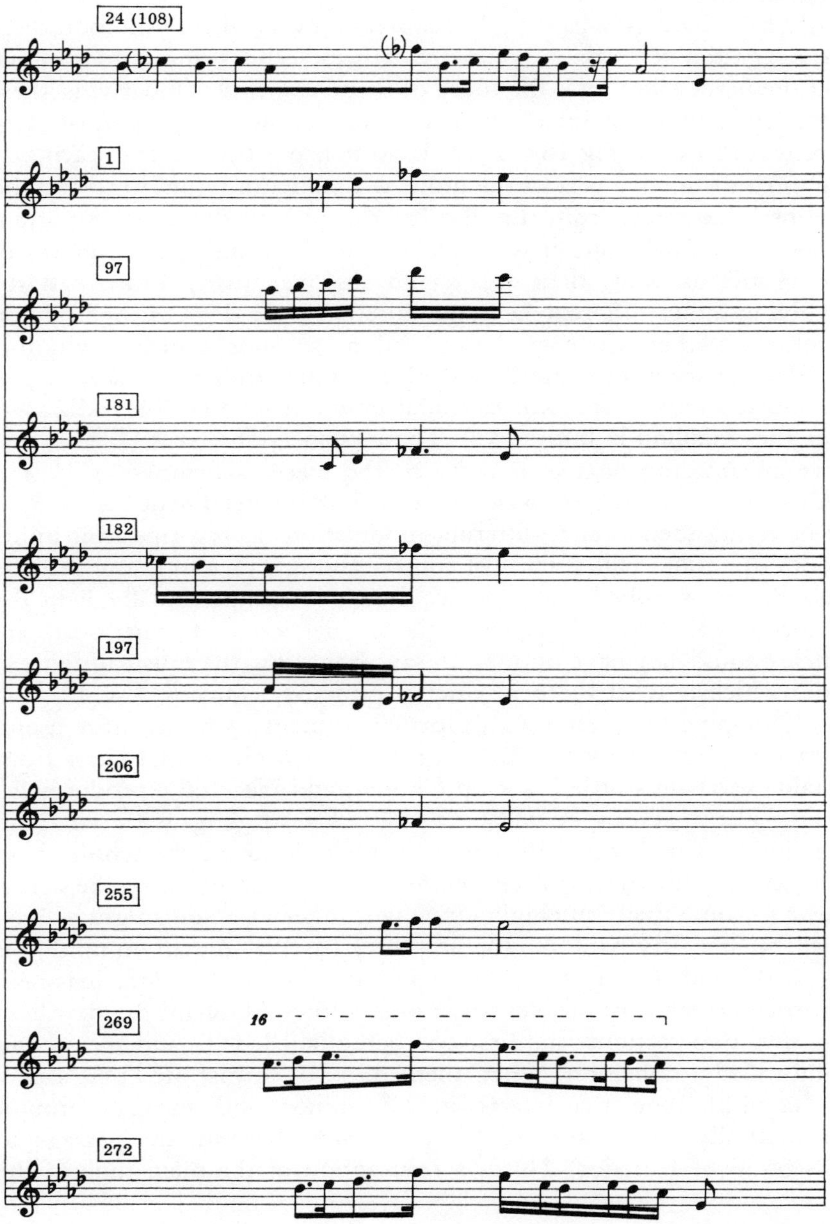

motivic analysis and formal segmentation. We shall look in turn at what each has to offer.

The *Polonaise-Fantaisie* is like a dream: everywhere you look there are suggested repetitions, veiled references, echoes and anticipations, and the harder you look the more of them you find. Underlying these are a few ubiquitous intervallic patterns. The most important of these motifs is shown in Fig. 165. There is no transposition here: in each case the most distinctive part of the motif is a fall from F (or F♭) to E♭, and the instances range from the first bar through all the most important tunes to the final page. If we were to consider transposed instances of the motifs as well, then we would discover many more patterns involving either different keys, or different scale-degrees, or both. In short: everywhere there are diatonic falling seconds, which is why it is so effective when they are dissolved into pure pandiatonic sonority at the music's most important cadential points (bars 199–205 and 272–7: note the pedalling in both cases). These connections, says Hamburger, 'give an amazing degree of unity to the piece, a firmness of design which, in the actual composition, can without detriment be overlaid by hovering themes and glittering modulations as is a ripe fruit by its bloom' (p. 108). This is true, of course, and it is nice to know that the piece is motivically homogeneous, but it does not actually help the performer a great deal. Motivic connections of this sort are synchronous; they have nothing to say about how the music unfolds in time, which is what the performer is primarily concerned with.

Chopping the piece up into formal segments is much more useful from this point of view. Hamburger borrows his formal chart from Gerald Abraham's little book on Chopin, and Fig. 166 reproduces it.[1] Charts like this can be very helpful when dealing with far-flung Romantic forms because they make it possible to see the whole thing at a glance. But they will be helpful only if they relate to the actual music in some easily intelligible manner; otherwise you might as well label the first fifty bars 'A', the next fifty bars 'B' and so on until you get to the end. Let us concentrate on bars 181 to 241, since it is here that the performance problems are most acute. Abraham divides these bars into two sections, the first one being labelled 'E' and the second being called a transition. What, then, does 'E' consist of? First, a new (or newish) tune that starts in G♯ minor and moves through chromatically falling keys to V of B major. Second, the passage of trills on V of B major. Third, a resumption of the main tune of the

---

[1] With the addition of bar numbers and a correction under E (33 bars not 34).

Fig.166

Bar 1	Introduction: 23 bars, mainly on A: various keys
24	A: 42 bars; in A flat
66	B: 26 bars; A flat but modulating
92	A: 24 bars; A flat
116	C: 32 bars; B flat but modulating
148	Poco ⎫ D: 33 bars; B major, etc.
181	Più ⎬ E: 33 bars in G sharp minor and B major –
	lento ⎭ 2 bars as in the introduction –
	final 10-bar reference to E
226	Transition: 16 bars
242	A: 12 bars; A flat
254	D: 35 bars; A flat

central section over a tonic pedal in B major. Fourth, a return to the opening bars of the entire piece, moving from B major to C major. And fifth, an abbreviated version of the newish tune with which the section began, now in F minor. This is a complete jumble of different keys and materials, some of them purely local and some having the strongest structural implications; the section even manages to span the most emphatic structural break in the entire composition, namely the pause at the end of bar 215. I have no idea how all this can be performed as one integrated section; and if it cannot be, then I see no point in lumping it together and calling it 'E'. As for the 'transition' that follows, this seems equally unperformable. What does a transition do? It links two structural areas, primarily (but not exclusively) in terms of their tonality. Here this means linking F minor with A♭ major. But these keys are practically coextensive in Romantic style – certainly they are much more closely related than the B major and F minor which are both included within the 'E' section. And in any case, the whole modulatory course of bars 226 to 241 is perfectly unintelligible as a way of getting from F minor to A♭ major. Where does the B♮ at bar 226 come from? (Hamburger is uneasy about this: 'bars 222–6 need careful dynamics and rubato', he says, 'if the resumption of harmonic movement away from F minor is to be made palatable'.) And above all, where does the B♭ at bar 242 come from? It seems completely unprepared both tonally and registrally; and the effect of all this will be that the whole 'transition' passage is played in a hurried, breathless manner, with the return of the main tune and key at bar 242 being blurted out without any warning.

Fig. 167 Analysis of Chopin's *Polonaise-Fantaisie*

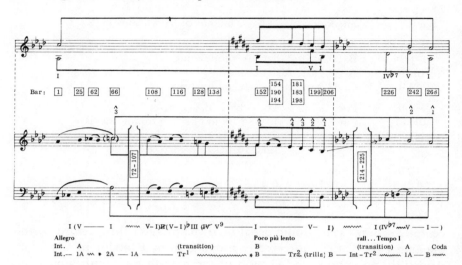

The reason why Gerald Abraham's scheme confuses rather than clarifies the music is that it consists of structural and surface formations all mixed up together. If we want to sort these out from each other, which is the only way we will achieve a scheme that does clarify the music, then we need to establish which segmentations are supported by the music's linear and harmonic structure and which are not. This is what Fig. 167 is intended to do. It reduces the entire piece to a two-part linear and harmonic graph and it shows two levels: background and middleground. The background level looks odd in Schenkerian terms because it consists of two quite independent fundamental structures embedded one within the other, each in a different key. (In terms of Schenkerian aesthetics that would mean that it really consists of two seperate pieces, which seems quite a reasonable conclusion since this is merely a translation to background level of what Chopin did in his Polonaise Op. 44, which has a complete Mazurka for its middle section.) One consequence of this is that at background level the primary tone of the B major fundamental structure is completely unprepared. However the other graph shows that there is a linear and harmonic connection between the two fundamental structures at middleground level. In particular, the B♮ on which the central section cadences is held over to bar 226, where it is harmonized as the flattened seventh of the IV chord with which the A♭ fundamental structure resumes. This gives the overall I – IV♭7 – V – I fundamental progression that is marked under the background graph: as it happens, precisely the same one that we found in Bach's C major Prelude, except for the flattening of the seventh. But is this middleground interpretation supported at surface level? At first glance you would probably say not. After all, the B♮ completely drops out from bar 215 to bar 225; the most prominent note is C, harmonized as V and I of F minor and then as I of A♭. Would it not be more straightforward, then, to regard this C as the resumption of the A♭ fundamental structure, rather than the B♮? It would: but I do not think it would be correct. Let us consider just what is being implied at the pause in bar 215. The use of the opening idea in bars 214–15 is the clearest possible sign of a structural return to the key and thematic material of the first section. When instead the tune from bar 182 is repeated, now in F minor, it is not at all what was expected: and it is not just the wrong tune, it is tonally wrong too. Hamburger feels this, though I do not think his explanation is correct: 'in a good performance the return of E in F minor may give momentary pause to the listener (it's the adding of the seventh, B flat!), but after half a bar, the ear feels secure' (p.112). But then why do both the tune and the F minor tonality fade out after six bars? In any case, my ear does not feel secure until the B♮ at bar 226: it is at that point, which after all coincides with the resumption of Tempo I, that the directed motion leading to the end of the piece gets going for me. And if you interpret the chord at this point as a structural IV♭⁷ – referring back to the B of the central section, and forward to the V and I of the fundamental progression – then the whole passage from bars 226 to 241 ceases to be redundant, as it was in Abraham's chart. Instead it really does function as a transition, and it clearly implies the B♭ of bar 242; so that this in turn becomes the destination of a musical process rather than an unforeseen accident.

I do not claim that this analysis makes everything about this passage clear and straightforward. In fact it would not be a good analysis if it did. An analysis should aim to be as straightforward as the music will allow it to be; but where the music is itself complicated (which perhaps is not that often) then there is something wrong with an analysis that makes it appear simple. And bars 181–241 of the *Polonaise-Fantaisie* are not simple. It is not just the way in which the introductory chords and the tune are interpolated between the B♮s of bars 213 and 226. This is only part of the larger formal overlap between the end of the central section and the beginning of the transition that follows it. I have included a formal segmentation in Fig. 167 which is based on the linear-harmonic analysis there and which shows this overlap. ('Int' stands for introduction and 'Tr' for transition.) Thematically and

tonally what is going on is rather like the sort of intercutting technique
that film editors use, and the effect is to create a kind of prolonged
caesura, if one can apply the concept of prolongation to caesuras. That is
what makes the *Polonaise-Fantaisie* seem such a big work, despite its
relatively modest dimensions; the sense of being in limbo up till bar 226
is as intense as anything that Beethoven created on a far bigger scale –
say for instance in the development of the first movement of his Fifth
Symphony. Naturally such compression makes for heavy demands on
the performer, but an understanding of the directed motion underlying
these intercuts makes it easier to cope with these demands. And that is
why I said that some of the analytical problems created by the
Polonaise-Fantaisie do reflect real musical problems.

Others do not, though. It is very difficult to produce convincing
foreground graphs linking the middleground of Fig. 167 with the actual
music Chopin wrote. You can find linear connections all over the place,
but they often are not supported harmonically and this makes it impossible to distinguish what is more important from what is less important;
register does not help much either. One reason for these difficulties may
be the intensive use Chopin makes in this piece of keys which are
implied but without there being actual cadences; as I mentioned in
Chapter 2, this Wagnerian technique is awkward from the point of view
of Schenkerian analysis because a Schenkerian graph works by showing
relationships between things that do actually happen, rather than things
that might have happened but do not in the event. But the main reason
for the difficulties is that in the *Polonaise-Fantaisie* prolongation
frequently seems to work by interpolation rather than by the normal
kind of Schenkerian embellishment. Usually when in Schenkerian
analysis you think of a note being prolonged, you mean that the prolonged note exerts some kind of influence over the entire passage that
prolongs it. But this often is not the case in the *Polonaise-Fantaisie*. The
entire central section is an interpolation into the main A♭ fundamental
structure rather than an embellishment of it; the influence of its primary
note, the C, cannot possibly be felt through this section, and that is why
(in contravention of Schenkerian dogma) I regard both A♭ major and B
major as structural keys at background level. The same applies on a
smaller scale to the interpolated passages I have marked with brackets in
Fig. 167. This technique of prolongation by means of interpolation is
simply an application at higher structural levels of the type of interpolation that Chopin uses a great deal at foreground level, the most
obvious example being in bars 249–52 (again involving A♭ major and B
major, incidentally). Musically this technique is perfectly straightfor-

ward at whatever level you apply it. The problems it creates if you want to make a detailed harmonic-linear analysis are analytical ones, not musical ones, and I am not really convinced that they are worth solving. Perhaps we just have to accept that some pieces of music work better under analysis than others.

II

Fig. 168 is the third of Schoenberg's *Six Little Piano Pieces* Op. 19. It is typical of the atonal repertoire in general in that it seems to have been written quite intuitively and, possibly as a result, is more or less intractable from the point of view of traditional techniques of analysis. Hence the invention of techniques such as set-theoretical analysis, which is guaranteed to give you some kind of analytical result under any circumstances.[1] There is a certain danger, though, in launching into sophisticated analytical procedures of this sort when you have no idea how a piece works. Any such method has a set of presuppositions about the nature of music built into it and you do not know whether or not these presuppositions are going to be appropriate to the particular work you are looking at. It seems to me that the less you understand how the music works, the more open and inductive your analytical approach should be. In this section I want to show how you can achieve this by devising a set of practical experiments into the piece you are analyzing.

You have to begin somewhere; so let us use a simple observation about Op. 19/3 as a starting point. It doesn't sound like Brahms but it does look like Brahms. In other words the Brahmsian rhythms, phrasing, dynamics and texture are all there; it is just the notes that are wrong. In particular the music seems to imply cadential patterns of tension and release. Let us make these explicit by changing the notes but leaving everything else undisturbed (Fig. 169).

What does this tell us? It shows that the borrowing of phrasing, dynamics and the rest from tonal style is very direct; nothing has had to be changed in order to turn it into a piece in F♯ minor. And this means

[1] Alan Forte has published a set-theoretical analysis of Op. 19: 'Context and Continuity in an Atonal work: a Set-theoretic Approach', *Perspectives of New Music,* I/2 (1963), p. 72.

Fig. 168 Schoenberg, Op. 19/3

Fig. 169 Op. 19/3, variant (1)

one of two things. Either the tension/release quality built into Op. 19/3 has to do purely with what are sometimes called its 'secondary features' – the phrasing and so on – and has nothing to do with its pitch structures; or else Schoenberg has created some kind of atonal equivalent of the harmonic tension you get in tonal music. But we cannot tell which of these alternatives is the right one simply by looking at Op. 19/3. We need a further test (Fig. 170).

Here the notes are the same as they were in Schoenberg's original but the way in which they fall into musical phrases is quite different, as you will see if you compare the two. Yet the music still sounds perfectly coherent in its new form: it makes sense as a waltz. Now it is not likely that you could do this so easily with a tonal piece; the harmonies would imply definite cadence patterns and if these now did not coincide with the phrasing, the result would be nonsense. The fact that this isn't the case here suggests that Schoenberg's harmonies don't have strong cadential implications in themselves. Instead it suggests that they make sense simply as a series, each relating coherently to its neighbours (and though I don't mean 'series' in the sense of serialism, it is quite an appropriate analogy). This means that any analytical method which chooses segmentation as its basic procedure – such as set-theoretical analysis – is not quite going to hit the nail on the head. It is going to tell us about the pitch structures of Op. 19/3 as if they were quite different from the pitch structures of Fig. 170, which obviously is not the case.

Next we want to find out more about how this coherent series of pitches works. Schoenberg lays out the music by means of fairly consistent part-writing, so it would be useful to discover how far the effect of the music derives from the linear coherence of individual lines rather than the harmonic aggregate they make up together. This is the purpose of Fig. 171. Putting the left hand up a semitone obviously is not as catastrophic in Op. 19/3 as it would be in a Mozart piano sonata. It still does a good deal of damage, though. Bars 1–2 are not too bad, though there is a loss of harmonic cohesion and also the music does not seem to move forward as strongly as it did before. That's interesting because considering the bitonality of these bars in the original (the left hand is in A♭ and the right hand suggests G) you would have thought that putting the bass out by a semitone would not have made so much difference. Bar 3 sounds nice but the harmony is no longer in character: it sounds like Debussy. The effect on the last three beats of bar 4, on the other hand, is disastrous; obviously the left hand needs to make a consistent aggregate with the right hand. Bars 5–6 lose in cohesion though at least the end of the phrase is satisfactory. Bars 7–9 are bad; the dominant seventh at the end has an effect like pulling the plug out of a bath, and this shows that maintaining a consistent level of harmonic tension is important in this piece.

Op. 19/3, then, depends for its coherence on the overall harmonic formations formed by its various lines. How important a part of this is the particular register in which notes occur? Fig. 172 provides the answer. This time the first four bars lose both cohesion and sonority. The music still

Fig. 170 Op. 19/3, variant (2)

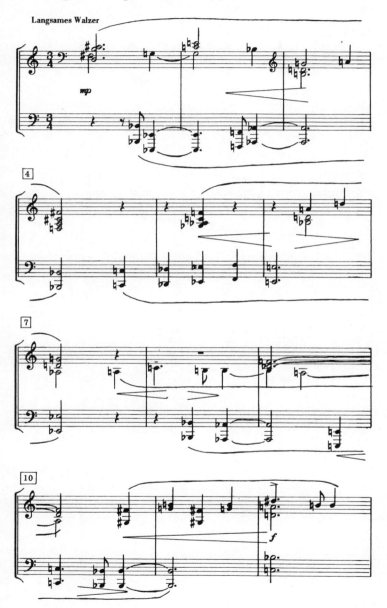

Fig. 171 Op. 19/3, variant (3)

makes sense, but it sounds like an arrangement – nobody would actually write it like that in the first place. As for bars 5–6, the only way you can make them work at all is by playing the new upper part *pianissimo*, in which case it functions as a Messiaen-style upper resonance; if you play everything at the same volume – so as to give an overall harmonic aggregate – it turns into complete nonsense. And the same applies to the remaining bars. The fact that the damage is so bad here shows what a very important role choice of register plays in this piece, and this is a serious criticism of any analytical method that assumes the functional equivalence of notes in different octaves – which is one of the basic axioms of set-theoretical analysis. What use is an analysis that cannot tell the difference between Op. 19/3 and Fig. 172?

More specifically, Fig. 172 has shown that Schoenberg's bass really is a bass and not simply the line that happens to be at the bottom of the texture. It has a special function in gelling the sound together. Actually you could guess this from the special way Schoenberg treats the bass in the first four bars; the *pianissimo* left hand is barely audible in itself behind the forte right hand, but it has a very audible effect upon the right hand's harmonic cohesion (you can try this out if you play the right hand by itself). And though the bass is just about as mobile as the other parts (it has 23 note-attacks on new pitches as against the top line's 25) it is different from the others in being simpler harmonically: it is rather more diatonic and is constantly harping on A♭, E♭ and B♭, especially at the beginning and ends of phrases. All this, then, is traditional. And the loss of harmonic cohesion in the final chords of each half of the piece (bars 4 and 9) when the bass is put at the top makes one want to call it a root in the traditional harmonic sense – so that each half of the piece would finish on some kind of B♭ chord.

The harmonies are not, however, so traditional as to make a conventional harmonic reduction feasible. It's true that Op. 19/3's chordal vocabulary is pretty homogeneous (this is something you could quantify in terms of interval vectors, if you wanted to) and this means that any selection of chords from it yields a rather consistent 'sound picture'. But it also means that there are no convincing criteria for deciding which notes have harmonic functions and which do not; and if you do not know what notes to leave out then obviously you cannot make a reduction. One possible way out of this difficulty is suggested by Schenkerian analysis, and this is to see if the harmonies are supporting some kind of slower-moving middleground line, probably at or near the top of the texture. If you look for this sort of line you will probably come out with the analysis shown in Fig. 173.

Fig. 172   Op. 19/3, variant (4)

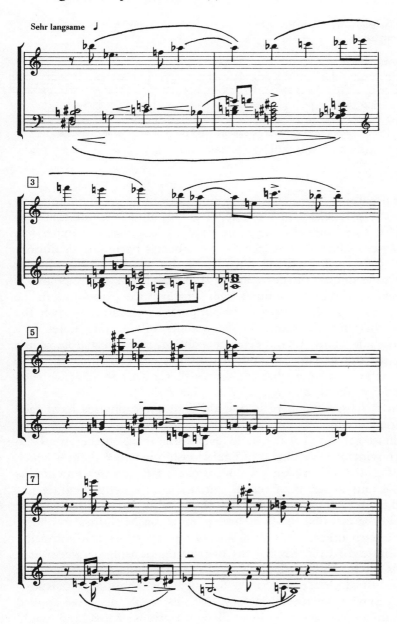

Fig. 173

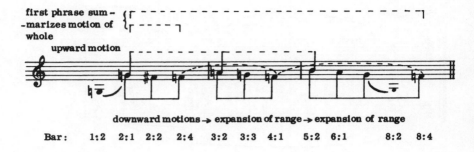

The harmonic formations coinciding with these notes do not have any specially privileged function; at least, they do not sound that way if you pick them out. At the same time I think that the upper-line notes do have some significance for the music's harmonic evolution. You will see why I think this if you play through Op. 19/3 while at the same time singing the notes in Fig. 173 at the appropriate points. It is very easy to sustain these notes over whatever the piano does in the meantime, because they seem to be supported harmonically over the whole of their length, rather in the manner of the long notes in a chorale prelude. This, then, seems to confirm the special role of the notes picked out in Fig. 173. But it does not necessarily confirm the connections *between* notes that are shown there. To test these we need a further experiment, and Fig. 174 supplies this.

What is happening here is that the first three phrases have each been shifted down a semitone in relation to the previous one. The fourth phrase continues at the same level as the third one because I can find no convincing way to alter the relationship between them – which is a significant discovery since it means these two phrases function as an organic unit in terms of overall pitch. (That is why they are not separated from each other in Fig. 173, as the other phrases are.) On the other hand the fact that the first three phrases can be shifted around in relation to each other, without any very apparent loss to the music's sense, indicates that there is not any organic relationship between them as regards pitch. This particularly applies to the junction between the second and third phrases (at bars 4–5) where just about any transpositional relationship seems satisfactory. All this would not have applied to the F♯ minor version, of course: there alterations of this kind would have made the music sound obviously wrong. And that means it

Fig. 174   Op. 19/3, variant (5)

would be a mistake for the analyst to assume that Op. 19/3 has the kind of overall continuity in pitch structure that the F# minor version has. In particular, it means that the otherwise plausible connections shown at the top of Fig. 173 – the ones in dotted lines – have to be discarded; at least, they do not seem to contribute to the psychological effect of the music. That would not necessarily mean that they are totally spurious, it's true. It might be that Schoenberg consciously chose to arrange things in such a way as to give these logical connections between phrases, though I would not have thought this too likely. But whatever the truth of this, it is important at least to know which of your analytical observations have something to do with the way the music sounds, and which do not.

The above is very far from being an adequate explanation of Op. 19/ 3, of course. As I said, the more experimental a piece of music is, the harder analyzing it tends to be. And Op. 19/3 is very experimental; that is why it seems appropriate to adopt equally experimental techniques when analyzing it. And if such techniques do not get that far in explaining the music, they do go quite a long way towards establishing what the *facts* about the music are. This seems a better starting-point than rushing in with imposing interpretational methodologies when you don't really know what you're trying to analyze. Besides, it's more fun.

III

Stockhausen's *Klavierstuck III* has this, if little else, in common with the *Tristan* Prelude: it has generated a quantity of analysis far exceeding the original music's bulk. The whole piece is shown in Fig. 175. Some analysts have seen this as all derived serially from the first five notes; but in order to do this you have to invoke transformations so complicated as to make the music's serial origins practically unintelligible. Paul Griffiths, on the other hand, suggests that the piece is in some way based on

> the operation of the Fibonacci series 3 – 5 – 8 – 13 – 21 – 34 – 55, which is undoubtedly important to the construction of much of Stockhausen's later music: there are 55 notes, 34 different pitches,

Fig. 175 Stockhausen, *Klavierstuck III*, with Maconie's rhythmic analysis

and a total pitch range, traversed at a stroke between the last two
notes, of 50 (=3 + 5 + 8 + 13 + 21) semitones. Furthermore,
intervals of three, eight or 13 semitones often appear at significant
junctures; examples include the chordal minor 3rds in bars 7, 10
and 13.[1]

Robert Maconie has a completely different interpretation. According
to him,

> Piece III, deceptively simple in appearance, is as hard to analyse as
> it is to perform. Its pitch organization is based on three abutting
> groups of four adjacent pitches: D – F, F – G sharp, and G sharp to
> B, an arrangement leaving C and C sharp as 'free radicals'. The
> order and octave transposition of pitches within each four-note
> unit is serially varied; occasionally at first, more frequently as the
> piece progresses, notes from adjacent groups are interchanged (the
> D in group 1 anticipates group 3, for instance, and the B flat and F
> in groups 5 and 6 have been exchanged). At bar 8, which begins
> with a 'wild' D flat, the substitution process becomes more
> difficult to follow, but it eventually leads to a merging of pitches
> into the compass of a tritone G – C sharp. The final sequence of
> seven pitches, measuring in semitones from the C sharp of bar 13,
> forms the interval series 3 5 6 1 4 2, but this seems to have little
> bearing on the intervallic construction elsewhere.[2]

Fig. 176 shows what I think Maconie means – though, as so often with
this kind of verbal analysis, one cannot always be sure.

All these analyses are basically trying to get at the sort of information that Stockhausen himself might have given you if you had
questioned him while he was composing the music: they are
speculations about his compositional procedures. That is why the fact
that none of these explanations quite works does not wholly invalidate
them: it is possible to think that Stockhausen started with a serial
scheme in mind, or one based on chromatic wedges, but that he started
deviating from the scheme as the work progressed. But whether they
are right or wrong in this sense, none of these analytical approaches is
going to tell us much about the way the music is experienced. If we
want to know more about that, then for all that it matters the music

---

[1] *Modern Music: the Avant Garde since 1945*, Dent, 1981, pp. 85–6.

[2] *The Works of Karlheinz Stockhausen*, Marion Boyars, 1976, p. 63.

Fig. 176 Maconie's intervallic analysis of *Klavierstuck III*, bars 1–7

Fig. 176 Maconie's intervallic analysis of *Klavierstuck III*, bars 1–7

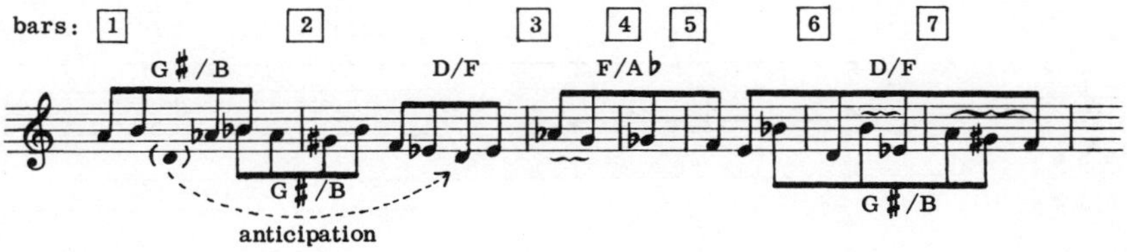

may be some kind of transcription of the Cologne telephone directory. We have to think about what the music does to us rather than how it came about. We need to describe it rather than speculate about it.

When you are faced with a piece in a style you know nothing about, the best starting point for analysis is usually to try chopping it into segments. Maconie's analysis, of course, involved segmenting the music into chromatic wedges, but while there clearly are chromatic wedges in it, they do not seem specially privileged as against the other motivic types. Fig. 177 shows some of these. Both these analyses give us some measure of the music's intervallic homogeneity, but not a lot else; after all, they simply see the music as a non-rhythmic sequence of pitch classes, and this really does not have a lot in common with the music as we hear it. Maconie also gives a rhythmic segmentation of the music into groups of three or six notes – this is shown in Fig. 175. But this segmentation does not correspond to the music's flow – I cannot imagine any performer finding it an aid to memorization or interpretation. So Fig. 178 shows a way of chopping up the music into five sections, which I find does aid performance, and which forms a convenient basis for more detailed analysis. As it happens, this segmentation receives some independent support from the fact that it creates a neat durational scheme: the sections last for 8 + (8 + 8) + 11 + 11 + 11 semiquavers, and this makes one speculate that Stockhausen planned the piece as five sections . . . But whether this is true or not (and I don't suppose we shall ever know, because Stockhausen has probably forgotten what he did), it does not affect the main point of this segmentation, which is that it should be useful. So here it is in action.

Segment I: bars 1–2:4. This is a closed unit: it opens and closes like a clam, which means that it does not create any specific expectations as to what will come next. Its arch-like shape comes both from register (peaking with the high G♯ at bar 2) and from dynamics. There is repetition of pitch classes but not of pitches; the different registers in

Fig. 177   More intervallic motifs in *Klavierstuck III*

which the A, B and D recur mean there is not a sense of patterned recurrence (as there otherwise might be). Fig. 178 shows how much the music is made up of rising contours, including one that rises continuously from the lowest note in this segment to the highest; in all there are seven rising intervals between adjacent notes in this segment, as against three falling ones.

Segment II: bars 2:5–7. The first chord in the music comes at the beginning of bar 3, and because of the linear continuity within each hand the effect is definitely polyphonic; this leads directly to the contrary-motion expansion of register with which the segment ends. This time the registral shape of the segment – a stepped increase – is not the same as the shape given by dynamics, which is an inverted arch; but both shapes coincide at the end and this creates a strong cadential feeling. There is a very definite sense that the music has got to move on to somewhere – and specifically that the registral expansion already initiated will be completed later on. All pitch classes are used in this segment except C and D$^\flat$; that possibly suggests that some special role attaches to these notes, in which case it may not be an accident that the third and fourth segments begin with D$^\flat$ and C respectively. Repetitions of notes within the same register, however, continue to be avoided – except for the B, D and E$^\flat$ which occur

358

Fig. 178 Formal segmentation of *Klavierstuck III*, with linear motions

together in bar 6 and echo the previous occurrence of these same notes in bar 2. Repetitions of pitches at the same register become much more frequent in the rest of the piece (from bar 8 there are 31 notes in all, 16 of which are repetitions) and this is a measure of the developmental character of the second half of the piece in contrast to the more expository character of its first half.

Segment III: bars 8–10.3. This is made up of three subsidiary groups; the pause after the first group is in fact the longest rest in the piece so far (or at least it will be if the performer controls his note-releases as accurately as Stockhausen asks him to). Nevertheless the three sub-groups cohere because of the inverted arch shape that is outlined both by register and by the density with which the notes occur in time; also there is a kind of rhyme between the final chords of this segment and the previous one, simply because of their registral affinity, and this again helps to establish the three sub-groups as a single segment. But it is a very fragmentary one; for this reason it strongly implies continuation.

Segment IV: bars 10:4–12. This is the most complex segment, partly because for the first time there is a suggestion of three-part counterpoint (see Fig. 178), and partly owing to the conflicting shapes outlined by different parameters. There is no clear overall shape either in dynamics or register, though there is some registral expansion; note-density declines, but unevenly. And the diminished-seventh chord in bar 11 seems to create harmonic implications of some kind, even if it would not be possible to say where the music is going tonally. The effect of all this is that the phrase as a whole functions as a particularly distinct upbeat: imagine how unsatisfactory it would seem if the piece stopped here!

Segment V: bars 13–16. This final phrase seems a very satisfactory conclusion to the piece and several independent factors combine to give it this cadential quality. It returns to the monodic texture with which the piece began, which makes for strong contrast with the previous segment. It includes the longest uninterrupted note of the entire piece (the dotted crotchet of bar 14) and this creates maximum contrast with the final expansive gesture that follows it; the contrast is dynamic too, since the dotted crotchet is marked *piano* while the final note is the only *fortissimo* of the piece – or at least it is meant to be, though getting a proper *fortissimo* at that register is barely more possible than limiting its duration to the dotted quaver Stockhausen asks for. Again, the final two notes of the piece echo the first two; at least, they are the same pitch classes, but they are now registered as the lowest and highest notes of the entire piece, and this provides the expected conclusion to the long-term process of registral expansion.

If the ending sounds conclusive, then, this is because it fulfils expectations established in the course of the piece as a whole; the music's form is to this degree organic. Furthermore I think that the segments into which I have divided it can reasonably be seen as part of the formal structure and not simply as an analytical convenience. After all, segmenting the music like this is tantamount to saying that it consists of a series of separate 'nows': each segment constitutes a single, but expanded, moment of time. And this kind of musical organization was very much in Stockhausen's mind at the time he was writing *Klavierstuck III*; he was reacting against the totally pointillistic style of *Punkte*, written the year before, and instead organizing his 'points' of sound into 'groups'. And if each group, or segment, projects a single musical quality within a single moment of time, then it is reasonable for the analyst to ignore temporal distribution within groups and look at the profile each segment makes when the pitches or intervals in it are totalled. Fig. 179 does this: it shows how many times each pitch class occurs in each segment. You can immediately see something unique about the last segment: it uses a chromatic wedge of eight pitch classes, and each of these pitch classes appears once and once only. Why those particular notes? I don't really know, but you can see that the pitch classes that don't appear in the final segment have all been used in each of the three middle segments, whereas only two of them (F and E♭) appeared in the first segment; what is more, neither of these appeared in the first half of the first segment. In other words, there is a similarity of profile between segments I (especially its first half) and V on the one hand, and segments II to IV on the other; and this reinforces the other ways in which the final phrase of the piece functions as a kind of return to the opening with what is in the middle forming a contrast. You will discover similar profiles if you look at the distribution of interval classes in each segment, too.

But my main reason for saying that the segments into which I have divided the music are a real part of the formal structure and not simply an analytical convenience is that each seems to act as either upbeat or downbeat within the form as a whole. Fig. 180 shows what I mean. Overall, the piece is directed towards its ending point; segments III and IV are upbeats to the final segment, while at the higher level all these three segments constitute a single downbeat in relation to which the first two segments function as upbeats. Fig. 180 simply expresses graphically the pattern of implications I described verbally earlier on,

Fig. 179 Distribution of pitch classes in *Klavierstuck III*

Segment:	I	II	III	IV	V	Total
C♯	0	0	1	1	1	3
C	0	0	0	1	1	2
B	2	1	1	1	1	6
B♭	1	1	2	0	1	5
A	2	1	0	1	1	5
A♭	2	2	1	1	1	7
G	0	1	1	1	1	4
G♭	0	1	1	1	0	3
F	1	2	1	1	0	5
E	0	2	2	2	0	6
E♭	1	1	1	2	0	5
D	1	1	0	0	1	3
Total	10	13	13	12	8	55

Fig. 180

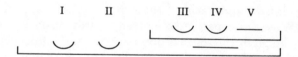

and I think it clarifies something about the way this piece is experienced; it seems to result in a better-controlled performance, too. Above all, it demystifies the music; whereas the kind of 'cracking the code' approach I illustrated at the beginning of this section makes it seem remote and incomprehensible, more like some ancient magic spell than a living piece of music.

Actually the thing that makes *Klavierstuck III* seem difficult to analyze is not so much the music: it is the score, with its precise mathematical notation of rhythms. Inevitably this encourages numerological rather than musical analysis. But musically Stockhausen's rhythmic notation is a kind of science fiction: what actually happens is that the performer improvises the rhythms more or less in accordance with Stockhausen's specifications, and the result is a rhythmic fluidity and independence of any fixed beat that probably could not have been easily achieved in any other way. In other words there is a glaring discrepancy between the fearsome mathematical complexities of *Klavierstuck III's* notation (and these are nothing compared to others of Stockhausen's piano pieces) and the way in which the music is actually performed and experienced by the listener. And in general I would say that it is discrepancies between score and experience that, more than anything else, make a lot of contemporary music problematical from the analyst's point of view.

Let us consider another piece by Stockhausen: *Stimmung* for six vocalists. This consists essentially of a single dominant major ninth chord on B♭ which is sustained for something over an hour. Stockhausen's original score (Universal Edition 14805) is much more concise than the length of the composition would normally lead you to expect. Really it is a sort of performance kit. It consists of two main things. First there is what Stockhausen calls a 'form scheme'. This is shown in Fig. 181 and it is a single sheet of paper which represents the entire piece as a sequence of fifty-one sections; the sections do not have fixed durations, but they specify which voice is to sing which note of the dominant ninth chord, and which voice is to lead within the section. And second, there are various materials which the performers use to fill out these sections: there are some poems and a large number of 'magic names' culled from the world's religions, but the most important group of materials are what Stockhausen calls 'models'. These consist of rhythmic patterns of nonsense syllables, each of which is repeated over and over again during the course of a given section. But the allocation of materials to formal sections is up to the performers, which means that the sequence in which they come and the way they are superimposed on one another varies completely from one performance to another.

But in any case, all this is only a minimal framework for the performance, because the music's effect derives very much from pauses, dynamic variations, and timbral modifications within parts as well as from the way the performers interact with each other; and these are all things that the singers have to improvize in the course of performance. So there is a complete contrast between the score and the very different pieces of music that arise from performing it on different occasions. You could not possibly work out what the score was like by listening to any single performance; you would have to do it by listening to many different performances and working out what they had in common. But this is not of course what someone listening to *Stimmung* normally does. What he experiences is not 'the piece' represented by Stockhausen's score: it's the particular performance he is

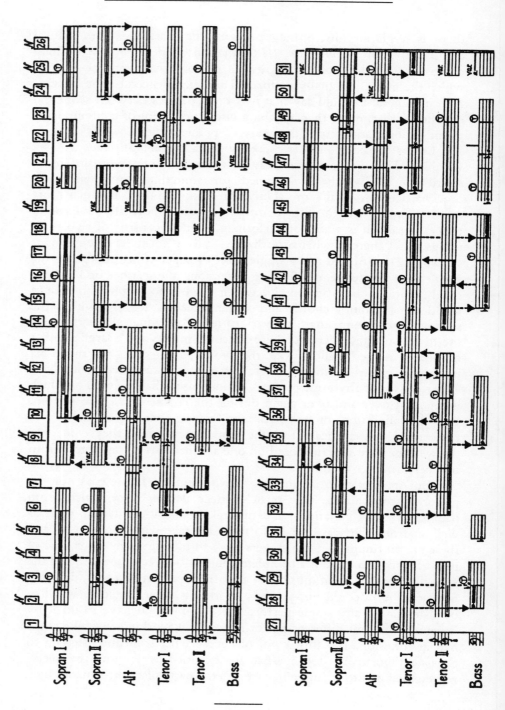

listening to. (You will remember we encountered much the same thing with the *Song of Simeon,* in Chapter 7.) And this means that if you want to understand the music as it is experienced, then it is no use basing your analysis on the score. Instead you need to use a sound recording as the basis of the analysis, and what I shall talk about in the rest of this section is the passage from 11'03" to 15'48" of the commercial recording by the Collegium Vokale Köln, sometimes known as the 'Paris version' of *Stimmung.*[1]

When you base an analysis on a sound recording, there is usually no point in trying to transcribe everything you hear: it may be impossible, and in any case an analysis that is not selective is not an analysis. So we shall try to pick out the more striking things as we go along. How shall we notate them? It would be possible to use graphic symbols, but there is a certain danger in this when you are dealing with an unfamiliar type of music: if they are to mean anything, graphic symbols must measure some specific variable (pitch height, dynamic level, density of attack or whatever), and at the beginning of an analysis you may not be in a position to know what are the right variables to be measuring. For this reason I think it can be better to reserve graphic notations for the presentation of analytical conclusions, and instead begin the analysis with an informal verbal commentary – just as we did with *Klavierstuck III.* As before, we shall find that what begins as descriptive observation turns almost of its own accord into analytical interpretation.

Segment I: 0'0" – 0'13". A unison D plus a B♭, that is barely perceptible in itself but alters the way in which the D is heard. The pattern of timbral change (that's to say, of the syllables being sung) is not very distinct, so that the overall effect is of gentle pulsation rather than of definite repetition. This short passage is static overall.

Segment II: 0'13" – 1'23". The whole of this section is marked by the rhythmic incantation 'aum aum aum kala': it is regularly repeated and establishes a triple metre. All the male voices take this up quickly, moving down from D to a unison B♭, so that the effect is of rapid rhythmic crescendo; a female voice, though also moving to B♭, con-

Opposite page: **Fig. 181** Stockhausen, *Stimming:* form scheme.

---

[1] Though currently deleted, this extract was available on two discs: first the complete recording of *Stimmung* on DGG 2543003, and second an anthology called 'Stockhausen's Greatest Hits' on the Polydor label.

tinues with the syllabic pattern of the previous section, singing it with a pronounced nasal twang that imitates the syllable 'aum'. She moves in and out of prominence, the irregularity of her pattern contrasting strongly with the regularity of the men's. At 0'55", by which time the 'aum aum aum kala' pattern is firmly established, one of the men recites a poem ('nimm Dich in acht . . .') in a sing-song, triple-metred manner; he begins quietly but becomes louder as the other voices give way to him (it is not possible to tell whether this is an effect of amplification or not). Soon after the poem ends, a female voice enters on A♭, singing in rhythmic unison with the lower voices; this is repeated without change for some time, with the nasal twanging still continuing, until the rhythm dissolves in a sustained 'aum' from which the next syllabic pattern emerges almost imperceptibly.

Segment III: 1'23" – 1'48". This is a short section with little internal change, in which the higher voices sing a unison A♭ (the same A♭, of course, that was introduced in the previous section). The new syllabic pattern is not strongly rhythmic and this increases the contrast between this section and the previous one. From time to time all the voices pause together and this gives the first short breaks in what has been otherwise a wholly sustained sonority since the beginning of the extract: silence floods through the breaks.

Segment IV: 1'48" – 3'10". This section begins very definitely, with the bass introducing a strongly rhythmic pattern on low B♭; the tenors rapidly take it up, one on the upper B♭ (this is particularly prominent in the recording) and the other on F. The female singers continue with the syllabic pattern of the previous section, but one of them changes immediately to C, and this means that this section gives the entire spread of pitches used in *Stimmung*; what is more, this spread of pitches continues until the end of the extract, so that what happens from 1'48" to the end seems more unified than what has gone before. There is some obvious interaction between the performers in the irregular changes of balance between the upper and lower parts – which also means between the weaker pulsations of the upper parts and the stronger pulsations of the lower ones. There are also synchronized dynamic surges at 2'17" and 2'47"; after the second of these, two 'magic names' are enunciated, one loudly and rather menacingly ('Hera', at 2'50") and the other more *sotto voce* ('Rhea', at 2'58"). At this point, and in strong contrast, the other voices are producing a particularly sustained, organ-like sonority with the various notes and syllabic patterns they are singing integrated with each other in the manner of a mixture stop.

Segment V: 3′10″ – 4′45″. The syllabic pattern of the previous section started emphatically but became less emphatic as the section progressed; this section again begins with a pulsating pattern and, though it is not the same as the previous one, the effect is of a renewal of rhythmic energy. The pattern begins on the upper B♭ and is quickly taken up on D; twice the singers with the new pattern cut out together, along with the bass, leaving only the sustained notes held over from the previous section and apparently unaffected by what is going on. At 3′45″ there is a marked change of character in all but the outer two parts: one of the women again intones the name 'Rhea' and this time the other singers take it up in a highly dramatic manner, with irregular flurries of intensity. Gradually the intensity dies away and the name is recited more regularly. The F sung by one of the tenors, which dropped out before the 'Rheas', re-enters from 3′50″, mimicking the other parts' pattern of articulation without actually pronouncing the name. With the 'Rheas' the rhythmic pattern with which this section began disappears, so it would be possible to regard everything from there on as a separate section.

Where are these observations leading us? The basic constituents of the musical form are obviously the repeated patterns of syllables that define each section and give it its particular rhythmic character; each section is experienced as a single prolonged 'now' and so there is a sense of temporal transition between each section and the next. And when one rhythmic pattern persists underneath a new one, this creates an effect of temporal overlap; two different 'nows' are superimposed on each other. This effect is particularly striking when one of the temporal strata falls out to expose the other – and most of all at 3′21″, where the contrast between time strata is reinforced by the registral contrast between upper and lower parts. Although, as I said, the syllabic patterns define the sections as a whole, the sections tend to be more rhythmically definite at their beginnings than at their ends; in other words, they tend towards relaxation, which means that they do not really have any clear implications as to what will come next. The performers' choice of syllabic patterns seems to be guided by the relationships of similarity or contrast in pitch between the various sections: thus rhythmically definite and indefinite patterns alternate in the first three segments, corresponding to the contrasted pitches of these sections, while the last two segments are similar to each other in both respects. And the syllabic patterns have yet a further role in that they provide a link between the sung pitches and the spoken words; this link becomes explicit in the fourth segment, where the 'he-a' of the syllabic pattern and the magic name 'Rhea' rhyme with each other.

How do these observations of a particular performance tie in with

Fig. 182 *Stimmung*, numbers 9–12, as performed by the Collegium Vokale Köln

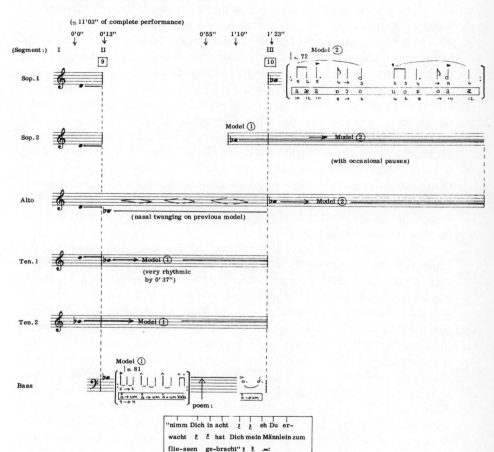

Stockhausen's score? Each of the segments into which I divided the music corresponds to one of the segments in Stockhausen's form-scheme, and each of the syllabic patterns corresponds to one of his 'models'; Fig. 182 is an annotated version of the relevant part of the form-scheme, showing what the Collegium Vokale Köln did in this particular performance. Everything I commented on can be conveniently located in this transcription. But unlike my comments, this transcription includes things that cannot be determined purely from the

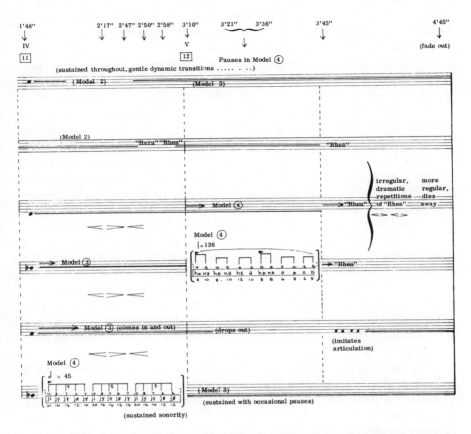

sound of the music, such as some of the assignments of pitches or magic names to particular voices; sometimes these can be deduced from Stockhausen's score, and sometimes they have to be guessed.[1] So the transcription is an idealization of the sound you hear. It doesn't directly describe the effect of the music: rather it makes it possible to *imagine* the music more clearly. And, as I said in Chapter 6, this is one of the things you look for in a musical analysis. In fact even Stockhausen's original score can serve as an analysis in this sense, provided that you *read* it in the sense that you read any other analytical graph, rather than staring at it as if it were a mandala.

[1] Hence the occasional discrepancies between my transcription and the one Stockhausen himself has recently published (Universal Edition 14737).

369

There are two particular respects in which the score of *Stimmung* is more analytical than performance scores usually are. The first is that it directly shows procedural and organizational aspects of the music, whereas performance scores usually only show the *results* of serial procedures, tonal organization or whatever (that is one reason why they need analyzing); in that it shows what different performances of *Stimmung* have in common, Stockhausen's score is analytical in just the same way as, say, Elisabeth Morin's chart of the variations on 'John, come kiss me now' (Fig. 86 above).[1] The second respect in which the score of *Stimmung* is analytical is that it is not possible to make any further reduction of the music – unless you count the most background level of analysis, at which you view *Stimmung* as simply a dominant ninth chord that is subject to timbral variation. Looked at this way, everything in *Stimmung* is a matter of timbre. The notes which the performers sing are harmonics 2, 3, 4, 5, 7 and 9 of the implied but absent fundamental, the B♭ below the bass clef.[2] And the syllabic patterns, which consist predominantly of vowels, project various overtones of these notes – in fact Stockhausen specifies the overtones he wants projected this way, and asks the singers to practise doing this as clearly as possible. So at this level the whole piece consists of a single source sound which is filtered in all sorts of ways, the filtering being done through the resources of the human voice rather than by electronic apparatus. It would be very tempting to say that *Stimmung* could only have been written by a composer of electronic music, if it were not for the fact that Wagner did almost exactly the same thing long ago in his *Rheingold* Prelude.

By now we have quite a lot of analytical material on *Stimmung*, but it still needs tying together. It will help if we bear in mind that analyzing a piece of music means simplifying it in such a way that it continues to make some kind of sense in its simplified version. And what we have said suggests that there are four levels at which we can make some kind of sense of *Stimmung*.

First there is the background level, the single sustained chord with constantly changing timbres. This is the level at which the 'tuning-in' which Stockhausen's title refers to happens: listening to the piece, or with its sound ringing in your ears after a performance, you lose track of time and enter a kind of trance. Then there are two middleground levels, in which time appears, but in a more or less schematic manner: Stockhausen's original

---

[1] Conversely it would be quite possible to use Morin's chart as a performance score (it looks quite like some of Stockhausen's scores), and this shows that the distinction between an analysis and a performance score is not necessarily a totally hard-and-fast one.

[2] Not harmonics 2, 3, 4, 5, 6 and 7 as Maconie says (*The Works of Karlheinz Stockhausen*, p. 239).

score, in which distinct materials appear but their order is not fixed, and the annotated version that shows the order in which things were done in a given performance. And finally, at the foreground level, there is the music that is performed, with all the real-time interaction and improvization that is involved in performing it. So in spite of the special problems it poses, it is not altogether impossible to interpret *Stimmung* in terms of the familiar kind of multi-layer analysis in which each level incorporates details that were omitted at the previous level. But of course it is no use pretending that we know how to analyze *Stimmung* in anything like the sort of detail that we know how to analyze, say, a Beethoven sonata. The reason is that, though we can distinguish various levels at which *Stimmung* is intelligible, we do not have an understanding of the relations between these levels that is even remotely comparable to our understanding of how foreground levels in tonal music prolong background levels. For example, though it allows of many different combinations, Stockhausen's score of *Stimmung* picks out only a tiny proportion of the timbral possibilities inherent in the background chord: how does one explain the rationale behind this selection? I have no idea; I do not even know what kind of explanation this question might be asking for. Or again, what principles govern the relationship between the annotated score, in which the sequence of models is determined, and the actual performance with its particular durations, dynamic variations, pauses and so forth? As before, no satisfactory answer seems possible.

Actually this last question is one that applies to the performance of more conventional music too. Music critics talk a great deal about interpretation, about the way in which a piece is projected in any given performance by means of finely-judged tempi, rhythms and dynamics. Yet nobody, and certainly not the music critic, really knows what the principles governing this sort of interpretation are; there are informal rules of thumb, but nothing more. But this does not, and should not, prevent people from making critical comments on interpretation; you can praise or condemn a singer's intonation or a pianist's rubato, and rightly so, without having a theory as to what would constitute correct intonation or rubato in any given situation. *Stimmung* puts the music analyst in just the same position, because it represents a massive expansion of the interpretational component found in all musical performance. And the appropriate response to this is not to resort to extravagant theorization, nor to give up in despair, but to listen critically to the music. That way you at least end up with a better idea of what you are talking about.

INDEX

Page numbers in italics refer to music examples